The Fun Mover Chronicles

Biking the Northern Tier

Tim Fahey

ISBN: 1986899136
ISBN 13: 9781986899130

po·et·ic li·cense

noun: **poetic license**; plural noun: **poetic licenses**

1. License or liberty taken by a poet, prose writer, or other artist in deviating from rule, conventional form, logic, or fact, in order to produce a desired effect
   "He used a little poetic license to embroider a good tale"

TABLE OF CONTENTS

Chapter One

ROCKY MOUNTAIN SIGH

A few summers ago I had the chance to bike four thousand two hundred miles across the United States from a middle-aged standing start, so I did. I got up off the couch, flew across the country, pointed a fully loaded touring bicycle towards home, saddled up, and headed out. I didn't train or plan much before I left; I just decided I had to go, so I bought what I needed and went—simple as that.

For ten weeks and two days I travelled in near complete anonymity over bike friendly roads and scenic landscapes that served as a gigantic stage set chockablock full of various and interesting characters from all walks of life. I met farmers, politicians, nuns, doctors, electricians, cops, high school beauties, financial advisors, granddads, moms, business owners, meth addicts, construction workers, and truckers. Thanks to them I saw more with my ears than I did with my eyes. How could I not? I met Donny the ex-con tailgating in a cheap motel parking lot. I met Short-Leg Lisa, the kindest hotelier alive. I met Guy, the self-appointed Cyclist-in-Chief and his jumpy sidekick, Dan. I met a terminally ill grandmother enjoying a cigarette with her morning coffee. I met a waitress named Daisy who carried mace, a knife, and an iPhone "for protection" in a town of fewer than nine hundred people. I met Joan and Bill, friendly folks who saved me from an uncomfortable night of camping in mosquito infested squalor. My bike put me in front of folks I would not have otherwise met and I was better off for it.

After seventy-two days of riding and seventy-one nights of sleeping in tents, motels, barns, basements, and strangers' homes, my sides were sore from laughing and my legs were tired from pedaling. We call ourselves man*kind*, not man*mean*, for a reason, right? Switching out my office chair for a bicycle seat was certainly not the best career move I ever made, but it allowed me a sabbatical of sorts and the chance to ingest some of the nourishment that only weeks on end of non-stop travel can provide. By the time the trip was over, my faith in a greater good had been rekindled and a new set of friends had been met.

Like many other straight through sea-to-shining-sea bicycle adventures, mine officially began the moment I dipped my back tire into the Pacific Ocean and ended the moment my front tire tasted the salty brine of the Atlantic. The direction? East. Like most other Northern Tier riders, I rode from west to east to get the major climbs over with and to put the prevailing winds at my back and in my favor. (A caveat: the jury is still out on the "prevailing winds" theory. I had more than my fair share of headwinds.) In addition, heading east gave me a major psychological boost: it was heartening for me to know that with each turn of the pedals, I was closer to home, not further from it.

I set out from Anacortes, Washington, and kept along the Canadian border through Washington, Idaho, Montana, North Dakota, Minnesota and Wisconsin. I crossed Lake Michigan and after a few days pedaling across central Michigan, I whipped out my U. S. passport and was allowed into Sombra, Ontario, Canada. From there I made my way along the beautiful northern shore of Lake Erie to Niagara Falls. I returned Stateside into Buffalo, New York, and merged back onto the Northern Tier bicycle route for a quick zip across northern New England. In just over a week I traversed the states of New York, Vermont, New Hampshire, and, finally, Maine.

My adventure ended at exactly 4:34 p.m. on Sunday, July 27, 2014, when I stood ankle deep in the cold brine with a clenched fist held high and with a smile as wide as a continent across my face. A small gathering of friends and family was there to witness my return and to welcome me back into the embrace of home. I set no trans America cycling speed record, but had not set out to; my cross country journey was a bike *tour*, not a bike *race*. Rushing headlong through a bike tour would make about as much sense as speed dating a supermodel. Who in their right mind would want to do that?

Biking across the States was by far the most physically difficult thing I had ever done and my "easy does it" approach to long distance cycling won the day. I started off with baby steps, riding thirty miles a day for the first week (though one day early on I had to ride over fifty miles, but I had no choice in the matter.) I methodically increased my daily distance over the next few weeks, until I reached the point where I could ride eighty or ninety miles in one day for several days in a row. Two things happened to make that possible: the terrain leveled out and my legs became stronger. A reasonable pace coupled with a sensible course strategy (that included stopping for ice cream every chance I got), helped me complete the ride.

I was biking a marathon, not a sprint, so I rode accordingly and knew I'd make it to Maine if I took my time. Some very close friends of mine (and even some close family members) questioned my determination. A few said they'd "see pigs fly before Fahey pedaled from Washington to Maine on a goddamn bike." Some thought the mental and physical challenges of riding the whole way across the States would be too much for me to handle.

Worse yet, many thought I was nuts to even try. Some suggested breaking the ride up over time.

"Maybe you should break the trip up into smaller bites, you know, Tim? Say, ride a thousand miles, return the next summer and ride a thousand more. You know, do it over four summers. Maybe that makes more sense."

"Ever think of just driving it?" another asked.

"See you next week, Fahey," was what one particularly cynical buddy said to me just before I left for the trailhead on the west coast.

I'm no bike hero or super human: lots of people ride the Northern Tier every summer, so I felt confident I could accomplish what I'd set out to do. It didn't make my ride any less difficult, though. I knew it was going to get ugly early and it did. I'd seen the Rocky Mountain elevation profile of the first three hundred seventy-five miles of the ride. Wow, was it tough. It depicted the severity of the climbing terrain as a jagged, soul-sucking silhouette of witches' hats and traffic cones. If my legs had eyes, they would have cried at the sight. A mere ninety miles into the trip, the happily horizontal asphalt floor I'd been riding for the first three days ended abruptly the moment I hit the foothills of the Rocky Mountain range, or, perhaps more accurately, when the Rocky Mountain foothills hit me.

Hard.

That fourth riding day was a back breaker. I had been pedaling along SR 20 in the shadow of Ruby Mountain near the Pasayten Wilderness Area for over two hours when I realized just how far in over my head I was. Several times over the course of that very morning I'd been forced to dismount and push my way up some of the steeper parts of what I'd thought was a mountain. (That steep incline sure registered as a mountain in my book: it was one of those pedal-it-if-you-can and push-it-if-you-have-to inclines that can turn a biking trip into a hiking trip just like that.) Passing cars whined and screamed like banshees as they, too, fought their way toward higher elevation. I had come across the very first long and steep incline of my short bicycle touring career and that incline was handing me my own ass on a plate. Hell, I never thought roads could climb that high for that long—the thing went forever up. I'd been more accustomed to the junior varsity hills found on the east coast and in New England. But, there I was, faced with the Division One Rocky Mountains of the Northwest and I was way out of my league. Ask any rider: the Rocky Mountains are not for the faint of heart.

I'd pulled over to the side of the road for a badly needed breather and a quick check of the map for the name of the Alp of Agony I'd been waging a climbing war against all morning. No male model at the ripe old age of fifty-three, I was rockin' a muffin top, a wince, and a face so flushed that it had caught the attention of a pair of Good Samaritans passing by in a pickup truck. They circled back and came to a stop right next to me. The guy riding shotgun draped a tattooed arm out his window and slapped the side of the truck with an open palm to catch my attention.

"Hey man, you OK?" he asked. His cute girlfriend leaned forward and into view from the driver's seat. With both of her hands on the steering wheel, she asked me if I needed "a cool drink of water or anything."

Too embarrassed to cry uncle, I thanked them for stopping and put up a front with a weak smile and a dismissive, "Nah, I'm good." In a prideful attempt to save face, I reassured them that "I got this" and offered up my "real" reason for taking a break: my buddy had fallen behind, delayed by his love for landscape photography. (I wasn't slowly dying slowly of oxygen depletion. No, I was waiting on a friend.)

"Yeah, we seen 'im takin' pictures back there," the guy said. He threw his thumb over his shoulder, pointing back down the hill. "You got him by a mile or two."

The guy with the tattooed arm wasn't buying my "just waiting for someone" tall tale. He looked me dead in the eyes and asked, "Listen, man, you sure? We got some water right here with your name on it."

I shook my head. My "No, I'm good on water, thanks" and their "OK, be safe." completed our roadside interaction. With a pair of waves, they were up and over the next rise in a third the time it would take me to cover the same distance.

Terrific. I'd reached the point where the very sight of me was enough to trigger the assistance response in complete strangers. I knew I had no business attempting to ride a loaded bicycle in the shape I was in, but I found it especially discouraging to also know my frailty could so easily be spotted and considered worrisome with a mere glance at speed.

"Oh, that's just great," I said aloud to myself after determining my exact location on my map with the sweat dripping off my nose like water from a leaky faucet. Bad news: I had not traveled as far as I'd thought, and what was worse, the incline I'd been battling for the past hour or two wasn't even part of a real mountain. According to my cartographer, it was a "slight rise."

A mere foothill was beating me to a pulp.

And that foothill was *nothing* compared to the massive set of snow-capped tsunamis that towered over the trees along the road up ahead of me. I swear those Rocky Mountain ridges stared down and snickered at the very idea of me attempting a summit. I may have mistaken a molehill for a mountain that morning, but I wasn't wrong about one thing: I was in deep climbing doo-doo and would be for the next couple of weeks.

I was being tossed around by an angry, cresting sea of dirt and rock and all I had was my bike for a lifeboat.

As soon as the kind strangers were out of sight, I regretted not accepting the water they'd offered. I wistfully replayed our conversation in my mind, dubbing in a request on my part for a ride. How relaxing a ride in their truck would have been. Trees would sail by at fifty or sixty miles an hour and my tired legs could rest for a bit while an internal combustion engine did its work.

Though tempted by the comfort a ride would have provided, I dismissed the idea just as quickly as it came. Hitchhiking is cheating when you are on a bike trip. What's more, if I'd hopped a ride, I'd have marooned my buddy Dave in the middle of that scenic cellular dead zone and would have been long gone by the time Dave could make a call.

I wiped my forehead with the back of my hand and turned my head back down the hill for a look. The word "Wow!" involuntarily fell out of my gob as a knee jerk reaction to what I saw. Tree-covered hills and rock-faced cliffs stood whisper still as dozens of tiny white jigsaw puzzle piece clouds hung suspended in a crazy blue sky. Though the view was certainly worthy of an Ansel Adams shutter click, it began to dawn on me what climbing big hills on a fully loaded touring bike was all about. The parkway we pedaled may have appeared painless from the seat of an automobile, but from my bike's saddle, the road looked more like a torturous substrate of endless suffering. I was huffing and puffing without access to the single most important piece of climbing equipment I owned: my car keys.

After getting slapped around by that first nameless incline, I caught myself wondering, *"How in the hell am I going to do this?"* Even the relatively flat terrain along the coastal plains that lead up to the foothills of the Rocky Mountains had managed to leave some pretty sizable boot marks on the backside of my bike shorts. During my "planning" for the trip, I'd grossly underestimated the cumulative physical toll that even the first three consecutive days of riding would take. Over the years my body had successfully adapted to the challenges of sitting on my ass all day in an office environment then sitting all evening on a couch or in an upholstered chair; you'd swear I was bowling pin if you saw me standing on a nude beach from fifty yards away. My backside was used to sitting in chairs, not saddles. What was I thinking? I wasn't a college kid running the Boston Marathon on a lark like I'd done a couple of times in the early eighties: I was a fifty-three year old guy swimming in delusions of grandeur.

Delusions or no, Day Four's riding assignment was a brutal task. Unfortunately, it was the most vertically challenging riding day of the entire trip. Ahead of us lay Rainy Pass (elevation 4,855 feet) *and* Washington Pass (elevation 5,477 feet). With no services, no campsites, no nothing but woods and bears between us and two big bumps in the earth's crust, we absolutely, positively had to get there (a campsite on the far side of Washington Pass) before nightfall, or we'd be forced to "camp in place" somewhere in the middle of nowhere. It was fifty-four miles or bust.

Worse yet, that fourth day's climbing task was just the opening salvo in a two and a half month long distance riding and climbing campaign I'd volunteered for. Later that very week we were scheduled to face Loup Loup Pass (4,020 feet), Wauconda Pass (4,310 feet), and Sherman Pass (5,575 feet). I tried not to think about the challenges of crossing the Continental Divide (Marias Pass, 5,200 ft.) sometime later that month.

Mercifully, the Rainy/Washington Pass combination, a brutal one-two punch to the neophyte cyclist's gut, would be the only time two passes would have to be attempted on the same day.

Exhaustion. Distance. Hunger. Beautiful views. Unknowns. Brutal climbs. Bears. Chilly descents. Quiet moments. Disappointment. Elation. Only 4,198 miles to go… Welcome to the wonderful work—I mean wonderful *world*—of bicycle touring.

And what a wonderful world it was. Over the course of the trip my daily mileage totals varied widely anywhere from zero miles (on my days off) to 114.5 miles, the farthest distance I covered in a single day. I completed a total of five "century" rides—that is a cyclist's term for one hundred miles (or more) biked in a single day. A "zero day" is a day when zero miles are added to the odometer: I had a handful of those rest days as well. No one shadowed me in a support vehicle full of clean clothing, chilled water, happy thoughts, and fresh food. No, this was an unsupported bike trip that had me saddled with everything I required to camp, clothe, consume, communicate, and crank my way across the country. My steel-framed bike weighed 27 pounds bare naked and over 70 pounds fully dressed. Me? I weighed 178 pounds before the ride and 158 pounds after. I camped about twenty-five percent of the time and spent most other nights at cheap motels—mostly for the shower, the bed, and the bug-free environment. My top speed on my fully loaded bike was forty-one miles per hour. I will never, ever, go that fast again on a bike. The slowest? Well, one day I was blown to a full stop by a particularly nasty gusting headwind, so I suppose the slowest speed I achieved while riding a bike was zero miles per hour.

Early on, way back when I was still flirting with the idea of actually going on the trip, I dialed up an old buddy of mine who I knew had ridden the Northern Tier in the early 1990s.

I told Steve I'd been receiving some pretty strange looks from people. He listened to me hem and haw about the pros and cons of my go or no-go decision.

"Am I nuts to do this thing?" I finally asked him, point blank.

Ever-the-wise Steve replied with a question of his own. "Did you ever think the people who are telling you *not* to go are the ones who are nuts? Tim," he continued, "you'll never, ever, *ever* regret going on a bike trip. *Ever.*

He was right. I have never, ever, *ever* regretted going on the bike trip. As a matter of fact, I am forever grateful that I was fortunate enough to be able to go on one in the first place.

Order up: one ladle's worth of warm bicycle travel soup that will include tall tales from the road and insights from a cornucopia of characters randomly met during a Herculean effort to ride a bike all the way from coast to coast.

Chapter Two

One Spin Class, Many Reasons to Ride

N ow is as good a time as any to fill you in on a few things that may help explain why I found myself soft bellied, flushed, and winded on that hill four thousand plus miles from Maine with a bike as my "soul" mode of transportation. You should know about the spin class, a loss in the family, and the gun guy before hearing more about how my buddy Dave and I met and ended up as cycling tourists on that Friday morning in mid-May, 2014.

As the spring of my departure approached, my wife Eileen began to openly question my sanity. She was worried that I'd suffer a fatal heart attack in the middle of nowhere and live out my final moments on a lonely road far from the needed access to medical services. In her mind, the odds of me returning home *in a box* and not *on a bike* were much better than even. (At one point she actually asked me if "we" were current on "our" life insurance policy.) To assuage her fears and to demonstrate to both her and myself that my heart could take a beating (no pun intended), I took *one* spin class to prepare for my ride across America.

Spinning totally sucked.

I arrived late to the Tuesday morning "Spintense" class. I parked my car amongst the minivans and ran inside. There were four women idly pedaling their stationary bikes, chatting amongst themselves. They took one look at me and I guess they didn't like what they saw on the man menu: after giving me the once over, they returned to their chat.

Not a moment later, a five foot four inch tall guy wearing white spandex bike shorts, a torn Dirty Dancing T-shirt, and a spray-on tan bounced into the room. One hop and he was on the stationary bike that faced the class. He reached for his cordless headphones before he noticed me standing there, unsure of what to do.

Realizing I was a spin class newbie, he pointed to a stack of towels on a table and said, "Grab one of those and take five."

I thought 'Take five' meant take a five-minute break, so I did exactly as I was told: I took a towel from a stack and sat down on a nearby bench along the wall.

The instructor looked at me like I had two heads. "No, take *bike number five*, silly," he said.

Embarrassed, I hopped on bike number five and noticed a glowing red '0' under the words "Pedal Tension." I snuck a quick peek at the pedal tension level on the bike next to mine: it read

'23.' I changed my bike's pedal tension from zero to *thirty*-three just because I was so awesome and in such wicked good shape.

"What's your name?" our instructor asked me through the microphone. I heard his question quite clearly: his voice was booming out of the walls and ceiling.

"Tim," I answered. I did not have to shout my response. The guy was right there, maybe ten feet away.

"I'm Mike, a.k.a. Mike the Bike. FYI...a.k.a. stands for *also known as*. I just learned that the other day. Imagine all those years not knowing? I always thought it meant *in other words*, but that would be 'IOW', right? Anywho, these are our lady regulars— Mary, Michelle, Connie, and Pam."

Four heads obligatorily turned right and nodded 'hello' in unison, then they all turned back to face the tan man.

The horses were at the gate.

Mike the Bike said, "Tim, I am *soo* sorry we don't have time to set your bike up in fine-tune fashion, but it looks like you have the hang of it."

He turned to the rest of the class and asked, "Are we ready to rock and roll?"

"Fuck, yeah!" shouted Connie, the blonde thirty something with the pig tail two down on my left. Hearing her drop the f-bomb was as unexpected as seeing a factory-installed tramp stamp on a Barbie doll. "*What in the hell is this world coming to?*" I asked myself. Had I accidentally stumbled into another dimension where men dress like strippers and women swear like sailors?

Mike the Bike gave the class a big wink and flicked a switch on the wall. All the lights in the room went out. A moment later a laser light show flashed alive in step with some terrible '80s pop music coming at us from all sides. I was not ready to participate in a spin-class rave with Mike the Bike and the Minivan Mommas, but there I was, pedaling madly along with everybody else. A short, muscular orange oompa-loompa in a torn t-shirt was verbally whipping us along and the Four Horsewomen of the

Apocalypse were running at full gallop. Through the din and out of the darkness came Mike the Bike maniacal scream, "Let's do this! You own the mountain!"

So that's how it was in the Spintense class; no nicey-nicey warm up—just a full-on spin-a-palooza with Mike the Bike barking orders and four out of five of us following his instructions to the letter. "Pedal faster!" and "Crank it like you mean it!"

With laser lights flashing and with Mike the Bike yelling and screaming at us, I started pedaling like someone was coming after me with a butcher knife. Two minutes later I was sucking wind. I dialed my pedal tension down to twenty-five, and then twenty, and then I determined that my "oh screw this" number was actually '7'. Embarrassed, I used my towel to cover up the glowing single prime digit.

Not that it mattered much. No one else cared what my pedal tension was set to. I stole a quick glance over at the lady regulars. They had stern looks of angry determination and their legs going spinning so fast I couldn't see their feet. It was clearly 'go time' for the Minivan-Momma set. If my heart stopped and I collapsed onto the floor, I expected the emergency response time would be either 'too late' or 'never.' Nothing personal and no offense taken, but all the ladies were there to crush a workout, not bring Mr. Pedal-Tension-Set-to-Seven-Sissy-Pants back from the dead. Sure, we were all going nowhere together, but they seemed to be going nowhere much faster than I was.

Finally, after what seemed like a forever and then some, zero-fat, barely sweaty Mike the Bike screamed a grand finale that included additional pithy shout-outs like, "Be the bike!" and "There ain't no mountain high enough!" and my favorite, "It's only a hill!"

The music died, the lights went up, and I dismounted like I was being pushed off a gurney in post op. I swung a leg over and bent forward, which allowed the momentum of my lower body to swing me off the seat. Both feet landed flat on the floor and

I stood up, steadying myself with one hand on the handlebar. I was using a stationary bike as a cane. I was a dizzy, swaying, sweaty mess.

Unlike me, the lady regulars regained composure quickly, proof of their overall superior state of health. As I stood there with a white knuckled grip on my stationary bike, they toweled off and congratulated each other with their "Way to go, girl!"s and their "Fuckin' A, that's what I'm talking about!"s. High fives and butt slaps were being passed around like nachos at a Super Bowl party and I wasn't getting served any. You gotta earn that spin class high five, and clearly, I hadn't.

With the overhead lights back on and my eyes returning to proper alignment and focus, I was horrified to see my stationary bike and the floor beneath it drenched in my sweat. I grabbed another towel or two off the table and started hand mopping the floor and bike. While doing so I accidentally caught a look at myself in the full-length mirror along the wall. Deathly pale and bloodshot in the eyes—I looked like a guy at his *own* wake, although I was standing upright with my eyes open and was holding a towel in one hand, not a Rosary in two.

Sensing dehydration occurring somewhere in the vicinity, muscle-bound Mike the Bike spotted me and bounded over with bottle of water like some sort of human St. Bernard rescue dog on its way to the scene of a tragic accident. Mike asked me if I was feeling OK and if I planned on "driving a vehicle or operating heavy equipment anytime soon."

I smiled at him as if he was joking, but Mike the Bike was dead serious.

In response to his question and in an attempt to show just how heavy equipment capable I was at that point, I jump shot my towel toward the used towel bin. Instead of the perfect "screw you" arch into the bin with a proper *swish* sound, the towel flew out of my shooting hand like an intoxicated duck with a broken wing and sprawled flat dead on the floor, far short and to the left of its mark. I swaggered toward the towel and told Mike the Bike that I was fine and that his class had been a good "break-in workout" on account of the fact that I'd be leaving soon for a trip across the country on a bicycle that actually moved when you pedaled it.

He asked me my start date, and I answered, "May sixteenth."

"Of this year?" he replied, astonished I was due to leave in less than two weeks.

I was tempted to retort, "Yes, Mike the Bike, this year, a.k.a., I.O.W. two thousand fourteen hash tag ASAP in, like, two weeks," but I bit my tongue. Given the shape I was in, Mike's question "Of this year?" had been a reasonable one to ask.

I took no offense to his response, but I'd never forgive him for calling me silly.

Fortunately for me, my physical fitness test was a self-graded exam, so, even after suffering through a measly forty-five minute spin class that left me feeling like I'd been tasered in both legs, I award myself the grade of "A" which stood for Awesome.

When I got home Eileen asked, "Well, how'd spinning go?"

"Fine." I replied, "Never felt better. I don't need to spin ever again. Check the box, baby, I'm good to go. "

"Bullshit," was all she said.

Sometimes women have an uncanny ability to see right through me.

At that point, any reasonable person would have asked, "If you suck so much at spinning, why in God's name would you want to ride a bike across the country?"

Fair question. First of all, biking is not spinning. Bicycles take people places, spinning machines don't. Bikes give riders the opportunity to experience the world at the perfect speed—not too fast, not too slow—while providing mental, physical, and social benefits. Personally, each time I climb on a bike it takes me back to better days. So let's see: bikes provide non-impact exercise, stress relief, social opportunities, a sense of fun and freedom, and, yes, let's toss in the fact that bike riding also inspires deeper, more prolonged sleep and higher levels of concentration. That's a lot of win-win right there. Biking is two-wheeled therapy for whatever it is that ails you.

Me? I rode for all of the above reasons and more. I rode in hopes that the physical atrophy that had naturally occurred over the course of my little-to-no-exercise forties and early fifties could be reversed. The sedentary lifestyle I had practiced with a monk's devotion had taken its toll. In my early fifties, I was plagued by constant lethargy and had a case of chronic lower back pain that had worn me down over time and had left me cranky, tired, and physically half the man I used to be. At one point my back was so bad the only way I could get out of my car was to swing my feet onto the pavement and pull myself up into a standing position like you see all the old guys do in the blue parking spots. Basically, I had reached the point in my life where I was sick and tired of being sick and tired. At the age of fifty-three I considered myself too young to be old and I wanted to do something about it. I figured I used to have a lot of fun riding a bike as a kid, so I thought a bike tour might be a way to kill two birds with one stone: have fun and get in shape. I was betting big and hoping high that bicycle touring would provide all the serendipity, exercise, and adventure I'd been missing out on for years. I wanted more life out of Life, and I thought a long bike ride would be the best way to get it.

Also, and perhaps most importantly, I rode to help process the grief I was facing with the recent loss of both parents. My father went first; he died of a FOX news overdose in 2013. My mom died less than a year later after an eleven-month long battle with ALS. Her death came suddenly, as far as I was concerned, and in the end, ALS robbed us all of a strong woman long before her time. The worst thing about how she went: she left us piece-by-piece, day-by-day, for nearly a year, and yet the whole time we knew she was still clear of mind and well aware what was happening to her. You could tell by her eyes that she had a lot of life left. Naturally, we all did what we could do to make her comfortable.

The ALS wrecking crew, assigned to the task of dismantling my mom piece by piece for unknown reasons, completed its ugly task on April 3rd, 2014.

I must be a bit of a momma's boy because I sure cried like a baby at her funeral after barely shedding a tear at my old man's. I surprised and humiliated myself the day we buried her by losing all composure in front of a couple of hundred people when trying to read a hastily written eulogy from the pulpit. Before the service I'd been so cavalier about things. Perhaps I was in denial when I told my brothers and sisters that I was going to put the "fun" back in "funeral." Yeah, right. I broke down and cried like a baby, drenching every word I uttered in tears. I stubbornly, stupidly, insisted on completing the eulogy even after my younger brother Matt rushed the pulpit and kindly offered to spell me at the task. I said no to the hook and finished my sad performance, determined to get through it at any cost. After it was over, I walked back to my pew and sat down. The church was quiet. I'd done something awkward. Normally I take pride in my ability to speak in public, but that time I had failed miserably in doing so. It was a humiliating performance, but there wasn't a damn thing I could do about it once it was over.

The reviews of my speaking performance came fast and furious. My sister-in-law wasted no time delivering her thoughts. Before I even left the church she suggested I "seek therapy immediately." She later recanted her statement, telling me she was just kidding, but her point was well taken. Therapy at that juncture wasn't a bad idea, perhaps, but thankfully, just after receiving her two thumbs down review, I received more comforting words from a brother-in-law who had suffered a similar loss of his own a couple of years prior. It made me feel better to learn that "There is no wrong way to grieve and everyone grieves differently."

At the luncheon reception after internment, a lifelong friend of my mother came up to me and said, "Don't feel at all embarrassed by your performance today, Tim. I'll never live to see it, but I would be proud if any one of my four boys cried as you did up there. It was a testament to your love for your mother. Any mother alive or dead would love to have what you gave your mom up there today." I thanked Mrs. McFadden. She made me feel a whole lot better about being the reigning Momma's Boy Champion.

With my mom so recently departed, my brothers and sisters and I recognized, chronologically speaking of course, that we were next up for the dirt nap. That little inconvenient factoid—knowing you're rounding your last turn on life's happy little carousel ride—can play with your head and force you to take stock in your life and get a good long look at how you spend the time.

Looking back on it, I see now how my cross-country bike trip was purposed by grief and initiated by a new and urgent sense of my own mortality. I reached a decision as a newly minted orphan that I may not have reached otherwise: come hell or high water, I was going on a bike trip.

Is anyone else up for a midlife crisis or a life transition?

After witnessing what ALS had done to my mom over the past year, I was in a lot of pain and the only way I thought I could expel the grief, hurt, and devastating sense of loss was through my legs. Hey, there is no wrong way to grieve, right? At that point, all I wanted to do was get on a bike and ride, ride, ride a never-ending road. "Life's a trip, enjoy the ride!" was a mantra of the 1960s that still rings true today. The older you get, the more you come to realize you only go around once.

They say, "Bike travel takes you further." I hoped my bike would take me away from all the pain I was feeling.

For me, the next order of business was to go—to actually go—on a long bicycle ride I'd once dreamed of doing as a kid and had long dismissed as pure folly once I grew past the age of twelve.

The day we buried my mom was the day I knew I *had to* follow through on a decades' long dream. I was going to take a bike clear across the U.S.

So, for all those reasons, I rode.

Chapter Three

RAMBO FOR NO REASON, I
FIND A BIKE BUDDY

Some people (like me, unfortunately) are full of unsolicited advice. When the word got 'round that I was thinking about taking a cross-country bike trip after my mom died, friends and family came a-running my way with their condolences about my mom's ALS diagnosis (and subsequent death) and their "What you should do's" about the trip.

The most memorable unsolicited advice I received prior to leaving for the ride was from a rather colorful buddy of mine who always considered himself an honorary member of Seal

Team Six, though he never spent as much as a single minute in the military. I jokingly nicknamed him 'Rambo for No Reason' because he had absolutely no reason whatsoever in the world to keep his hair jarhead short or to wear camouflage on weekends. A non-hunter, he drove around town in a camo-covered pickup truck that never left the pavement. Irony is everywhere: he stood out *because* he wore camouflage.

Rambo for No Reason usually ran Saturday morning errands in tactical gear and used military jargon ("Copy that," "Stay Frosty," and "What's your sit-rep?") whenever he could. He dressed for *Ser*bia, but lived in *Suburb*ia. One look at him and you'd imagine he'd be used to having his coffee black, but oh no, not Rambo for No Reason. He was a Venti Iced Skinny Hazelnut Macchiato, Sugar-Free Syrup kind of guy. Go figure.

"Dude," he said to me at a dinner party, "heard the news. Bike trip, huh? Sounds badass, man, I'd love to do that... Got a question for ya: are you packin' a nine to cover your six?"

Military lingo translation: Are you taking a nine-millimeter handgun along with you for protection? I replied, "No." His face got all squeezed up as if he'd just bitten into a lemon. He told me to "Cowboy the fuck up and get with the program."

"Dude," he urged, "you gotta be ready when the shit goes down. Seriously. You know, God made man, but Sam Colt made all men equal. Booyah!"

He followed up his "Booyah!" cheer with a chest bump and somehow managed not to spill a single drop of his martini. He took another swig from his shaken, not stirred big gulp and continued. "Shit, man, you're on the road, minding your own made in A-freaking-Merica goddamn-business, when some bad guy comes along and tries to take your wallet, your watch, or who knows? Maybe that particular bad guy is some sort of perv looking for some ass and he wants yours. I am talking man-on-man heavy spooning sick shit here, dude.

How you gonna defend yourself in that rather touchy situation, huh Ponyboy?"

(A quick aside: I was impressed with Rambo for No Reason's ability to reference a character from S. E. Hinton's book *The Outsiders.* I hadn't heard the nickname 'Ponyboy' since I'd read the book in eighth grade. In 1975.)

He continued. "So, whatcha gonna do, huh? Gonna give the bad guy your wallet? The watch? Gonna let him kiss you on your forehead and call you Carol? Hell the fuck no you ain't! I say just pop pop pop the motherfucker three times, tight cluster, center mass, no questions. And after the boom-boom stick goes off, you gotta ghost it outta there before the coffee-and-doughnuts crew shows up with their bullshit questions and their one-size-fits-all stainless steel bracelets."

I paused for a moment. Then I admitted that I was reluctant to kill.

He gently threw an arm around my shoulders in a conciliatory fashion as if I was actually Ponyboy at an important crossroads in my young adolescent life. I thought he was going to tell me to "Stay golden, Ponyboy."

But he didn't.

"No one *wants* to kill, man!" he reassured me.

He looked both ways and leaned in closer.

"No one wants to kill…*at first,*" he whispered. "Just get over it. Bitch up for Christ sakes. And after the shit goes down, Casper the fuck out of there pronto. And don't run. You gotta walk— or bike—away, I guess, in your case, so you don't attract any attention. Act *completely normal* and get on with your day like you are Mr. Happy Horseshit Wonderful out on a bike ride, enjoying your happy little ignorant life where everyone in your social set has straight teeth and granite kitchen countertops."

I looked at him. I was speechless.

He delivered every word he said in his next sentence with a poke of his finger on my chest, just above my sternum. "Your

legal name is actually 'Mr. Happy Horseshit Wonderful' if anyone asks. Got that, buddy? Take my advice."

Frankly, I was a little taken *aback* by his advice. He was talking
'tight clusters' and 'center mass' at an otherwise cordial social
gathering, insisting I "Bitch the hell up" (I still don't know what
that even means).

He turned away from me and mumbled quietly to himself
while he absentmindedly stirred his martini with an olive stuck
on the end of a toothpick. His martini glass was huge, roughly
the size and shape of a bright-yellow YIELD traffic sign; I imagined him getting his camo covered Super Duty Ford F-250 home
that night was going to involve some tree bumping along the way.

"A bicyclist...no one would suspect...freaking brilliant. No
self-respecting cop would ever chase down some spandex-clad
dude on a bike. A bicycle tourist is the perfect cover of all time."

He looked at me and said, "Shoot to kill, though, man, shoot
to kill. Anything short of that, you're a Democrat. No shit. I don't
know about you, Bike Boy, but I'd rather have twelve men judge
me than have six men carry me, if you know what I mean." He
pointed his index finger/pistol barrel at me and synchronized a
"Booyah!" with a thumb/hammer drop on his mimed gun.

I half-heartedly mimed right along with him and faked like
I'd caught one in the right shoulder. I waved a goodbye to him
and he made one of his many return trips to the bar.

Though I appreciated his concern for my safety, there was no
way I was going to carry a loaded handgun on a bike trip across
the country. I knew there was always a statistical chance that I'd
be confronted by a bunch of freaky forest folks trolling slowly
down blue highways in rusted pickups hunting for people with
higher IQs to eat, but the chances were so small that it wasn't
worth the worry or the weapon. I knew the best defense against
bad outcomes was having both a heightened sense of situational
awareness and a burning desire to stay clear of any trouble in
the first place. A pair of sharp eyes on the lookout and a pair of

strong legs ready to flee at a moment's notice had served me well at keeping trouble at bay.

What is even better, though, is having a *second pair of eyes* on the lookout.

Enter the Buddy System.

As much as I wanted a buddy to tag along with me on the ride, I was having a hell of a time trying to find someone, anyone, to join me. Most people I knew were tied up (or tied down, depending on how you look at it) with kids, careers, mortgages, aging parents, you name it. Life tends to prevent people from having any time off. I was having an especially tough time because my departure date was up in the air. Sure, the bike route itself was in set in stone (I had maps), so I knew where I was going, but I didn't know when I was going or when I'd be back. The start date and duration of the trip were uncertain, as I honestly had no idea how long it would take me to ride across the States. And I wasn't going anywhere near a starting line until after my mom died.

With so much uncertainty surrounding the trip, I had no takers for the second spot. So, as the spring of 2014 approached and as my mom declined more and more each day, I became more desperate to pedal away the growing sense of pain and loss. Even before she died I'd decided that when the time came, I was going to throw caution to the wind and head off alone if I had to. If I postponed the trip "until later when someone could join me," I'd never go.

Because I *had* to go and couldn't find someone to go with me, it was looking like I was going to go alone.

That is, until I met Dave Wilbur, a twenty-six-year-old Yale fine arts graduate student and landscape painter who just happened to be heading out west around the same time I was planning on going. What a coincidence we were "going to head west to do some riding sometime in the spring-ish." We met as buyer and seller on Craigslist when he answered my bike for sale ad. My

Raleigh Sojourn never really fit me well and I had a hankering for new bike anyway, so I posted it for sale.

Dave was the one and only person to answer my ad. We agreed to meet in the parking lot of the local train station. He stepped off the train and I showed him the bike.

While he looked the bike over, he gave me reasons for his interest in it: he needed a bike to ride through some of the national parks in the Pacific Northwest for the landscape research he had in mind. I could not believe my ears. Here was a guy heading to the same region of the country at roughly the same time I'd planned to. We spoke more: it turned out he was broke and I was desperate, so I make him an offer he couldn't refuse. I offered to cover his food and camping costs if he agreed to join me for the first, say, ten days or so of my trip. If he got himself out to Seattle, I'd rent a car and drive us both up to the trailhead in Anacortes, Washington, about hundred and ten miles north of Seattle on the coast. A couple of days later after some Google vetting done on both our parts, we came to an agreement. I'd pay his way and he'd make sure I didn't die on his watch. We were a go. Eileen was delighted: now she'd have someone "on site" to "help make the arrangements" if needed.

In addition to the food and camping fees, Dave agreed to give me a painting of my choosing sometime in the future. By supporting Dave I was finding a buddy *and* funding the arts. Win-win.

I did not know Dave well at all at first, but he seemed normal enough and he could certainly pull his own weight as an outdoorsman. What made him an especially strong candidate for the position (besides his pulse) was that Dave had through-hiked the Appalachian Trail (more commonly referred to as "the AT" in camping circles) in five and a half months. For those of you not familiar with that staggering feat, what Dave did was tantamount to winning the gold medal at the hiking Olympics. Anyone who had *walked* 2,168.1 miles through wilderness was jake in my book. I further came to learn that Dave's lifetime total of nights slept outdoors was somewhere north of 450. His mental toughness and camping experience quickly won him top spot (well, the only spot) on my buddy-system-candidate short list.

I was glad he accepted my invitation. Without Dave along at the start providing humor and sharing his camping, food preparation, and outdoors experience—and his Buddha-like sense of patience—I doubt I would have covered as much ground right out of the gate.

Mr. Inside had met Mr. Outside!

A friend of mine once told me, "The real heroes are the ones that stay home." I understood: just because I was the one riding didn't mean that I was alone in the effort. Eileen and our son George kept the home fires lit and the dog fed while I was away, and I remain forever grateful for their support.

Were it not for their understanding, encouragement, and blessing, the following story would never have happened.

Chapter Four

SEE SEATTLE AND MEET THE MONA DORIS

Five weeks after my mom died I found myself forty thousand feet in the air going 550 knots per hour en route to an airport to meet a bearded dude I barely knew. While sitting seven and a half miles above the earth, I was struck by the contrast of how much technology and how little time it took me to reach the west coast and how little technology and how much time it would take me to reach Maine. Jet engines, fuel, pilots, co-pilots, radios, runways, security checks, taxis, and satellite navigation on the way out, two legs and one bike on the way back. Five hours after catching an early morning flight out of Boston's Logan airport, I arrived in Seattle in time for lunch. Modern technology and aviation are amazing things.

But then again, so is a seventy-two day bike ride.

The first thing I did after stepping off the plane in Seattle was get a cup of coffee. Not surprisingly, coffee was readily available at the Seattle airport, so I stepped right up to the first counter I saw and asked for a small black. I noticed the young woman who took my order had a nametag that read "Doris." She did not respond to my "Good morning" greeting, so I left it at that—I learned long ago no matter how many "good morning" pulls on the old conversation-starter cord I try, some people are as reluctant to start as a rusty lawn mower.

I noticed Doris had a block-letter tattoo on her forearm that read "Lisa." That tattoo was hard to miss; the block letters were an inch high. While she poured my cup of the hot stuff, I wondered if Doris had the wrong nametag or if there had been a terrible mistake made at the tattoo parlor. Or neither: maybe her name was actually Doris and maybe she thought highly of a woman named Lisa. Who knew?

Well, I had to know, so I asked her.

Her response? "Saving money for the portrait and the *MONA* part. I love Da Vinci's work, and last time I saw that painting with my own eyes, my nana was still alive, standing right there next to me at the Louvre. I miss my nana each and every day."

Boom. There you have it. File that under: *You won't know if you don't ask.* It turned out that reticent Doris had a story literally up her sleeve. All I had to do was ask her about it. Doris was not a chatty young woman by any means, but she delivered information without wasting a word. I admired her for that and wished I could say the same about myself. Doris was also darn good at her job—she delivered a serious cup of wake-me-the-fuck-up coffee that kept my eyes from blinking for the next fourteen hours straight. Grateful for her help, I tipped her enough money to pay for all the ink in the *MONA* part.

Wow, after just one sip of her kiosk kickass, I felt like crowd-sourcing startup funding for the Next Big Thing. I banged out some disruptive, change-the-world computer code right then and there on my coffee napkin. I wanted to grow a close-cropped beard and wear torn jeans and a loose-fitting black hoodie sweatshirt and run around the food court manically waving my napkin around and shout at the top of my lungs, "This changes everything! *This changes everything!*"

But after taking a good look around me, I noticed there were at least forty hipsters doing exactly that, so I thought the better of it. I'd keep my world changing shit on the down low.

With an overnight bag slung over my shoulder and a cup of hot coffee carried with the same caution as a full glass of nitro glycerin, I managed to dodge my way past all the slow walkers and airport gate dashers and made it to the car rental counter unscathed, with every drop of hot coffee accounted for.

Dave was there and ready to go.

"Hey man."

"Hey."

Off we went.

A short few hours later, we were in Anacortes, Washington, assembling our bikes in our room at the Majestic Inn and Spa, which wasn't exactly majestic and wasn't exactly a spa. The view out the window of our room was also non-majestic; a dirty parking lot and brick wall stared back at us with a bland indifference. Majestic? My ass. And the spa? The spa door had a sign taped to it that read, "SPA BROKEN."

How do you break a spa?

The place wasn't a palace, but it didn't matter; it was close to the trailhead and to a couple of bike shops, so it fit the bill nicely. We spent that afternoon on last-minute preparations, one of which for me was securing a seat post clamp. Mine had somehow disappeared during transit and without it I was stuck. Were it not for a local bike shop that just happened to have a properly sized seat clamp in an odd's and ends box, our departure would have been put on hold until one could be sourced. After I secured that one small part, my bike was ready to roll.

New to bike travel, I had made the mistake of over packing. It turned out that most of what I had shipped out had to be returned home, as there was no way my bike or my legs could handle it all. So, as Dave and I assembled our bikes and sorted the gear, I got busy creating two different piles, a SHIP HOME pile and a TAKE WITH pile.

The fact that bicycles demand minimalism was not news to Dave, the more experienced outdoorsman. He'd brought a more reasonable and appropriate amount of gear. With fewer things to load on his bike, he was all packed up hours before I was. While I sorted, Dave propped himself up against his bed's headboard and kept himself busy by studying the maps. I noticed him steal a furtive glance or two my way over the course of that afternoon: I think he was assessing my mechanical and organizational skills.

I don't think I wowed him. He managed to keep his opinions to himself, but from the looks of it, he wasn't impressed. I knew I'd made the over packing mistake, but I was working hard at a fix.

Somehow Dave managed to stifle a laugh or two at the newbie in front of him until I busted out the frying pan and stood over the SHIP HOME and the TAKE WITH piles pondering my next move. I stood there for a full minute internally debating the pros and cons of taking a frying pan. Its fate and my lack of understanding of the weight/worth principle were on full display.

For Dave, the frying pan was the clincher.

"Dude, a frying pan? Are you seriously considering bringing a frying pan on a bike trip?"

"Why not? It's a camp pan," I explained. I turned around to look at him and morphed into an infomercial salesman and defended my pan purchase. I put on a frying-pan show-and-tell: "It's light. It has a folding insulated handle that cuts its packing profile almost in half, making storage a breeze. You have to admit, that's handy, yes? Also, this pan is both aluminum and nonstick...you know, for easy cleaning and weight savings while on the trail. That is very important when water is dear."

I tapped my finger against it, and it rang like a dull aluminum gong.

Dave said nothing.

I shrugged my shoulders in defeat, and casted my infomercial salesman enthusiasm aside. "The guy at the camp store said he had one and took it camping all the time."

"Yeah, he had *one left* to sell to some yahoo who just happened to be you. Dude, eighty-six the pan, you'll never use it."

Swallowing my pride, I reluctantly went with Mr. Outside's advice and dropped my awesome, brand-new, nonstick aluminum frying pan with the collapsible handle onto the growing SHIP HOME pile.

I had to save face somehow though, so naturally I went with the old wisdom of *an extra pair of socks is always a good idea.* Mr. Outside could not argue with that one.

"Screw it, I'm bringing extra socks, then, " I declared.

"Yeah, sound packing move, Malibu Barbie," Dave replied, not looking up from his map.

I was unsure how to respond to the 'Malibu Barbie' reference. Maybe his comment was some sort of an AT hiking trail put-down. I chuckled and let it go. Well, I sort of let it go. I promised myself if I ever cooked bacon in that pan when Dave was around, he wasn't going to get any.

Malibu Barbie, my ass...I'm way more G. I. Joe than Malibu Barbie.

Anybody knows that.

One of the last things I did the night before we left the Majestic Inn and Spa was send an open social-media invite to any and all who'd might be interested in joining me for all or part of the way across. I emphasized people wouldn't actually need a bike to join me—they could just rent a big wide van and drive in front of me to block the wind.

Chapter Five

THE STARTING GUN GOES OFF, WE MEET SOME GUY

Departure day dawned and Dave and I were not up, not packed, and not ready to go by the time the clock struck our soft target departure time of 7:00 a.m. We also missed the 8:00 a.m. start time by a country mile. Then we missed the "nine o'clock 'fur shur' this time" start time.

It was no big deal, really. Neither one of us was in any huge rush to leave the Inn and hit the road; the weather was iffy and overcast and both of us were pretty beat from the previous day's cross country plane rides and otherwise long drive and bike packing and assembly efforts. Besides, we had plenty of time to grab breakfast and cover the 35.5-mile shakeout tour over flat terrain that made up our first day's ride from Anacortes, Washington to Sedro-Woolley, Washington.

And, of course, this was a bike *trip*, not a bike *race*.

It was clear to me from the very first that I'd been lucky to have Dave along. His easy-going demeanor and his company were both welcome over the course of the miles we rode together. Having a buddy like that along for the ride made the tough parts go more ease-y and the easy parts go more please-y. Dave had all the characteristics of a good traveling companion: the dude was value-add.

Towards ten o'clock we were finally ready to get going. We headed to the front desk to drop off the room key and settle up with the Majestic Inn and Spa. I noticed the clock on the wall read 9:40 a.m. and I pointed that out to Big Dave.

"Not too bad, huh, Big Dave? We are, like, twenty minutes early for our ten o'clock start time. Man, we are crushing this shit."

Dave shrugged his shoulders in a laid-back way. "Chillin' it while killin' it." We soft fist-punched and executed a perfect hand explosion takeaway. As dorky as we were, Dave and I were already in bike sync. That is to say, we had successfully regressed back to our twelve year old selves and had a solid trail vibe going, evidenced by the fact that we'd both laughed at the "Pull my finger" fart joke and neither one of us was troubled by day one's late start.

I noticed the desk clerk snarl as she looked out the front window of the not-so-majestic Majestic.

"Typical," she seethed. "Damn clouds come in all the damn time. It was sunny earlier, and now this." She pointed accusingly at the weather outside as if Mother Nature herself had done something wrong by bringing life-giving moisture to the area.

"Well, here's hoping those clouds leave just as quickly as they arrived," I said in a futile attempt to bring a little sunshine into her miserable little front desk world.

She rolled her eyes and would have none of it. "There is no chance in hell of *that* ever happening."

She thanked me for dropping off the room key, adding that she hoped we'd enjoyed our stay. "Management communicates its sincere apologizes for the busted spa. We hope you enjoyed your stay and that we will see you again real soon. Have a good day," was the last thing she said, without a modicum of either sincerity or empathy in her voice.

With her duty-bound apology and half-hearted farewell complete, she pointed her doughy face back into the steady glow of her computer screen. It gave her pouty mug a bluish hue. I noticed that the potted plant next to her was brown and dead.

A minute later, Dave and I were out the door, on our bikes, and headed for the Pacific.

The first order of business was to get to the trailhead—the Anacortes Ferry Terminal—and dip my rear tire into the Pacific Ocean. When I suggested to Dave that he dip his back tire in, too, he declined.

"Dude, back tire dipping's for through riders only. I'm just heading to East Glacier then south to Yellowstone. Once you dip, it's a cross country trip."

That being the case, my bike party had to get started off on the right foot by giving my rear tire a baptism of sorts, one that marked the ceremonial and celebratory beginning of a cross-country bike trip four decades in the dreaming. Back tire in the Pacific, front tire in the Atlantic. Dem's dah rules: that's the only way you know you rode the whole way.

So, on a chilly and overcast day, on a rocky beach in Anacortes, Washington, we documented the inauspicious moment with a quickly captured cell-phone photo. It wasn't the best weather; rain threatened and a raw wind blew a steady ten knots. A dog barked in the distance while seagulls scavenged neck deep in greasy fast food containers that had been flushed out of open dumpsters by chilly gusts. The whole place had a doom-laden, industrial-wasteland sort of feel to it. It was not how I'd pictured the start of my bike tour. The tired, low-lying, rusty commercial buildings spotting the shore didn't serve to brighten the scene.

But who cared? I was at the start of something bigger than that day's forecast. There I was at the ferry terminal in Anacortes, Washington, where the Northern Tier bicycle route begins (or ends, depending on which direction you are going). None of the early-season tourists and commuters boarding the Super-class ferry *MV Elwha* took any notice of the two men making their way down to the water, one with a bike, the other with a phone. The ferry's fog horn blasted a long '*boo who*' as it prepared to leave the dock, providing a gloomy narrative to the whole scene that, along with the pall of leaden skies, seemed pretty damn bleak and dreary to me. I did not realize it at the time, but that mournful sound of the ship's horn was my starting gun going off and the very beginning of a long ride that would take me to places not found on any map, places I could leave pieces of my grief behind and places I would experience the generosity and kind-heartedness of complete strangers.

With my back tire in the drink, I turned and asked Dave if he was ready to document a piece of bicycle-touring history.

"I'll bet you feel like the photographer who documented the Wright brothers at Kitty Hawk when they became the first humans ever to fly in a controlled aircraft, right Dave?"

"Yeah, it's crazy man. Smile Asshole—I mean, smile, Orville."

I cracked a smile, threw Dave the bird, and put my hand back on the bike seat just before he took the picture. With that, our shoreline business was complete. I stumbled a few times as I pushed my fully loaded bike over wet stones and clawed my way back up over the loose rocky beach to the pavement. By the time I returned to level hardtop, I had broken into my first flop sweat of the ride and I hadn't even pedaled once. I was at sea level standing in a cold breeze and sweating like I'd just stepped out of a sauna. I did not want to think about what pushing a bike up a hill at altitude would be like.

With the soles of my shoes a little sandy, I stepped from beach to pavement and shook hands with Dave. I mounted up and began rolling.

We were off!

The weather got better fast. A mere four miles into the trip we slipped out from beneath the cloud cover that stubbornly hung over the front desk clerk at the Majestic Inn and Spa. Our first lesson in bike travel was learned: you never know what's coming around the next turn, weather-wise or anything else wise. Bike touring is a little like Life itself in that regard, you gotta keep going 'cause you never know what's coming. Things change. (Hey, I know this is getting deep after a measly four miles in, but I didn't come up with that rather obvious realization until a few thousand miles later.)

That very morning both Dave and I were happy to discover an unexpected added bonus that further eased our introduction into bicycle touring: not only were we riding into sunshine and perfect temperatures, but also we were effortlessly navigating along a plethora of protected sidewalks and bikeways, part of a network of bike paths that made the majority of the first day's route a traffic-free jaunt. We even managed to catch up to a couple of other touring cyclists we'd spotted ahead of us. They were a friendly pair and invited us to join them for lunch down by the water at the Bay View State Park. We accepted.

Their names were Dan and Guy, and they were both heading north toward the Canadian border for a few days of bike camping. Experienced riders eager to share their knowledge of the area, they provided us with invaluable riding tips gleaned from dozens of their own bike tours over the years (watch your water, fix flats fast, stay alert), bike tours that took them mostly in and around northwestern Washington State.

The duo was affable until we told them we were heading east-bound on the Northern Tier. At that news, their mood went from lighthearted to cautionary. It was like watching two happy-go-lucky clowns turn into somber homicide detectives investigating a particularly gruesome crime scene. They told us in no uncer-tain terms that we needed to secure three days' supply of food and water in Marblemount, WA, prior to attempting to climb Washington Pass, eighty miles to the east of where we stood.

"Marblemount is your last possible stop for supplies," Guy warned. "No services after Marblemount. If you don't have enough food and water when you leave Marblemount, you'll be asking for trouble. You'll find yourselves mighty hungry and possibly tragically thirsty up near the top. And, if things go side-ways anywhere near the summit of Washington Pass with a fall or a broken bike chain or some other unforeseen mechanical or physical mishap or, worse yet, catastrophe, you'll get to see firsthand how quickly trouble finds you."

"If you get stuck up in them hills for any reason at all this time of year," he continued, "you'll be fucked."

"Is that a bike term?" I inquired with a smile.

Guy would have none of my attempt to lighten the mood. That was the first time I got the hairy eye from a guy named Guy. So funny I thought I'd die...

Guy was looking over the map that Dave had spread out on a picnic table for discussion and reference purposes. He looked like some battle-hardened WWII four-star general socked away in a smoke-filled underground bunker, analyzing death-toll es-timates and best routes over varying terrain as bombs exploded above him. The problem was that we were not looking at a map of Normandy in early June 1944; we were looking at the Sedro-Woolley, Washington environs in mid-May of 2014. I imagined there weren't any Nazis for us to worry about where we were go-ing. Full of bravado, Guy seemed to savor his self-appointed role as the Cyclist-in-Chief, sternly warning touring neophytes like us about the dangers of ill preparedness. Personally, I thought Guy was overdoing it a bit with his dire warnings of impending death, but he was right to urge caution when attempting any summit.

There's trouble in them thar hills!

"No services from here," Guy said, pointing to map panels and dragging his finger across it, "to here." It was as if he were drawing an invisible line through a highly militarized zone full of trigger-happy snipers in ghillie suits. "That's about sixty or sev-enty nasty miles of nothing but up," he said.

Dan joined in for the second part of the sentence, "...noth-ing but up."

"And the downhill, Guy," said his sidekick Dan excitedly, jumping up and down like a kid anxious to go pee or to hear the end of a scary story. "Tell them about the downhill, Guy!"

"Yes, thank you, Dan, good point," Guy replied in measured tone, full of self-importance.

"You two," he continued, disco pointing at us with both in-dex fingers through his bike gloves. "Just because you summit Washington Pass don't mean your problems are over. What goes up must come down."

Who *was* this guy, Guy, this Knower of All Things, this Captain of the Obvious?

He continued, "After you reach the top, you gotta safely make your way down to a campsite on the other side, and that ain't no easy thing to do. You got three choices, three campsites located here, here, and here." Guy steadied his reading glasses on his nose with his left hand as he punched his right index fin-ger down dramatically onto the map with each 'here' for extra emphasis.

"Don't go for door number one. The first option on the other side, here, the one closest to the summit, is still too damn high and too damn cold at night. Go to the second, or ideally, the third campsite on the far side, lower down the mountain, that is, if you have enough strength left to reach it. Reaching that second campsite should give you half a chance, anyway."

"Half a chance?" I thought. "Half a chance at what? Living through the night?"

Guy ignored my telepathically delivered question, my tilted head, and my quizzical look. He continued lecturing, allowing his bike wisdom to flow as freely as the tidewaters of Padilla Bay located only a few yards away from where we stood.

"But if it gets too late and you find yourself running short of daylight and/or water, don't try for the third campsite. You boys would be surprised to the point of shitting your asses in two just how fast it gets dark and cold up in them mountains once Mother Sun goes down."

A moment of silence followed. No one dared speak. It was as if Guy were telling us all a ghost story and we were at the edge of our seats, eagerly anticipating his next utterance. Would the inexperienced cyclists make it to the other side of Washington Pass? Would they? could they? survive alone, stranded in the darkness, on the very hill that had killed so many? Or would our two bike touring heroes succumb to the cold, cruel elements, their remains never found, perhaps cast asunder by the scavengers like bear, wildcat, fox and vulture known to populate the area? Join us next week for the thrilling conclusion of *Bike Hard, Take Chances*.

Come on! Guy didn't scare me—he *confused* me. How in tar nation can you shit your ass in two? Hasn't everyone's ass already been cleft right down the middle by the Almighty hand of God? And what's with the "Mother Sun" reference? Who made the gigantic thermonuclear furnace in the center of our solar system female?

But Guy was on an unstoppable roll. He turned to Dave; it was time for a pop quiz.

"What insulation level is your bag?" he asked.

Mr. Outside, my boy Dave, knew the answer and came right out with it. "I got a negative five, and my buddy Tim here's got a twenty." How Dave knew I had "a twenty" was as beyond me as what "a twenty" meant.

Guy looked us both over. He pointed to Dave with grudging respect. "You'll be OK." Then he pointed straight at me, and his forehead crinkled up just a bit with disdain. "You'll be fucked."

Great. Just great. We'd stopped for lunch on the very first day of a wicked long bike trip I'd waited my whole life for, and not even four hours into our ride, I was informed that I was likely to die of exposure while *in my sleeping bag*. By Guy's estimate, I had a week to live, maybe less. I wondered if I should fill out my own toe tag just to save the recovery team some time. Why didn't my sleeping bag come with a free toe tag and a Sharpie?

Guy continued. "So don't neither of you boys get caught at night up in them hills anywhere near the summit of Washington Pass, or rest assured, you'll be fucked. Shit hits the fan up there, and you boys might want to consider getting two in a bag. For warmth."

Full stop. "*Two in a bag?*" I am sorry, but it would have to be cold enough to freeze a housecat solid before I would even consider pulling some survival Hot Pocket move with a dude.

Oh, but it wouldn't come to that. Dave and I would be fine. I remained confident we'd be able to manage any adversity we were faced with because this was a *bike tour*, not a *bike trek*. We were not attempting to bike across the Bering Strait or anything; we were just pedaling the Northern Tier Route for God's sake. Tons of people do it every year and this was the first I'd ever heard of the "two in a bag" survival technique. Worse case scenario, if I got too cold, I would ride my way back to civilization and to all the warmth it provides.

Personally, I thought Guy was overdoing it with his "you'll be fucked" comment. Dave, however, took Guy more seriously and made a mental note to load up with a three-day supply of food and water prior to our summit attempt of Washington Pass.

I finished the rest of my peanut-butter-and-jelly sandwich and ambled over to the water to stretch my legs and skip some rocks, weary of the doom and gloom scenarios Guy was dishing out. I looked back at the Council of Three. They were standing shoulder to shoulder, hunched over the picnic table, nodding their heads, looking down at the map and pointing to things like a team of surgeons hard at work, trying to separate the conjoined triplets of Time, Distance and Road Conditions.

After lunch we parted ways with Dan and Guy. Dave and I continued riding, stopping sporadically to rest, snack, and make minor adjustments to our bikes. I had no idea how the thirty-five and a half miles would wear on me, and I was growing frustrated, as neither my body nor my bike had lived up to my expectations. I grudgingly admitted to myself that I should have probably taken more than one spin class to physically prepare for the trip. In addition, I realized that a more properly fitted bike would have been a better purchase decision as my neck, shoulders, back, and arms bore the brunt of an ill-matched frame geometry. The top bar on my bike (from the base of the seat post to the top of the front fork) was a little too long for me, so I had to lean a little too forward than comfortable to reach the handlebars. That took me out of my optimal, more upright riding position. My arms bore more of my upper body weight than they would have on a properly fitted bike. I was learning a hard lesson: denial and hasty purchasing decisions are both things you eventually pay for.

In addition—and perhaps more maddening—I realized that I should have done some break-in rides prior to flying out west. My bike shimmied violently anytime I went faster than seventeen miles per hour. I desperately hoped pilot error was to blame and not some structural imperfection of the bike itself. In an attempt to improve stability at speed, I'd played around with the weight distribution by shifting things around in my bags. I end-lessly fussed with the contents of my saddlebags and grew quite frustrated with the stubborn shimmy. Eventually, I arrived at a manageable solution: I placed the heavier items at the bottom of the panniers and closer to the ground to lower the overall center of gravity and put sixty percent of the load over the front wheel, the rest in back. It took many days to come up with that solution, days filled with trial and error which included multiple roadside stops to unpack, redistribute, and repack all my gear. What a pain. So much for my fancy, pretty red bike. Dave played Bike Buddha the whole time and waited patiently as Malibu Barbie shifted things around in an increasingly manic search for en-*bike*-enment (that's enlightenment, but on a bike).

It was not the end of the world, but the first day's ride took longer than we thought it would. My multiple stops and weight redistribution efforts contributed significantly to our very late afternoon arrival in Sedro-Woolley, Washington.

By the time we got there, Dave and I were in search of two different things: he was in search of a campsite, whereas I was in search of a motel. There was no way on God's green earth I was going to camp that night; I was flat-out bushed and in dire need of a mattress. Similar to the way many arguments are settled in the US justice system, our difference of opinion on the camp-site/motel issue was resolved without having to go to trial. The outcome was determined by who had more money. In the case of *T. Fahey v. D. Wilbur,* I had the wallet, so I won the argument. Precedent had been set: Dave's search for a campsite came to a screeching halt the second I spotted a motel vacancy sign in Sedro-Woolley.

"Home sweet home," I yelled up to Dave, who was riding ahead of me, as usual. I broke trail etiquette and a buddy-system best-practices rule by turning off route without first making cer-tain Dave had my twenty. ("Twenty" is Rambo for No Reason-speak for "*location.*")

I rolled into the motel parking lot and shot straight over to the office manager's door. It was only after I dismounted and propped the bike up against the outside wall that I checked around to look for Dave. I found him on my first visual sweep of the area. He was about a hundred feet away across the street, straddling his bike, palms to the sky, shoulders shrugged—a five-foot-nine-inch-tall bearded human question mark wearing black adult diapers, gloves with no fingers, and a bike helmet.

Pointing to the motel, I offered, "Pull an Appalachian camping move if you want, but I'm staying here," pointing to the building that would be my home for one night. "Thirty-five and a half miles…I'm done." I signaled *safe* like a baseball umpire would.

Dave shook his head in disappointment and reluctantly joined me at the front door of the motel.

"You're such a motel pussy."

"Call me what you want, but I'm Mattress Man tonight, pure and simple."

"OK, I get it, but you are still a motel pussy."

He leaned his bike up next to mine against the building. Moments later, my wallet had less money in it, but I had an entirely platonic motel ménage à trois all set up and ready to go. It was going to be a hot shower, a soft mattress, et moi. I was tired and looking forward to spending tons of time with both.

After thirty-five and a half miles of stops and starts, I was hoping for something better than the view I got out the motel window. A pileup of old couches sat next to a pool one fifth filled with decomposing leaves and browned rainwater. After all that riding, that's the view we got in Sedro-Woolley, Washington. Sweet. Day one's mileage was in the books, and the first panel of the first of a dozen map sections had been fully traversed. We were on the second panel. Progress was being made, but at what cost? It was a Pyrrhic victory: I was wiped out.

I tossed my stuff on my bed, grabbed a shower, and got dressed in the only street clothes I had. The hot shower made me feel better, but I was still exhausted. Dave was up next for the shower, so I stepped outside into the sunlight while he did his thing. I sat down on the concrete path that led to the pool area and basked in the warmth of the late afternoon sun.

It felt good just to sit there.

I gave in to a wave of exhaustion and spread out flat on the sundrenched cement, and didn't move a muscle for the better part of an hour. I could feel gravity pull me into the walkway as if I weighed five hundred pounds and had no internal skeletal structure. It felt like I was pulling Gees just lying there. The weight of my body pressed into the warm cement while I slowly deflated and pancaked onto it. I got a sense of how a balloon felt after all the air was let out of it. In all my life I had not felt that tired while awake. It was the first time I experienced the nearly overpowering and strangely satisfying wave of exhaustion that comes after a long ride.

After lying motionless as a cemetery resident for some time, I saw Dave step out of the room and into the sunlight. And that, my friends, is the difference between being in your twenties and being in your fifties: Dave was ambulatory after a thirty-five mile ride, I was not. Sprawled flat on a patch of concrete that felt like a bed of feathers, I was down for the count and stuck to that pavement like a magnet stuck to a piece of steel.

Dave was on the phone with his girlfriend, Heather. A word or two of his phone conversation may have made it to my ears, but my brain hadn't the strength to process sound at that point. When I wasn't dozing, I was staring straight up into a deep blue sky streaked with contrails of the jets flying high above me, pointing their way toward landing strips or the next vector points in their trips to Elsewhere.

Dave blocked the sun intermittently as he absentmindedly walked about in circles between the sun and me. He kicked my foot. "Hey, dead dude, Heather says 'hey'."

"Say 'Hey' right back at her," I replied unenthusiastically and in a tired voice. "Man, I don't even know how you can walk at a time like this. Thirty-five miles. I am wiped out."

Dave replied, "Come on, Malibu. We'd better start thinking about getting some dinner."

"Or what?" I asked.

"Or you can die right there."

"I'd die in a Zen state, at least," I said. "Everything is fine, except I can't move. I'm happy...nothing hurts, but I cannot move." My eyes were closed. The sun felt warm on my face when Dave wasn't blocking it.

He laughed. "Come on man, you'll get hungry soon. You'll want to eat before you get hungry, believe me."

I went with the wisdom Dave had accumulated from his experiences hiking the AT and peeled my sorry self off the ground. I rolled over and propped myself up on one elbow. I rested in that position for a minute or two while I mustered the strength for my next effort to lift myself up off the ground. My heart had to get used to pumping blood to eyes, ears, head, and shoulders again while I was in my on-one-elbow resting position. I finally rolled over and put both palms on the ground and, in a pushup motion, stood up.

We went out to grab some food at the Forgettable Restaurant, where a forgettable waiter served us forgettable food. I had the "Give me a second and it will come to me" appetizer and the "I completely forgot" entrée for dinner, followed by "I have no idea what I just ate" for dessert. Dave had been right: a few minutes before the food arrived at the table, I had grown uncomfortably hungry. My body required fuel, and as exhausted as I was, I ate like a contestant at a competitive eating event as soon as the food got within reach.

Dave just laughed as I shot up sparks with my knife and fork.

"Been there, buddy" was all he said.

We returned to the room with our bellies full and I was fast asleep before my head hit the pillow. The muscles that had kept my eyelids open through dinner tossed in the towel sometime after I stepped into the room and sometime prior to the time my feet left the floor.

Our first full day of riding was complete.

The following morning—Saturday, May 17—sunlight splashed in through the sliding glass doors and onto my face. Unable to ignore the incessant shine of sunlight any longer, my eyes popped open to a new day.

The first thought that came to mind was that I was alive. The second thing I became aware of was that some shirtless dude with a big-ass beard was walking around my motel room in bike shorts with a cell phone pressed to his ear. The third thing that happened was that I remembered I was on a bike trip and the guy walking around was a friend, not a foe.

Dave spoke into his phone. "Yeah, he's still asleep. Either that or he's dead. I figured the sound of me packing up for the ride today would wake him up, but nothing has moved on that side of the room since last night when we got back from dinner. What do you call that sleeping disease? ...Yeah, Tim might have that...I'll give him a few minutes before I throw his tent at him, the one he didn't use last night because he insisted we go for the motel option...Yes, I did call him a motel pussy...Well, he deserved it...Oh, did I tell you about the frying pan yet? Tim was going to bring a fucking *frying pan* on a bike trip... Yeah, I know, right? What are we, on a cattle drive with John Wayne? Do we cook beans and bacon over an open fire? Right? Hey, what time is it? ...Really? Is that your time or my time? OK, gotta go. Gotta get breakfast going and hit the road. I'll talk to you later, Sweetie. Bye."

Dave tossed his cell phone on his bed and found a T-shirt.

"I'm awake," I said.

"Good morning, Sunshine. Heather says 'hey' again."

"Hey back. What time is it?"

"Half past butt crack. Let's get some breakfast and do this thing."

"OK, OK, fine," I said, adding, "And by the way, I loved that frying pan more than Life itself. I never should have mailed it back."

"Come on Malibu, let's get going."

I got out of bed and followed what would become a daily routine: I took two of the little blue pills that make bike travel possible for the over fifty set and went for coffee.

"Viagra?" Dave would usually ask when I popped those blue pills.

"No, wiseass," I'd respond. "Aleve."

Anti-inflammatory naproxen sodium capsules kept the wheels turning in my world all the way across the country. Without them, my late middle-aged body and pre-existing chronic lower backache would have barked all the louder and the longer and slowed my snail-like progress all the more. Reducing inflammation and pain were two crucial things for me to be able do in order to continue riding. So, as a preventative measure, I usually fed my tired, sore neck, back, legs, and arms some blue in the morning and I always fed my grey matter some black. Black coffee and blue pills: if you are over fifty and riding your ass off every day, it's what's for breakfast.

It took a while to get breakfast, change into riding gear, and lube up with sunscreen and butt butter (more on that chafe preventer later). The combination of the previous day's ride on an ill-fitted bike and the previous night's sleep on a mattress built by a band of angry sadists aggravated my lower back pain to new levels. Throughout the morning Dave had continued to wait patiently for me to get it all together. His bike was packed up and ready to go by the time I first put my feet on the floor. Dave had skills: he was always ready to ride long before I was, but I never heard him complain once about my slow-motion mornings.

We eventually got going, and the creaking and cracking sounds my body made actually stopped after the first five or six miles. My leg muscles, tight and sore with lingering lactic acid residue from the previous day's pedaling efforts, flushed themselves out after a while, and I felt biker strong enough to continue to ride throughout the second day. It didn't look like the shimmying problem was going to be much of an issue, as seventeen miles per hour was not likely to register on my speedometer at anytime soon. At that point, the chances of me going seventeen miles an hour were slim to none.

Fast forward to the end of the second day: In a stunning reversal, Dave won the camping argument (a case fait accompli, as there were no motels available), and I found myself sitting on a tree trunk, my first of many campfire chairs over the next few weeks. The sun was low in the sky, and I was waiting for my dinner water to boil. Unbelievably to me, we'd ridden a full five miles further on the second day than we had on the first. We'd biked along flat terrain and had gotten that much closer to the Rockies.

We were officially camping. I had my tent, sleeping bag, sleeping pad, and rain cover all set up before dinner. All I had to do at that point was unzip and climb in. While waiting for my dinner to cool down a bit, I reflected on the fact I'd never in my life pedaled seventy-six miles in the span of forty-eight hours before. I expected to beat that two-day total sometime over the course of the coming weeks, as I became a stronger and more experienced rider. I was proud of myself and a little amazed at how far wiggling my femurs for a few hours a day could get me. I may even have been worthy of a high five from Mike the Bike and the Minivan Mommas at that point and wondered if they'd think I was still "silly" after learning about my daunting two day mileage total. Mike the Bike might still think I was not ready to drive a car or operate any heavy equipment, but I was feeling pretty confident after riding seventy-five miles in two days' time.

After polishing off a delicious just-add-water meal, I rinsed my dish out with canteen water. A sharp eye was kept out for the bears that were undoubtedly drawn to our campsite by the fetching scent of my yummy dinner. I hadn't seen any sign of a bear yet, but I was certain they were out there, somewhere, just waiting for a chance to attack.

After Dave finished his dinner, he got up and walked over to the only other campers at the campground. A friendly Canadian couple, Romeo and Louise, were staying in a rather sizable old Airstream camper that looked like the Taj Mahal to me. We accepted their kind invitation to join them around their campfire for a beer. We sat and chatted for a bit, each of us with a bottle of beer in our hands, hands that had been holding onto handlebars for the better part of two days. Over the course of our conversation, the sun set, the wind picked up, and the temperature dropped, yet I remained reluctant to hit the sack; I didn't want to be defenseless in a tent should a bear stop by. Personally, if I were a bear, I'd see every tent as a rip-stop nylon wrapped 98.6-degree ready-to-eat meal of thigh, breast, arms, and brains that tasted like chicken, or maybe pork. I'll never know.

The time came to leave. I thanked Romeo for the beer and left the comfort of their campfire's warm exhale and used the dancing shadows of the firelight to help navigate my way through the chilly darkness to my nylon cocoon. I removed my shoes, unzipped the tent, turned around, got low, and dropped into my tent butt first so as not to drag any dirt into the tent with me—a cool AT tent move Dave had suggested. He also suggested being quick with the zipper in order to prevent bugs from gaining accesses into the inner sanctum. The fifteen-knot winds had grounded the bugs: I imagined all the bugs in the area were holding onto tree branches and leaves with their sticky little bug feet so as not to blow away.

I settled into my sleeping bag for the night and thought back to the first time I'd ever slept in a tent. I was a kid back in the late 1960s when my parents let my brothers and me sleep out in the backyard in Belmont, Massachusetts after warning us to watch out for the killer grizzly bears some neighbors had just called to warn him about. Of course we kids didn't know there hadn't been a bear sighting in suburban Boston since the Revolutionary War. We were all under ten years old at the time and excited to camp "in the wild" right there next to Route 2, the six-lane highway that abutted our property.

The complete lack of bears in the area didn't stop my dad from sneaking outside about fifteen minutes after saying goodnight. He snuck up to the tent and growled like a bear to scare the crap out of all of us. Screams and giggles erupted from inside that tent and they continued long after the first "bear growl" was heard. I hadn't thought about my first backyard camping trip in years, and the memory of it brought a smile to my face. Holy smokes, that was a thousand years ago now.

With the wind blowing and the night chill settling in, I thought the ground seemed harder, less welcoming, than I'd remembered it.

"Sleep well Mom and Dad," I said for no reason that I could think of and rolled over on my side and fell asleep.

As the waters of the Skagit River gurgled and shushed by, my tent fluttered in the wind. I knew just such a soundscape would provide ideal cover for an approaching man-eating grizzly. With a sleeping bag preventing me from executing my best Kung Fu moves and with a pair of arms that would finish third place at a grade school arm wrestling tournament, I knew any attempt at self-defense on my part would be fruitless against a super predator like a grizzly bear. No matter. I went to sleep comfortable in the knowledge that I'd done an extra good job of cleaning my dinner plate and that the actual number of bear versus human confrontations was low. Not absolute zero, mind you, but low.

Things turned out fine. I awoke alive and just as bear-free as I'd been the night before. After some farts, burps, aches and groans, blue pills, instant coffee, trail bars and swigs of water, I reluctantly threw a leg over and started rolling into my third day of riding. Romeo and Louise must have been still asleep inside their Airstream trailer because when we passed by it on our way out of camp there was no sign of them. The campfire we'd sat around the night before was a cold, black dot in the ground. It looked like a great big period at the end of a sentence marking the end of a very long day. I'll bet Romeo and Louise hadn't felt the cold wind once all night in that Airstream of theirs, or heard the rain cover of my tent as it luffed in the stronger gusts. God, the second I unzipped my way back into the world that morning, the cold air poured into my little nylon cocoon and slapped me awake with all the subtlety of a cold shower.

The first little town we rolled up to after leaving our campsite was Rockport, Washington, population 109. It stood quiet and still, holding its breath, tiny and hiding as if it didn't want us to know it was there at all. Now, for those few of you out there who haven't been to or heard of the town of Rockport, WA, I'll save you the trip. Here are some facts I dug up from the 2000 census: Based on per capita income, Rockport ranks number 48 of 522 areas in the state. Geographically it is puny, with a total area of 0.4 square miles. Who lives there? Well, there were thirty-nine households tucked into the nearby woods, ten of which had kids living inside. Twenty of the households had married couples living together, and four had single moms. One-third of the households consisted of nonfamilies, and ten were made up of individuals. There was one person over the age of sixty-five, who lived alone. Dave and I didn't see or meet any of them. As I said, it was as if the town of Rockport wanted to be overlooked. It was so small a town you'd miss it if you blinked.

We blinked.

Chapter Six

Next up? Concrete, Washington.

We mid-morning rest stopped in Concrete for water and coffee, not knowing that Robert De Niro, Leonardo DiCaprio, and Ellen Barkin had visited the area to shoot a movie called *This Boy's Life* twenty-one years prior. Darn, we'd *just* missed them, or so you would think, as it remained the number one topic of conversation by the guy who handed me a cup of coffee across a linoleum countertop that in some places was worn down to the wood by years of use. He also told me about the robbery of the State of Concrete Bank, the historic grade-school fire, and the nearby hydroelectric dam.

"Highest dam the world ever saw for a while," he said.

I did some fact checking later and learned the coffee guy was a straight shooter, telling it the way it was, right down to the cast members of *This Boy's Life* and the world's highest hydroelectric dam.

Nothing much else since besides tough times seemed to be happening in Concrete; the town was lodged between a rock and a hard place. No truck on the road was younger than fifteen and every vehicle in the place, including cars, trucks, and quads, appeared to be little more than dirty, rusty, tired mechanical work mules whose sole purpose in life was to haul folks and things about. No status sleds were spotted. Car washes appeared to be as foreign an idea around those parts as debutante parties. When a shiny new car rolled into town, everyone knew whoever was driving was just passing through.

I stepped into a convenience store for some water and received a refrigerated reception from the cashier cop. By the look on her face, you'd think I was going through her pajama drawer at home. I looked around the store. It had more security cameras than my bank branch at home and the cashier's eyes only saw conspiracy. Her peepers bounced between the closed-circuit TV screens and me. She'd apparently grown tired of being held up by drug addled zombies and had decided to do something about it. Ten bucks said she had a loaded sawed-off within an arm's reach of where she stood at the counter. Welcome to running a cash business in crystal meth country.

"Hi, howareyouuu?" she asked, blending the three words into one and holding on to the "you" part for an extra second or two. "You finish shopping? Ring you up?"

I imagined she had seen more shoplifters than the local magistrate, so I couldn't blame her for wanting me to make a quick purchasing decision and move toward the register. One look at me, though, should have indicated I had no business being on her shoplifting threat list; bike shorts, muffin tops, and clingy cycling shirts don't make for good cloaking, and bicycles are notoriously poor getaway vehicles regardless of who is pedaling. I wasn't dressed, equipped, or inclined to shoplift, but that did not prevent me from feeling like a suspect under her watchful eye. Two waters and two dollars later, I got out of there and stepped back out into the sunlight a free man, away from her world of surveillance where everyone is guilty until proven innocent.

I handed Dave his bottle and took a seat next to him on a bench just as a female meth addict walked by. Late stage addicts are easy to spot: they look like ambulatory human skeletons with hockey player teeth and jumpy eyes caged in recessed sockets. I felt sorry for all of them and was old enough and wise enough to know that there but for the grace of God go I.

She said, "Nice sweatshirt. It's really, really bright. Does that bother you? I mean, how loud it is all the time?"

She was referring to my neon-yellow nylon shell. I told her it didn't bother me. "It serves a purpose," I added. "With this on, drivers can see me more easily. Wearing this reduces the chances of me getting hit by a car."

"'Getting hit by a car.' That's funny. Have a good day." She waved and stepped into the woods behind a dumpster, taking along her long blond hair, her "I lost the fight" teeth, and what was left of her weight and her mind after the crystal meth had pervaded her body. God only knows what was in those woods behind the store, but I, for one, was not curious enough to find out.

If anything much at all was going on in Concrete, I missed it. It was a pretty low-key place. While rehydrating, Dave and I managed a few hellos to passersby, mostly locals stopping in for this or that. No one seemed in much of a hurry. Most were already where they wanted to be.

The friendly spirit of the town stood in sharp contrast to the looming cement silos at Superior Avenue and Highway 20.

Those silos were more like an enormous tombstone marking the death of better days. It had the words 'Welcome to CONCRETE' painted across it in fading red block letters. I was told the "This Boy's Life" crew for the movie had painted it.

Apparent economic hardship hadn't dampened the spirit of the people in the area, however. Every single one of the people we saw from that bench that day busted out a big smile when they greeted each other and us. I could have sat happily on that bench for a month, as I've always enjoyed the company of fine, friendly folks. It was unfortunate for me that the one and only sneer I received in the whole town was on the face of the first person I met—the lady inside the store at the cash register ready to ring "youuu" up. I wished I hadn't seen her first; she'd given me an inaccurate first impression. Concrete wasn't cold and hard; people there were quite the opposite.

Yeah, I wouldn't have minded sitting there on that bench for a month—God knows I was tired enough to do just that. After a bit, though, Dave and I came to the conclusion that not only had we better get going, but a cup of the local java juice was needed to serve as liquid ignition keys to get our bike motors revved up again in order to do so.

One of us was to make the ultimate sacrifice and get off their ass and fetch coffee if we were ever going to get out of there. So, we decided to play rock-paper-scissors for it. Winner got to remain seated while the loser got coffee. I threw a rock down and Dave tossed a paper, so I lost and had to pull a Juan Valdez and come back with some Columbian coffee that would help get the bicycle benchwarmers back in the game.

I got up off the bench and headed around the corner and almost bumped right into a guy coming the other way.

"Sorry," I said, and stepped to my right.

I got a good look at him. His grease-stained baseball cap sat on a bird's nest of tangled human hair. Two placid brown eyes looked back at me from underneath the frayed brim of his baseball cap.

It was like seeing something peering at me from the other side of a hair hedge. The only parts of his face that didn't have a bushy beard growing out of it every which way were red splotchy patches stained by the sun. The rest of him matched his hair and his hat; he was an ambulatory totem of dirt and stain. He'd either slept in on a dirt floor the previous night or used a shovel to dig up his clothing to get dressed for the day. His overalls were torn in some places and duct taped in others. He'd been through the wringer.

Conversely, next to him was a dog that didn't have a speck of dirt on it. In a sitting position, the head of the dog came up to its owner's waist. I took a closer look at it. The dog appeared to be a wolf...a *smart* wolf. It looked up at me with a pair of eyes behind which I swore I could see the wheels of a hunter/predator turning. It had neither leash nor collar, so it was just as free as I was to do whatever the hell it wanted. I noticed the moment the guy stopped to avoid bumping into me, the dog also stopped and then sat down, flanking its owner on the right side, but looking over at me to its left.

Clearly (and thankfully) it was an obedient, well-trained animal. Not only did it look like a smart wolf, it looked like a smart wolf *athlete*. I sidestepped farther to my right to put more distance between it and me, because even though it was cleaner than a Westminster Kennel Club best-in-show winner, it also looked like it could kill me in a second if the owner snapped his fingers or uttered some secret kill command in Yupik.

After apologizing for almost bumping into the guy, I added, "That's a beautiful dog, mister. Clean as a whistle." It was a beautiful dog: well proportioned, clean, powerful, and intelligent looking in the eyes. Westminster Kennel Club blue-ribbon material, no doubt about it.

The guy responded, "Thank you for saying that to me. The nicest compliment you could have given me is to say that you think my dog is beautiful."

"You're welcome. I call them as I see them."

He was so grateful and appreciative that I wondered if I was the first person to throw a compliment his way. Ever.

I asked him what kind of a dog it was. "It looks like a wolf," I added before he could answer.

"Kettle here is one-quarter wolf, actually; her mother was a half breed." He went on, saying, "I got her mom from a guy up in the hills who is trying to breed the American gray wolf out of a line of mixed breeds. He's got twenty-two dogs right now and has some of them down to about 12 percent wolf, but he's still having some behavior problems."

He paused. "He's a good man. There's good money in selling the dogs, but he won't sell to any families with kids or to the dog-fighting people. He likes dogs too much for that, so he ends up working real hard every day just to keep them all fed."

"What's your dog's name again?"

"Kettle. She's fourteen. You can pet her if you like."

I declined, figuring that people who pet the offspring of half wolves run the risk of ending up with nicknames like Righty or Lefty—or worse yet, One Nut.

"Her mother lived until she was eighteen and a half years old. She died in the fall a couple years' back. That's a long time for a dog to live. I think the wolf part makes them live longer than normal. We both miss her mom a ton, don't we, Kettle?"

The hurt in his eyes was easy to spot as he looked down at his dog and thought back to another dog now gone. Kettle looked back up at him at the mention of her name. After a second, the owner smiled. It was a little forced perhaps, but it was there. He petted Kettle's head and looked at me.

"Thank you for calling her beautiful, mister, I sure appreciate it. I don't have a woman in my life, and this dog here is just about the only company I keep. Nice meeting you."

He extended a hardened claw of a hand that had a scar across the back of it. His skin, a vital organ, sure had taken a beating over the years protecting his insides.

I took his hand and shook it.

"You, too," is all I said.

"Come on Kettle, let's get on with it," he said and off they went.

My mind's eye has him standing ramrod straight and roughly dressed in filthy clothes with Kettle, his obedient wolf dog by his side. Despite his unkempt appearance and contused hands that evinced a hardscrabble life in the back hills, somehow he exuded the dignity of a true gentleman that I hadn't seen from many people, regardless of their station in life. Maybe you had to be there, but I had never been so happy to lose a rock-paper-scissors game, as that loss gave me the chance to get a quick peek inside a book that didn't at all match its cover.

By the time I returned with coffee, Dave was talking with three road cyclists who'd just pulled in. All three were lanky and stood over six feet tall. They had necks and legs so long they looked like some sort of spandex-clad bicycling giraffes. Their digital watches, aerodynamic helmets, cleats and carbon-frame bikes looked expensive. They wore matching shirts from the same Vancouver bike shop, spoke with Canadian accents, and had muscle sets on their thighs and calves that broadcast what they'd been doing with most of their free time for the past decade. They were road biking Vikings, complete with heart monitors and digital watches, out for a ride that would take them far and wide.

They told us that they had begun their day at four o'clock that morning *one hundred and sixty miles* from where they stood and were just past the halfway point of a loop ride that would put them *back home in Vancouver* sometime before dark. That's 400 kilometers—250 miles—in *one day*. As soon as they bought water from smiley-face lady, they were off again, clicking and snapping their carbon-soled bike cleats into their custom carbon pedal sets, waving their good-byes, and adjusting the little rearview mirrors that extended out from their bike helmets on thin wires like bike helmet antennae. During our short exchange, I'd decided to keep mum about our comparatively minuscule mileage total. You have to know your audience.

After we finished our coffees, we were out of excuses not to get going, so we went from the bench to our bike saddles and started cranking. During our next few hours we rolled under a swaying canopy of tree branches that arched high over the straight, flat, paved roads. The scene was spectacular, the weather perfect: it was seventy degrees, sunny, and clear. Days like that were what I'd imagined bike touring to be and one of the reasons I'd set out to ride in the first place. Little did I know then that equipment trouble was brewing slowly and steadily under my left foot and that I was less than a day away from nearly crippling myself and putting my whole trip at risk so soon after it had begun.

There are three types of pedals available to the modern day cyclist: platform pedals, pedals with toe clips (think "toe cages"), and clipless pedals. I used clipless pedals as they were (and still are) considered to be the most efficient way to transfer energy to the back wheel. In order to use clipless pedals, you have to be wearing bicycle shoes with cleats on the bottom of the sole. Those cleats are attached to the bottom of the sole by two tiny screws. The rider snaps into the pedal with a "click" as the cleat locks into the pedal and provides firm footing in a straightforward position. In order to free the shoe from the pedal at dismount, the rider simply has to twist his/her foot out of the locked position. Got it?

I ran into mechanical difficulties when the cleat on the underside of my left bike shoe came lose: one of the screws that affixed my cleat to the shoe fell out which allowed the cleat to swivel around the remaining screw.

At first I didn't notice it. After a while it was like my left foot was on slippery ice. What did I do? I tightened up the pedal's grip on the cleat by adjusting the springs on the pedal itself. That helped for a while. But gradually things grew worse. I could not keep my left foot pointed straight on the pedal, so I improvised by awkwardly turning my heel in at a certain point in every rotation. I compensated with my body to fix a mechanical problem. Stupid, stupid, stupid. A few thousand rotations later, the awkward movement had enflamed my Achilles tendon. That tiny tendon bore the brunt of my efforts to keep my left foot in the correct facing forward position throughout the entire rotation of the pedal. I had singlehandedly managed to hurt myself. I was such a dummy; it wasn't the *cleat* slipping from the *pedal*: it was the *cleat* slipping from the *shoe*. It did not occur to me to check the mounting screws on the underside of my bike shoe. Had I done so, a simple tightening of a couple of screws would have saved the day and would have prevented the whole disaster in the first place. By the time I realized what the problem was, it was too late. The damage was done and I did not have a replacement part on me. My left hamstring began to hurt.

After a few hours we stopped at a ranger station to get directions and suggestions on where the best campsite was up ahead. An affable park ranger a little down on his luck provided some color and some intel. His gripe? DC budget cuts had reduced his team from sixteen people to one and had shrunken his region of responsibility from six thousand acres to a mere seven hundred. However, the ranger remained optimistic about his position and still considered himself to be "blessed beyond belief to live a life in the woods."

Washington, DC, hadn't gotten around to turning off his water yet, so he was able to point us to a nearby spigot where we refilled our canteens. As we topped off, he suggested a campsite up ahead that would be his choice for the evening.

"There's a campsite in Steelhead State Park about twenty miles down the road. It'd be my choice ten times out of ten if I was going east and planning to spend a night inside a tent."

Dave and I pedaled the twenty it took to get there and were happy we did. It turned out to be nothing short of perfect, with clean, warm showers, fire pits, nice neighbors, and plenty of grassy, level tent lots to let. It ranked as one of the top two best campsites of the trip. Most exciting for us was that the people running Steelhead State Park had the good sense to provide refrigeration on the premises, and some genius had the further foresight to put beer in said fridge so that it would be cold and available for sale by the time we arrived. Their industriousness was rewarded: I bought a beer for Dave and one for myself. They did not disappoint. My left leg did, though.

Chapter Seven

Entering Into A World Of Hurt And Trouble

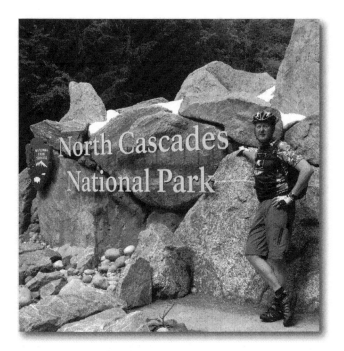

By the fourth day the pain in my left hamstring had really kicked in and my neck, shoulders, and back weren't happy either. Should I have been properly fit to a bike before the trip? Absolutely. And I missed my bed and my car pretty much in that order. At some point, Dave took a picture of me leaning on the entrance sign for North Cascade National Park. I might appear like some kind of conquering bike hero, comfortable standing

at ease in the picture with my legs akimbo, but that's the place
where things started to go sideways on me. Standing with hand
on hip wasn't a problem at that point. Pedaling a bike was.

In addition, the equipment and weight distribution problems continued to confound and served to exacerbate an already difficult undertaking. I must have stopped ten times the
first day and six times the second day trying to adjust things
so the bike would not shake uncontrollably at around twenty
miles per hour. My feeble attempts at weight redistribution
were only partially successful; I achieved a moderate amount
of stability at speed. The bike continued to wobble like a
drunken sailor every time I went anywhere near twenty miles
per hour, forcing me to slow down to stabilize. I had more
than four thousand miles to cover, and if I was going to be
limited to a maximum speed of seventeen to twenty miles per
hour, I knew I wouldn't get home before Halloween at the
rate I was going.

On the toughest riding day of the whole trip, the day we
had to summit Rainy Pass and Washington Passes, my cleat lost
a screw. It couldn't have happened at a worse time. I reached
the point where it hurt too much to pedal the bike, so I pushed
my bike uphill for a while in my bike shoes, then changed them
out for my sneakers. My clipless bike pedals were not designed
to work with sneakers, but sneakers were all I had. It was not a
perfect solution, but it was better than nothing. Besides, I was
walking next to the bike more at that point anyway.

(A week or so later I stepped inside a bike shop and threw a
bunch of money at the problem. I bought new cleats, new pedals and had some adjustment work done to my handlebars that
made them easier to reach. Basically the mechanic did his magic
on my headset spacers and voila! I could ride in a more upright
position.)

Pushing my overloaded bike up those hills that day with a
bum leg was a tough go. I wasn't the only one breathing heavily

and sweating profusely; Dave was pushing his bike for a while, too. I had to concentrate on steady breathing and steady stepping, and kept my eye on the front tire to remain in balance as I pushed. I knew my tunnel vision was a symptom of exhaustion and dehydration. It was not a good situation to be in. Our biking trip had turned into a hiking trip and I was running low on water. At the low point of our thirteen-hour-long effort to get over Rainy and Washington Passes, we were taking ten to fifteen minute breaks at every mile marker to catch our breath and rest up for the next mile long push to the next marker. We probably pushed fifteen miles in total that day due to the fact that it was way too steep for us to ride.

Don't ever mess with the Rockies. They mean business.

The worst part of the whole day happened after I finished the last of my water. It was getting dark and cold, just as Guy had warned us about. We were four miles short of the Washington Pass summit when my mouth got sticky and dry and my balance became noticeably off. I had to concentrate on shaping my words when I spoke if I wanted to be understood, but I wasn't talking much then anyway.

Saying something like, "I'm stopping here" took an effort. I had to stop walking, take a lungful of air, and then push the words out of my mouth, one by one. I. Am. Stopping. Here.

Dave would reply, "What?" and I'd have to take a deep breath and try again.

The sun was low in the sky and it was quickly getting cold and dark. The shadows stretched across the road as the sun sank. I walked more slowly and concentrated on not tripping. My feet felt drunk. To quote Guy, I was on the verge of "being fucked." In endurance sports like cycling and running, they call it "hitting the wall" or "bonking" when you run out of energy, when you have nothing left.

There I was, bonking. I knew what was happening and couldn't believe it.

When I heard a car approach from behind, I put my bike down and stepped into the road to wave it down. Fortunately, the car stopped and a lady got out to ask me what the problem was.

"Water," was all I could say.

Well, if you can believe it, the lady happened to have five-gallons of cool, clean delicious water with her in her car. What were the chances? I could have kissed her. She explained she always kept a five-gallon jug of water with her whenever she drove over the pass because "Washington Pass is no place to be without water."

Amen to that, sister.

She was an early and shining example of a trail angel, that is, someone who shows up out of nowhere—and oftentimes in the middle of nowhere—in the nick of time to lend a helping hand. Trail angels are miraculous: her car was the last car that day going our way over the pass. How lucky was that? And not only did she stop, she happened to have all the water we needed. After we topped off all our onboard canteens, she wished us well and drove off. I drank my fill, and after a few minutes, came back on line. With her water in my veins, my sense of balance returned and my tongue no longer stuck to the sides of my mouth. The water that woman provided enabled me to push on, to go up and over the pass that day, make dinner that night and enjoy instant coffee the following morning. Dave replenished his water as well. That Trail Angel's generosity was a real lifesaver for me.

It was past seven o'clock when we reached the summit. After a quick photo, Appalachian Trail Dave warned, "We gotta watch out for hypothermia, so put everything you got on before your sweat cools. Evaporation works too well sometimes. It will be night soon, and it's going to get much colder than it is now."

I quickly did as instructed. I wanted to get down that hill and into a sleeping bag as safely and as quickly as possible. We'd been riding for just over thirteen hours and I didn't want any trouble on the descent. Late day falls make for long nights.

"Stay close. If one of us goes down the other guy needs to be nearby to help. We're losing light. You ready?"

"Yeah, let's go," I told him. I could see my breath in my response.

I'd layered up with everything I had, just as Dave had done. Three pairs of pants and four layers of shirts were not near enough insulation. What I needed was a bearskin drape and a helmet with big horns on it. It was full on Scandinavian Viking weather and I was way under dressed for it. I froze my ass off on the descent even with everything I had with me on. Without properly insulated gloves or booties, my hands, feet, face and ears felt the brunt of the cold during a terrifying drop into the cliff-lined valley below, the valley on the far side of Washington Pass that we'd pedaled thirteen hours to see.

It was cold. It was steep. Even a few seconds off the brakes would get the bike up to speeds I was terrified of. The wobble had been reduced, but going twenty-five or thirty miles per hour was crazy. I had to constantly pinch the brakes to keep from going too fast. My fingers, hands, forearms and triceps were aching from the strain of riding the brakes before I was even one third of the way down. I thought about what someone once told me: "Don't ride the brakes too long on the steeps. If you ride the breaks too long on the mountain descents, your rims will heat up causing your tires to puncture."

A flat tire at that point would have taken precious time to repair and would have been a real challenge to do with frozen fingers in fading light. At that point a delay of any kind for any reason would really screw things up for us. Night was approaching.

We were running out of time and daylight. Shit. Shit. Shit.

The views in the fading light were no less than absolutely spectacular, though. The park ranger had warned us to be extra careful on our descent and not to get too distracted by the gorgeous scenery. He said every year a number of drivers, motorcycle riders, and, yes, even some bicyclists sometimes end up paying the ultimate price for not keeping their eyes on the road. I managed to steal several quick looks at the hard earned vistas on our descent. My hands and forearms barked louder and louder as they grew sorer from all the break squeezing. Riding that road alone in the cold, at that altitude, at that time of day after so many hours in the saddle would be super stupid to attempt. I was happy to have Dave on the hill with me as backup. The Buddy System works.

We continued down. The faster we rode, the colder it got. The slower we went, the longer it took. We sought a balance between speed and comfort, but there was none to be found. The day's water weep from the snow banks on both sides of the road began to freeze, so we were forced by a heightened sense of caution to ride in the middle of the road to avoid any chance of riding over any black ice. Fortunately for us there were few cars coming in either direction at that late hour, so we had the place to ourselves. We managed to navigate our way down without suffering any mishaps.

Massive granite cliffs on both sides of the road reached up toward a pale blue sky stained dark to the east. The setting sun scaled rocky peaks to the west as we descended ever lower into cooler air. Darkness pooled in the valleys as the rays of the setting sun left the valleys and climbed the snowfields of the peaks two thousand feet above us to the west. Bright snow reflected dying light into parts of the valley, the sun's last offering before moving further west and leaving us in darkness for the night.

After a hairy descent into what felt like a polar vortex, we spotted a sign for at the first available campsite and immediately decided to pass up that option for the next one farther down the road. Just as Guy had said a few days prior, that campsite would have been "still too damn high and too damn cold" for comfort. It was also too damn far off our route to even consider: the sign informed all who read it that the first available campsite was six miles off course.

We continued on down to the next campsite.

Klipchuck Campground was located just after the Cutthroat Trailhead. By the time we arrived the temperature felt like it was in the low forties at best and falling. We were the only people there, the only people crazy enough to venture out to Klipchuck campground so early in the season. After a long day of climbing, walking, pushing and sweating, we were both completely spent and had only enough energy to fire up the JetBoil stove to mix up a ramen-noodle dinner (that tasted five star), suspend a bear bag, set up our tents, and fall completely exhausted into them.

We didn't talk much that night during set up and meal preparation: nothing personal, but thirteen-plus hours in a saddle climbing and pushing up hills under a hot sun and then riding down them in the freezing cold tends to still the tongue.

I sure was lucky to have stopped that car and resupplied my water stores near the summit. Dave wasn't in as dire a situation as I had been: he still had some water on him and had some water purification pills ready for both of us if push came to shove. All we'd have to do would be to find a stream and use it as a spigot. The dude was a camel, though, a freaking bike camel. He ate like a bird, too. The Bearded Man, a.k.a. Mr. Outdoors, sure knew how to roll and ration.

Both of us confessed later that we were grateful to have both Rainy and Washington Passes in the rear view mirror. Guy had been right about another thing, too: I was surprised to the point of shitting my ass in two at how quickly the light left and the temperature tanked after "Mother Sun" dropped behind the rocky edge of my mountain world. I still didn't know what "shitting your ass in two" meant, but I was going with it. I crawled into my sleeping bag with everything I had with me on. It was not comfortable, but thirteen hours in the saddle? My eyes shut and stayed shut for pretty much the next ten hours. Insomnia didn't have a prayer that night.

After hours of solid shuteye, I awoke to a chilly, clear morning. I was beginning to understand how important the breakfast meal was to a good day's ride. Taste was not as much a priority as substance. I needed something in my stomach. Reluctant to face the chill, I lay in the comparative comfort of my sleeping bag. I needed breakfast if I wanted to get up and going, but that meant I had to get out of my sleeping bag...and I didn't want to get out of my sleeping bag.

The frost on my tent gave me an indication of how cold it was outside. If I was at home and there was frost, say, on the windshield of my car, I'd be sure to put on a winter coat and a pair of insulated boots before stepping outside.

But I wanted breakfast...

I went back and forth like that for a while before hunger pushed me out of my tent. Mr. Shit Together Camper Dave was just as zombie tired as I was the night before, but he was already up, fed, and on his third cup of instant coffee by the time I stuck my head outside my frosted tent for a look around.

"Hey man," I croaked.

"Hey."

"Your tent cold last night?" I asked, holding the tent's canopy tightly against my neck as I would a wool scarf in a raging snowstorm.

"Nah, I was good. Threw on the double long johns and slept like a baby after a tit dinner. Coffee?"

'Double long johns'? What the hell are double long johns, and who would have the foresight to pack them? The dude was hardcore. I had my entire wardrobe on—which included a short sleeve cotton blue Hawaiian shirt with palm trees on it—and my garb still came up way short of keeping me warm.

It totally sucks when you don't camp right.

I emerged from hibernation, eyes squinting in the bright morning sun. It took me an hour and a half to say, "OK, let's roll." I knew I would eventually get better at the camping thing, but I deserved a break, as it was only my second or third time camping in as many decades. And I was at a severe disadvantage: all my crap was in four bags, all the same color, two big, two small. Oh, and I had a handlebar bag, too, with some more crap in it. I had shifted things around so much to stabilize the bike that I had no idea where anything was.

Not so with Dave. In less than ten seconds he could find anything he needed. If I wanted to retrieve something from my saddlebags—saddlebags that all looked exactly the same, mind you—I'd have to dig through everything until I found what I was after. What a pain. Not having a place for everything and not having everything in its place compounded my frustration and lowered my efficiency rating to laughable status. At one point, Dave started to call me the Packing Princess. I called him the Bearded Bastard, but we both agreed that was a pretty weak retort. Besides, he was right. The fact that I had to dig through everything to find anything was camp-pathetic.

We got back up on two wheels after a time and rolled downhill for another few miles, freezing our asses off in the very chilly morning air. The views were still something to see, but they were a whole lot less dramatic that morning at lower altitudes than they'd been at the top the evening before. Six miles into our freezing morning ride, we passed the third campsite, the Early Winters Campground. Even though it was a measly six miles from Klipchuck, Early Winters Campground was not an option for us the night before: we'd never have made it. Hell, by the time we saw that Klipchuck Campground sign and hung a left into the entrance, we barely had the strength to hang that bear bag.

I hated to think of what would have happened without that timely delivery of fresh water near the top. Who knows? Maybe one or both of us would have taken a fall. I was definitely bonking and getting dizzy. Chances were good I'd have run a pretty serious risk of taking a header on the backside of Washington Pass. Dave could make stream water potable with his water purification pills: it was good to have them as a backup measure if we needed it.

There is no doubt about it. When the shit goes down Armageddon-wise, I'm-A-geddon my ass over to Dave's place and knocking on his front door.

Later in the day and lower off the mountain, we arrived at and enjoyed a warmer and sunnier clime and were able to finally rid ourselves of the chill that had followed us down the mountain most of the morning. We left all the cold behind by the time we got to Manama, Washington, and had a quick lunch followed by more pedaling that afternoon. When we stopped riding that day we were looking at dinner and camping in Winthrop.

Though I had been especially excited about reaching Manama for lunch, it was more important to me to visit a bike shop purported to be there. Word on the street (well, word on my map) was that there was a fairly decent bike shop in town and I was psyched to switch out all my equipment, including my bike if an appropriate replacement one could be found.

Boy, was I disappointed when we arrived to find no bike shop. Our intel was stale. The only bike shop in town had gone out of business two years before. Damn! I needed to replace my bike cleats and pedals a.s.a.p. My leg hurt, but my foot along with my toes started to hurt as well. Manama bike shop or no bike shop, I remained determined to do two things: reach the Atlantic Ocean by bicycle and not snap a tendon in the effort.

I doubled down on my "easy does it" strategy. It took some patience, but I worked the road and continued digesting the miles ahead with my sneakers on and at a slow pace. Pushing past your comfort level is one thing, pushing past your breaking point is another thing altogether. Sometimes there is a fine line between the two. But if you are really smart and you are able to manage it, try to do all the endurance stuff like going on a long bike ride, running a marathon, swimming the English

Channel, and walking the entire length of the AT or the PCT (Pacific Coast Trail) while you're still young…maybe like in your twenties young.

Have I said, "Getting old sucks" yet?

Well, it does. Getting. Old. Sucks.

When I think back about how close I came to snapping my left Achilles tendon, I wince at the thought of what a buddy of mine went through after he tore his while playing pick up basketball. After tearing his Achilles clean through, he went to the hospital and was initially misdiagnosed with a pulled calf muscle. Fortunately for my friend, things turned out well. Another doctor happened by and made a more accurate diagnosis before my buddy was discharged that day.

"That's no pulled calf," the second doctor said, "That there is a snapped tendon. You'll need surgery immediately. Can't wait. Nurse, get this man into the operating room STAT."

As I understand it, the proper way to fix a torn Achilles tendon that has rolled up a leg like a retractable curtain pull is to undergo immediate surgery. The tendon has to be pulled back down the length of the leg and it has to be anchored back to the heel of the foot. If the surgery is not done in a timely manner (within forty-eight hours of the injury), the tendon, a sticky string, will become irrevocably bound to itself. Months of bed rest, recuperation, and physical therapy are required for proper healing to take place. The tendon binds onto itself after only a couple of days. The only thing you can do at that point is consider changing your legal name to "Hop Along" because that's what you'll be doing for the rest of your days.

My buddy went under the knife that very night and his tendon was successfully re-attached to his heel. The following six months were full of bed rest and painful rehab sessions with someone he referred to as "Pam the Pain Bearer," but he made a full recovery. His basketball days are over forever, though.

In my case, I'd dodged a bullet when my Achilles tendon held. If that tendon of mine had snapped while I was on the road, I would have been in a real tough spot—the pain would be near childbirth levels and, with no hospitals nearby, I'd be faced with an uncomfortable commute to a surgeon and a rehab schedule that would prevent plane travel and thus ground me to the area without the ability to ride or travel, for a while at least.

I've never seen the inside of a medical school, so I could have it all wrong, but that's the way I saw things in the spring of 2014.

So let's see: my neck, shoulders, arms and lower back were killing me, my legs were woefully weak, I drank water like a drain and sweated it out like a sieve, and I was catching looks from concerned strangers eager to stop by to see if I required medical assistance. Oh, and I was achieving better living through chemistry with my intake of Aleve every morning and evening. What the hell was I doing out there?

I felt like a pacifist in a war zone.

Chapter Eight

We Learn About A Place To Stay Forever

I t had taken us the better part of five days, but by May 21st we'd made it through Skagit and Okanogan counties. When we passed the road sign "Okanogan county limit", we decided to celebrate the occasion with an early break for lunch. That day's roadside meal of peanut butter, Nutella, trail mix, and raisins wrapped up in a piece of pita bread was enjoyed and named the "Funky Chunky" before it was halfway eaten. I couldn't believe it: a mere five days into the ride and I was enjoying a pavement picnic, feasting on things that looked a lot like cow patties and sitting cross legged by the side of the road, happy as a lark. As unappealing as the Funky Chunky looked, that smash up of sugar, salt, protein, and bread tasted darn good and it served its purpose well. It fueled the legs for the rest of the afternoon. We were less than a week into the trip and I, never a picky eater, felt my taste receptors becoming even more open-minded about foods of all kinds. If eating large amounts of food guilt-free is what you are after and if you want all of your next meals to taste like the very best one you ever had, go ride a bike a long way, sit yourself down to a table, a bench, or even a patch of roadside and dig in. Bon appétit.

Or should I say, bike appétit?

Another unexpected thing I noticed less than a week into the ride was that I was spending most of my time free from digital distractions as my bike saddle was beyond the reach of the destructive and distractive electronic media that normally showered down upon me every waking moment. My brain began to reap the benefits of being left the hell alone for a while. No email, text, or phone service reached me, so for the first time since 2004 I got to enjoy some quiet time between the ears. Like many other people, I'd lived with TV's, radios, and thought killing cell phones that come with quivers full of electronic "app arrows" that kill one's ability to concentrate.

With so much information out there (I'm pointing to the sky) trying to make it in here (I'm pointing to my temple), is it any wonder that distracted driving deaths are on the rise?

It was fun to step away from the mighty and omnipresent messaging force that didn't exist twenty years ago. Take a look around for yourself: we have parking meters that talk, cameras that spy, phones that track, and frozen peas that yell out from grocery store freezers announcing they are on sale. Tollbooths blink THANK YOU as you roll by at twenty M.P.H. Highway billboards blink changing messages. It is crazy out there in Media Land.

So much had changed since I was a kid. Remember when skywriting was the shit?

I do.

Anyway, bike riding in dead zones (great name for a book, by the way) was re-introducing me to the way things once were: simpler. I realized that in today's world it is becoming next to impossible to avoid screens as you make your way through a normal day. The media industrial complex (if there is such a term) never stops spreading and never ceases bombarding us with impressions, messages, news, opinions, and facts, real or fake.

My unofficial survey of other road cyclists revealed that they, too, had experienced long and wonderful stretches of uninterrupted thought while underway. Perhaps more oxygen reaching the brain is the explanation or maybe it is simply spending more time in an electronically sterile environment that does it. Who knows? All I knew was that my powers of concentration were improving a mere week into the trip.

But my legs weren't. I couldn't walk very well and my left leg hurt all the time, in any position, moving or not. I was up to two Aleve pills both morning and night. I hobbled around camp the following morning in Twisp, Washington on a bum leg and felt iffy at best for that day's riding assignment: the 4,020-foot ascent of Loup Loop Pass. Two Aleve pills and a double shot espresso chaser went down the hatch on my way out of town along with a hefty dose of denial and male bravado. That triple combo of pills, coffee and denial made me bulletproof once again. I'd convinced myself I was ready for another summit attempt. Dave and I knew from the maps that the hard climbing would begin right after we left Twisp and it sure did. I held my handlebars in a new way that day: my fingers were crossed in hopes some more Good Samaritans would again happen by with real life offer of a ride, a ride I would have been very tempted to take.

It had been a tough few days on the road. In a vein attempt to prevent suffering any additional damage to the tendon in my left leg, I experimented with pedaling with just my right leg for a while, but it did not work out very well. I could push down and pull up with my right leg, but one-legged propulsion threw my balance off. It didn't work, so I ended up just taking it really easy on my left leg and kept my left foot on the left pedal only as a placeholder and something to gently lean on while my right foot came around for another turn at pressing down. Bikes are made to run on two pistons, not one. After many arduous hours on our bikes, we made it up and over Loup Loup Pass that day and to a campground that looked a whole lot like a parking lot.

No rest for the weary and no break for the good guys: no motel in sight. After a long day in the saddle, we were faced with a mattress free and shower free camping scenario. The Motel Pussy was not happy about the sitchu at all.

When we first rolled into the campground, we thought we'd made a mistake and missed a turn or something, but we hadn't: we were actually *in* the campground looking around *for* the campground.

To our eyes the place didn't look much different from a parking lot lined with a shit ton of baseball fields on one side and scrubby brush with woods behind it on the other. Pickup trucks and minivans overflowing with kids and equipment wound their way into the municipal recreation, camping complex. As soon as drivers spotted the team uniform that matched the ones their kids had on, they'd take a hard right and park their car at their designated field. Minivan doors would slide open and disgorge a clown car full of uniformed kids who'd jump out like paratroopers with baseball bats and gloves, ready to invade the field and win a victory for the home team. I noticed some kids had their faces pressed up against car windows as they passed us. I heard one kid ask his mom, "Where do the dirty bike people sleep when the sun goes home at night, Mommy?"

Classic. They were on a drive-through safari tour and couldn't quite recognize the migrating *Northeastern white-legged late middle-aged bicyclist* in its native environment.

I smiled and waved back at the few of the tikes that waved at me. One kid stuck his tongue out then ducked below the sill and out of sight. Good stuff man. I remember doing things like that at his age.

We arrived at our little patch of paradise for the evening. It was a twenty-by-twenty-foot-square piece of dirt sandwiched between two picnic tables and it cost me ten bucks. Forty cents a square foot was too high a price if you asked me. The picnic tables weren't anything to write home about; they were covered in parking lot dust just like everything else.

Dave and I set about to the now familiar work of setting up camp. We'd just completed erecting our tents when a guy about five sites over stepped out of an RV the size of a Wal-Mart with the words "Roadside Manor" painted on the side. The guy wore a blousy linen shirt, a pair of loose fitting Bermuda shorts, and weird gladiator sandals. His held had a cocktail in his right hand and a dog leash in his left. The pink leash led down to a fury softball-sized dog that looked like shag carpet remnant and could not have weighed much more than a deli sandwich. Did it ever yap.

The RV guy headed our way.

His words of greeting arrived about thirty feet before he did. He said he was a "Canadian from Canada" and hailed from the "beautiful, special city of Penticton," about 130 miles north of where we stood. Neither Dave nor I invited him over, yet over he came. As we prepared our dinners, the man went on and on about how the Indians discovered the "truly heavenly region of Penticton" and how three rivers and "a climate that only God could have arranged" made it the best place in the whole wide world "to work, to live, and to raise children and foodstuffs."

Honestly. He used the word *foodstuffs*. I love bike travel! Do you think you'll ever hear the word *foodstuffs* mentioned on a long car ride? There is no chance of that ever happening. You could drive a trillion miles and never hear someone in a sedan use the word *foodstuffs* in conversation. Me? I was traveling by bicycle and heard it less than a week in.

Seriously, "*foodstuffs?*" That's nothing short of awesome right there.

The guy went on. I mean, the guy went on and on about the town of Penticton as if he were the mayor of the damn place or something. He wound up his diatribe with the etymology of the word.

"*Penticton* means a place to stay forever. Native Americas came up with that name long ago," he assured us, then gave us a moment to let it all sink in about just how fan-fucking-tastic that whole concept was—finding the best place on the globe to live, work, raise children and foodstuffs—and to stay forever.

When he (finally) stopped talking his dog looked up in alarm as if someone had turned off the soundtrack of his little doggy world. It pawed an ear as if to check to see if it still worked and looked up at its owner with its head cocked sideways. I am no dog whisperer, but I'd wager my tent fees that the shag carpet pooch with the pink collar and matching leash was wondering, "Have I gone deaf, or has this fucking asshole finally stopped talking about the goddamn town of Penticton?"

The dog, Dave, and I stood there. The dog turned to me with a "Say something before he starts up again, you idiot!" kind of look. I nodded to the mutt and took advantage of the pause in the conversation to pop a glaringly obvious question his owner's way.

"If Penticton is a place to stay forever, what in the hell are you doing 130 miles south of it?"

"I just had to get out of town for a bit."

So much for 'forever.'

Someone inside the Roadside Manor yelled "Pookie, Pookie!" and the dog shot off like a fur comet back toward the mother ship. We all watched that little dust mop cover the distance at a pretty good clip, its pink leash in tow. Once it arrived it scratched at the screen door and turned to look back to see if Mr. Penticton was coming. The Mrs. was calling, and both Pookie and our Mr. Penticton had answered the call.

"Yes, honey, Pookie is by the door," he shouted. "I'll be right there, too. Open up for Pookie," he said. The screen door opened a crack and little Pookie pulled a Houdini move and was there one second, gone the next. It wasn't a perfect disappearing act, though: old Pookie's pink leash got caught in the door. One yap later the door opened up a second time and the pink leash receded inside the RV quick as a snake tongue.

The Penticton guy thanked us for "our nice little chat," pulled a 180, and beat it back home to his camper. Pookie tasted freedom a few more times before nightfall for a piss and a sniff of the Dumpster, but that was the last we saw of his owner that night.

The conveyor belt of camping characters and mini vans had slowed down by the time dusk settled in over Camp Dumpy, but we still had one last and very special guest yet to arrive.

A terribly odd looking young woman appeared as if out of nowhere from behind a scraggily group of trees and undergrowth which stood about forty yards away from our tents. Once free of the entanglement of the scrawny scrub from which she'd emerged, the woman stood up and revealed herself in full regalia. Her clunky hiking boots looked capable of climbing El Capitan. She wore the same canvas pants you might see on an arborist, and a blaze orange bucket hat that you might see on a rapper or a hunter. She carried a wooden walking stick. If Mother Earth had spawned a bastard child with Johnny Appleseed or the Cat in the Hat, our new neighbor was it.

As she made her way over to the unoccupied tent site adjacent to ours, she kept looking back at something in the bushes. I couldn't figure out for the life of me what it was or why she'd come from that direction in the first place. There was no road, or path, or trail on that side of camp.

She made herself our new neighbor with a chin wave and a
"Hey, s'up?"

With a practiced shrug, she let slip her knapsack and it fell
dead at her feet just behind her. She set about to erecting her
minimalist tent in a New York minute.

Her outfit was a rather odd mix of Massachusetts Pilgrim
from Colonial Times, the Matrix, and L. L. Bean store closeout
sale. To my eyes, she was just another average hiker looking to set
up camp and call it a day, but to Dave, she was a real knockout,
bushy armpits and hairy legs notwithstanding. Her tent-setup
moves registered as sexy to Dave.

"Gee-sus," said a gob smacked Dave. "I haven't seen a tent
like that since the AT. That's a Thomas Johnny tent. He makes
about twelve a year. I wonder how she got one...she must have
some serious camping skills. Did you see that? Man, she set that
thing up in, like, forty-five seconds. That's a handy skill to have
in a rainstorm."

I looked at Dave, then at Little House on the Prairie, and
then back to Dave. I waved my hand in front of his face. "Your
eyes working, Dave?" I asked, and flipped him the bird. "How
many fingers am I holding up?" He brushed my hand away in
order to study her mad camping moves.

After setting up her wicked-awesome tent in record time, she
abandoned all dignity and plopped her butt straight down in the
dirt next to her knapsack. She sat cross-legged and unwrapped
her trail-bar dinner which she chewed facing away from us. Her
head moved up and down as she ate. I didn't understand: there
was a perfectly good picnic table about ten feet away from her,
but she'd opted to stuff her pie hole full of trail bars sitting on
dirt. She had kind of a "raised by wild dogs" thing going on and
had a couple of tattoos—I think the one on her left arm was of
a G clef. The other tattoo was a tramp stamp peeking out at us
between her pants and her shirt. It was located just above her
coin slot, which, by the way, was showing. I couldn't make out if

the tramp stamp depicted a dolphin or a unicorn, but either way it served to confirm to me that, in my humble opinion, she had the ability to make bad decisions concerning skin stains.

I closed my eyes and tried to shake the image of her butt crack out of my head.

Unfortunately shaking the vision out of my head was easier than shaking the nose off my face. I was maybe about twenty-five feet or so downwind of her, so I was still well within nose shot of her body odor. After riding all day, I knew for a fact that I did not smell pine tree fresh myself, but being downwind from that woman almost put me off my food. Her scent came close to hog barn levels. She stink, stank, stunk like she had recently bathed in an open sewer and had splashed copious amounts of Ode de Large Urban Transit System on after toweling her nasty self off with a wet dog blanket.

She turned to us suddenly and pushed half formed words through her partially masticated trail bar asking, "Hey, do you guys know where we are?"

Dave let out a groan—he will deny it to this day, but I heard it with my own ears—a groan of disappointment. Alas, though the sexy beast had crazy camping-tent-setup skills, she had no idea where the hell she was. What a massive letdown for my boy Dave. Thomas Johnny Tent chick went from being Miss May on Dave's Hot Camping Chicks 2014 Calendar to being just another name on his ever-growing list of women he'd been wrong about.

"I'm done," he said.

"What, so soon? What about raising children and foodstuffs?" I inquired.

"Situational awareness is key to any relationship."

He turned away distraught and with no interest at all in further engagement. He was pissed about the tent, I think. It must have bothered him to no end knowing that a Thomas Johnny tent had somehow fallen into the wrong hands. I think Dave was tempted to take it away from her and keep it for himself.

It so happened that near the spot where our new neighbor had materialized from were half-dozen little brown-and-black bunnies. I eventually spotted them hopping about and chewing on grasses. They must have been what had caught her attention earlier and why she had kept turning around to look at them as she made her way to her tent site. The bunnies must have been from a recent litter because they were so small and still hanging out together. She could not take her eyes off those kittens. (That's what you call baby rabbits—kittens. I looked it up.)

She talked to me about those little bunnies as if I, too, wanted to adopt and name them all. She didn't ask me what I would call them, but if she had, I would have told her I'd name the first three 'Breakfast', 'Lunch', and 'Dinner'. That might have pissed her off, but the fact of the matter is, I like my rabbit best on a plate.

(Now dear reader, don't you be hatin.' Come back to me after you've had a taste of the bunny and tell me I'm wrong.)

Mother Earth continued. "The cute little bunnies. They're all black and brown. There are so many of them and they are all so cute. I think I would name the one over there 'Reese's Cup.' I think they're feral rabbits. Do you think they're feral bunnies lost in the woods? Is there a rabbit farmer near here? Where do they go at night? Do you think bears eat bunnies? Do you know anyone who will be driving on Route 20 tomorrow?"

Dave had no interest in even looking her way. Me? I had to know more about the young woman traveling alone who had walked out of the bushes and hadn't a clue as to where she was or that some rabbits are born free.

I ignored her questions and asked a couple of my own. "Is that a G clef on your arm? Are you a musician?"

She cocked her head and thought about it for a second and said, "That's a weird question. Why would you ask me about a G clef on my arm? I'm not a musician, although I've never turned down an invitation to drum circle... Oh! On my arm you mean? That's not a G clef," she said, reaching over and touching it. "A lot of people think that. No, it is a tattoo of the stick I used to kill a rabid squirrel that attacked me on a training hike I took last year. I felt badly about it, but it was going to be either him or me, you know? I will spare you the details, but it was a Life or Death situation involving a cooler, a folding camp chair, a stick, a squirrel, and a tent. And me, of course, it involved me. The better man won," she added.

I didn't have the heart to inform her that there was no man in the fight, nor were there two men in the fight, so there was no way the "better" of two men won. I let things lie. I think I knew what she was getting at.

She continued, "After killing it, I later determined it was a male and it was, indeed, rabid and, thus, not thinking clearly. I keep its squirrel spirit with me, and the tattoo is a reminder of the day I took a life. Do you know how much a veterinarian charges to determine if a squirrel was rabid? Sixty American dollars."

OK then.

I asked her where she was headed. She replied she was following the path of her Great Spirit Mother. Bottom line? She was walking alone, God only knew why, to God only knew where. She was out to complete a 350-mile-long trek from Somewhere Else to Nowhere Still.

I forget her starting and finishing points, but when I later asked Dave about her route, Dave, who had a deeper working knowledge of such things, replied, "That makes no sense. Why the fuck would anyone want to do that?"

Come fall she'd be off to grad school in Fairbanks, Alaska to, in her words, "become a licensed geophysicist" which I thought was hilarious. If you ask me I think there are way too many unlicensed geophysicists running around talking trash about our earth mom. Something should be done about that.

She told me she intended to study the glacial iceberg melt and to come up with an accurate prediction when all mankind would drown in a global flood. She wanted to, in her words, "get a line on when the icebergs will knock over the Statue of Liberty in Boston."

Fucking awesome. I love my bike. I really, really do.

Alas, we will never know what eventually happened to our neighbor as she was up and gone by first light, long before I got the chance to furtively provide her with Dave's contact info. I'd planned on telling her that Dave was the shy but very well endowed type who'd be up for procreating with women interested in bunnies and global warming. Darn it! Maybe they would have fallen in love, gotten married, and gone to Boston to see the Statue of Liberty on their honeymoon before travelling east to San Francisco then north to Argentina.

I had to hand it to her, though; she sure had some mad camping skills. She was like a camping ninja with tricks up her sleeves that no one saw coming. I'm not talking about any serious shit like throwing stars made from last year's Girl Scout cookies or blowguns made from friendship rings. I am talking about a full-on, totally sick talent for executing a world-class furtive egress, otherwise known as the daybreak dash. No one heard Little Miss House on the Prairie pull up stakes that morning, including the guy who collected money for the tent fees.

I crawled out of my tent with a pain level of maybe a seven (zero being no pain at all and ten being birthing triplets). My leg was killing me to the point it where I had to re-jigger that morning's To Do List: it was going to be Aleve first, coffee second…if I could find the Aleve.

The first thing I saw when I stuck my head out of my tent was a perfectly quaffed tent fee guy in a pressed olive shirt with a clipboard standing on the very spot where the Thomas Johnny tent had been the night before. The guy was looking around at his feet as if he had been talking to her and she and her tent had just vanished into thin air.

When he saw me climb out of my tent, he put two and two together and came up with five. He looked at me like I was guilty of something: he thought I had aided and abetted a debt dodger. The guy adjusted his aviator sunglasses and began a conversation in a combative, semi accusatory way. There was no "Good morning" or "Nice day we are having, isn't it?"

"Where did your friend go to? Will she be back?" was his open.

"Huh?" I looked behind me for the guy I thought he was speaking to. There was no one there. "You talking to me?" I asked, pointing to myself with my thumb to my chest.

"Yes," he said.

"You mean the nutter who slept there last night?" I asked, blinking in the morning sun, raising my hand to prevent it from making me blind. "Fuck knows, man. Have you checked the local loony bin? Maybe the orderlies in white dragged her back to the rubber room she calls home. Or maybe she followed the little brown and black feral bunnies back into the woods."

The guy had no idea what I was talking about, but he still pressed his point.

"Well, I saw you talking to her at dusk. I meant to come over and get her tent fees last then, but I got to talking with the occupants of tent sites 14, 15, and 16." He pointed to the Roadside Manor that our Mr. Penticton lived in. "I saw you speak to her and that makes you her friend. And your *friend* skipped out without paying for her tent spot. These tent sites are not free, you know."

"Yes, I know. I have my fee receipt somewhere if you want to see it."

"Not necessary. I was looking *for her* tent payment." He stood there like a prison guard with his arms folded across his clipboard.

It took me a moment, but I, too, got to five with two twos. "Wait, you want *me* to pay *her* tent fee?"

He nodded yes.

"Never seen her before last night. We shot the shit for a while, then I turned in when I discovered she was crazy as a bag of cats."

"Well, sometimes friends have to pay their friend's tent fees."

I thought of something. "Hey, wait. You and I are talking right now, right?" I asked.

"Yeah."

"Well, then, by your logic, does that make us friends?"

He looked at me quizzically. I puckered my lips and winked at him with a come hither smile and a silent nod to my tent.

That did the trick. He got all creeped out. (I'd creeped myself out, too, but the pain in my leg helped me manage to keep a straight face.)

"Um…no. You have a good day."

"You too, my *friend*."

The guy took off like he'd kicked over a hive of bees.

I found my stove and water for coffee figuring caffeine might help me in my search for blue pills. I didn't know which saddlebag they were in, dammit.

Dave had heard the entire exchange from inside his own tent. I could hear him snickering, too. He said, "Nice going, Frying Pan. I couldn't see from here. Did you wink at the guy when you asked if you were friends?"

"Damn right I did."

"Classic."

"Hey, screw him. He tried to hustle an extra ten bucks of tent money outta me."

"Yes, he did, Tim. And you know he'd just spend it all on drugs."

I smiled as my water for coffee boiled and as I massaged my sore leg. I took a good look around. The campground was indeed a dump, but it was also a comedic stage upon which many characters had strolled.

"Children and foodstuffs."

"Where do the bunnies go at night?"

"Situational awareness is key to any relationship."

A good sense of humor is as important as tire pump on a bike tour: both can get you rolling again when things go flat.

Chapter Nine

MEMORIAL DAY, WAUCONDA PASS, SHERMAN PASS

After morning coffee, Dave and I set about to strike camp when we heard a screen door slam. Pookie had emerged from the Wal-Mart RV along with its owner, Mr. Penticton. I'll be damned if Pookie didn't shoot on over and start dry humping Dave's leg. Poor Dave had just gotten on the phone with Heather when he was blindsided by the early morning dry hump from a yapping shag carpet. In reaction to all the commotion below his knee, Dave made an instinctive reflex kick and sent Pookie into the air. Pookie sailed by me doing his level best to twist his legs around in time to stick the landing.

Freaking dog nailed it: all four paws tasted the dirt at the same time.

I spit up some coffee. God that was funny.

Old Pooks wouldn't take no for an answer, though. He took the kick like a trained doggie in a dojo and rolled back up and was back on Dave's lower leg faster than you could say, "What the fuck is wrong with this bat crazy yapper?"

Possibly the best line of the whole trip was then uttered by Dave who was looking down and still talking to Heather on the phone, trying to gently shake Pookie off his leg.

"Pookie, get off of me. No means no, Pookie. No means no."

Seeing Dave then gently shooing Pookie off his lower leg with slow motion kicks was another good laugh, another spit up of coffee, and a great to start my riding day. I wished him luck trying to explain to Heather who Pookie was.

"It's your beard, dude. It is Pookie-licious. Pookie finds you quite fetching," I laughed. Dave was still shooing the dog away. I laughed more.

With a wave and an immediate apology shouted from across a few empty tent sites, Mr. Penticton started heading our way.

"Here Pookie. Pookie, get off that nice man. He is not your ducky doll."

Dave and I looked at each other. What the hell was a ducky doll? What kind of weird shit was going on inside the Roadside Manor? We spoke quickly, and nodded knowingly.

Dave hung up after whispering to Heather, "I'll talk to you later, honey—gotta go."

We both wanted to go wheels up as soon as possible and we both saw Mr. Penticton as being detrimental to our efforts. Neither one of us was eager to hear any more about Penticton from its number one fan, so we staged an awkward moment / mock fight as he approached.

"Man, you snored so loudly last night I could hear you all the way from my tent!"

"Oh, yeah? Well, your packing skills suck. Honestly. You couldn't find your own ass with two hands. Hey, where's your toothbrush, huh, Mr. Organized? Locate your toothbrush or shut your trap."

Thankfully, our Mr. Penticton was conflict averse, so he gathered Pookie up, tacked left, and made his way to a guy sitting all alone at a picnic table a few sites over. Poor guy was just sitting there minding his own business, cutting through a morning mental fog with a cigarette and a cup of coffee. He had no idea what was heading his way.

Enter the Word Thrower. "Hey there," said Pookie's dad, "I'm a Canadian from Canada. Mind if I join you for a sit?"

Dave and I knew from the previous night's experience that we'd dodged a fairly large caliber Talking Bullet. We high fived each other, returned to our silence, and were outta there in less than ten minutes. Sure, we could have told the guy to go pound sand, but neither of us wanted it to reach that point.

We made our way to breakfast place named Magoo's that had all of the animated Disney characters drawn on the walls. I think Bambi was on the door to the women's bathroom and Dwarf Sneazey was on the men's bathroom door. Dumbo, Aladdin, Goofy, Mickey, Winnie the Pooh, Snow White and a shit ton of other favorite family fun franchises were represented on the walls of the place. I'm not sure how the owner managed to do secure permission from Mr. Disney, but I suppose if your are not selling tee shirts or coffee mugs with Disney characters on them, you can put them anywhere you want. It looked like the hand painted characters had been there a long time, maybe from the mid-1960s. Granted, the decorations might have been a little overdone, but the food was out-of-this-world delicious and certainly would be my hands down number one choice for a great breakfast place in Omak, Washington.

After breakfast I settled up and we saddled up and headed out for another day of riding in perfect weather. Omak being Omak, it did not take us a ton of time to leave it. Before we knew it we were in the middle of nowhere once again, pedaling at a leisurely pace, two abreast, on a scenic two-lane road without a car on it for probably twenty miles in either direction. We were slow rolling through paradise.

Pop quiz: what was the first lesson we learned about bike travel? Right. "You never know what's coming around the next turn." (Very good, you are paying attention.)

Too bad we weren't. We didn't see the German shepherd come tearing out from behind a rusted out doublewide trailer on the side of the road. That dog sprang at us from out of nowhere, hell-bent on tasting blood.

We'd just passed the place and hadn't given it a second thought. There was no way that derelict dump was lived in...or so we thought. The overturned broken three-legged white plastic deck chair in the front yard told a story of woe, the torn screen door hanging onto the trailer by one hinge suggested defeat, and the weeds growing five feet tall in some places indicated a suffocated sense of all future hope. A rusty Chevy Nova parts car with nothing but broken windows and a questionable past, was propped up on cinder blocks in the front yard with a small tree growing where the engine block should have been. Regardless, someone must have called that rusty hellhole home because the dog sure did.

The dog exploded from behind that trailer and careened around the corner at a full tilt; its deep barks the sound of a true Hellhound. We went from looking at the pretty trees and talking about road design, art, painting, and the role roads play in shaping the National Parks experience for the millions of people who visit each year, to asking ourselves, "Is this the day I'm going to die?"

A mean dog, it came at us as pure evil. I wish I'd had Kettle around to defend me at that point: my girl Kettle would have kicked that dog's ass right back to hell and slammed the gate shut right behind it. But alas, my favorite quarter breed wasn't available. The only defense Dave and I could come up with was increasing the distance between those teeth and us. We did our damnedest to create some.

The dog nearly caught Dave. For a good five or ten seconds the jaws of death kept an even pace within a half gallop's reach of my bearded buddy's left leg. Dave was pedaling for his life; his beard pushed flat against his chest by the wind, his eyes blue saucers, and his legs a flurry of activity. I'd never seen Dave open his eyes that wide before. It wasn't funny at the time, but it sure was funny as hell later. I almost pissed myself as the all nervousness and adrenaline worked their way out of my body through the laughter. Somehow we outpaced the dog and left it winded in our wake.

We stopped about a half-mile down the road to catch our own breaths. I *had* to stop. I'd done some pretty serious damage to my left hammy during the sprint and unfortunately, had felt it tear a little. My leg—what's that medical term? — was fucking killing me. Luckily for me, Dave had been the dog's main target, the second time that morning Dave had received unwanted canine attention. Granted, I just happened to be a little in front of Dave when Cujo the Hellhound bounced off the pages of *World War II Dogs* magazine, but Dave and I were virtually neck and neck with each other the whole time that dog ran after us.

So, there we were, straddling our bikes, stooped over with forearms on our handlebars, breathing hard, and coming down from the adrenaline rush, when I chanced a look behind us and saw the dog trotting our way, its step lively and silent, its triangular ears laid flat against its skull as it closed in. The damn thing hadn't given up on its prey just yet. It was in stealth attack mode, getting closer by the second.

"Dog!" I yelled, marking round two of another all-out sprint that included two bicycle travelers and a mad dog.

We bolted as fast as we could. Too far away to make a real go at us, the dog made a half-hearted attempt at a rush, but soon realized the show was over. It turned away, defeated, and it slinked back home to the rusted doublewide with no meat for dinner.

Dave and I put an unnecessarily large distance between the German shepherd and us before our feet touched pavement again. During our mad dash to get away from the dog the second time, I'd dropped one of my plastic water bottles in the road, but there was no way I was going back for it. My left leg was on fire and the rest of the day's progress was slowed as a result.

Our wheels rolled into Tonasket, Washington later that afternoon, leaving us with plenty of daylight for camp setup and supply replenishment. I popped in to the local hardware store and secured some mace to have on hand for any possible future dog attack. The only available mace they had left was a pink canister and it was a dead ringer for a tube of lipstick. I bought it anyway. Well, mace is mace, right? It didn't really matter what the canister looked like as long as the mace worked. Hell, I once met a Texas woman who carried a pink .45 cal. Smith and Wesson in her purse. Guns come in pink, so it wasn't a surprise to me that mace did, too. I stuck my Malibu Barbie mace/lipstick in my handlebar bag and never used it. It was more like a pink placebo than anything else.

Well deserved downtime ate up the rest of our afternoon. We visited a local ice cream store, twice. Bicycling is what happens between ice cream cones: we stopped in for an ice cream immediately after getting to town and laughed more about that dog. Between each spoonful of ice cream, we tried to recreate the looks of terror we'd worn on our faces as we'd pedaled furiously away from trouble.

Slowly but surely, we were making our way over the Rocky Mountains. It was great to know that Wauconda Pass, our next day's riding assignment, was going to be the last big bump we'd be faced with for the next few days. Flatter terrain meant fewer climbs, which meant we could start upping daily target mileage from thirty to forty miles per day. The double whammy of Rainy and Washington Passes in one fourteen hour-long day in the saddle with 54 miles logged had nearly wiped us off the map. With our trip odometers up around the two hundred and fifty mark, we were beginning to get some war stories of our own. Even though we'd only been a week or so on the road, we had more legs to work with than when we first started out. Well, in my case, leg…singular. Bad as it was after the dog attack, the pain in my left leg grew worse over the course of that afternoon. Even the ice cream wasn't helping much. The forced sprints away from that German shepherd had taken their toll on me.

Tim Fahey, welcome to Relapse City. Population: You.

It was going to take maybe three Aleve pills every morning and one or two every night with a bunch of pain in between to get through my recuperation period. I was keenly aware that prolonged use of anti-inflammatory meds comes at a cost—even if I stuck to the recommended daily dosage. Liver damage, heart problems, intestinal issues, and even increased kidney toxicity levels can result from regular daily intake. I was none too happy about the "damned if you do, damned if you don't" scenario I was facing.

After a second delicious chocolate-chip sundae, we located the free bike camping spot behind a municipal building in Tonasket, WA. With Tonasket so small, finding our way to the campsite was a cinch, and setting up our tents was a breeze in still air, in broad daylight, on level ground, and on freshly mowed grass. We knew we had Wauconda Pass in store for us the very next day, and we also knew the road started climbing just outside Tonasket. I guess people don't like living *on* the hills, just *next* to them. We had to get some good rest that night in preparation for the next day's climb.

Tonasket itself is a well-known waypoint and a popular stop for Northern Tier travellers, but that night we didn't see any. Most riders wait until later in the season to insure that the Going-to-the-Sun Road in the Rocky Mountains in Glacier National Park in Montana will be open for passage. But, as I am sure you might know by now, Dave and I weren't on the same schedule as other riders. Though our mid-May departure from Anacortes, WA upped our chances of being caught in a late season snowstorm, we had the road, the campsites, and the motels to ourselves.

That afternoon died a colorful death in a blaze of slow motion kaleidoscopic glory: the Sunset Show was spectacular. One half mile away from our campsite stood a big green Mexican food truck on the far side of a community park. Dave and I sauntered on over to that rolling kitchen and gave it a try. A scrumpdillyicious dinner was inhaled as we sat on a bench and listened to the steady hum of the refrigeration unit that kept the sodas cold. We watched another riding day get snuffed out like a used match by the gathering dark from the east.

All the cycling tourists that were to follow us later in the riding season had a good surprise in store: that unassuming food truck was serving up the food of the gods. So good was the food, we both teed up a second round of chicken burritos and another couple of cold sodas. God himself was in the kitchen that night, drumming up some pretty seriously delicious Mexican-food-truck burritos. Sure, some of you might not think The Almighty would spend His or Her precious time in a food truck disguised as a short order cook, but make no mistake: that Mexican man with the gold front tooth and the short hair and the stocky build who made us dinner was God in the flesh. Want proof? Only the Good Lord could manage to put a piece of paradise on a plate for five bucks a whack and a smile on every mouth that ate it. He's probably still there, working incognito and serving up tasty burrito miracles to anyone and everyone willing to step up to the counter of that big green truck in downtown Tonasket and hand him some cash for his efforts. If you go, stop by and tell the Good Lord I say, "Hola, y gracias" again. Best. Meal. Ever.

Between the Mexican food truck and our tents was a horse-shoe-shaped Founder's Day memorial park with portraits of some of the early Tonasket settlers who'd put Tonasket on the map in the first place. Tired as I was, I was curious about the history of Tonasket's founding fathers, so I lingered on my way back to my tent and ended up reading about every one of the town's founding fathers featured. Epitaphs were found below tacky airbrushed portraits; the park was like a large obituary page you could walk around in.

It was clear that the people who came before us had worked very hard throughout their lives to carve roads and build farms into the landscape and to bring Tonasket into existence. There was Chief Joseph Tonasket, 1822-1891, who was a rancher, a racetrack owner, and a lobbyist who went to Washington, DC to get more farm equipment to the area. There was Joshua Paul Douglas who built roads using horses and a slip scraper. Try that backbreaking work sometime. Had I not read about Mr. Douglas, I'd have not appreciated the roads I was riding as much.

Though the Founders' bones were nothing but dust in the cemetery just past where the Mexican food truck was parked, their history came alive to me with the reading of it. Even through the separation of time and space, the human struggle is the human struggle. The early settlers made something of themselves as a direct and sole result of their continued lifelong efforts. To paraphrase Pogo, "We have met the Tonasket Founders and the Tonasket Founders are us."

Tonasket settlers were once living beings just like you and me, dealing with the struggles of daily life, experiencing adversity, love, success, hardship, loss, and pain. Their 'at bat' in the game of Life came a few generations ago in the late 1800's and early 1900s while a brand-new country was stretching its arms towards the Pacific. Aside from the fact they faced different types of problem sets in their everyday lives, I was struck by the similarities of the human struggle over time. Maybe it was because I hadn't been an orphan for very long, but reading their histories was fascinating and the commonality that connects us all through time was hard for me to miss. Everyone born gets a go at Life. The founding fathers lives were much different than mine, but we all ride that same carousel and are all part of the cycle of life. (That's where the term, "Same carousel, different day" comes from in case you were wondering.)

What? You've never heard that saying?

I ambled back to my tent for some shuteye, happy to be living in 2014 and not 1883. It is not the cell phones that tip the scales for me. It's the Aleve.

All told we had completed seven days of riding, covered 230 miles, summited Rainy Pass, Washington Pass, and ridden through such notable towns as Anacortes, Bay View, Sedro-Woolley, Concrete, Rockport, Newhalem, Mazama, Winthrop, Twisp, Okanogn, Omak, Tonasket. Up ahead of us lay Wauconda Pass, the town of Republic, Washington, and then the dreaded Sherman Pass, with its 5,575 feet of vertical climb. We had enjoyed stellar weather ninety-eight percent of the time. My legs were stronger and my lower back pain and tendon ache was not as bad the next morning when I woke up (maybe a four pain level). I hopped on one leg to get some black coffee and blue pills. I smiled at the irony. Black coffee and blue pills were put on my insides to help me deal with the black and blues on my outsides. I had not discovered the fountain of youth or anything, but I can report with some measure of confidence the Canteen of Contentment can be found in any water bottle cage attached to any bike frame. All I knew for sure was that the best drug in the world comes with two wheels, a seat, handlebars, and a long stretch of road.

Bike travel must be something else on a bike that fits you. My bike didn't fit me and I was *still* having a blast.

We left the lovely town of Tonasket and started climbing Wauconda Pass the minute we got out of town, me in much better shape after two chicken burritos and a rock solid night's sleep. Also, I'd lost nine pounds of clothing off my bike as I'd mailed some items home the day before. Yes, you read that right. Nine *pounds* of stuff I really didn't need was pushed up over the Loup Loup, Washington, and Rainy Passes. Nine *pounds* came off my bike. Even with a lighter load, though, it was still a tough ride. Wauconda Pass made us work hard. The good news? With less weight to carry, my bike was more stable.

Something of note happened on the way to the Wauconda Pass that you might learn something from, so I might as well mention it.

We pedaled under a clear sky for most of the morning and early afternoon. We managed our food and water supplies to last just as far as what we thought would be our next supply point: for us, it was a convenience store about twenty-eight miles into our day. The convenience store was a low-slung building on a slight hill, so we could see if from afar. Having that convenience store in sight gave us a visual on our next pit stop, and we were looking forward to taking a break, having a bite, and enjoying a nice, cool drink in the shade.

A jab awaited us up ahead, however. We got our first inkling of trouble when, as we drew closer, we noticed there were no cars in the parking lot. Our worst fears were realized when we arrived to find the store closed. Their summer schedule (that included being open on Sundays) was to begin the following week. For Dave and me it was like being turned away from the international space station after we'd just burned our last gallon of rocket fuel to reach. No water, no food, and over thirty more miles of climbing ahead of us. We were sitting there dumbfounded, trying to process the drastic, mind-boggling turn of events, when a car pulled up and a woman got out and made her way to the CLOSED sign on the front door.

I thought she might be the store manager or an employee who could provide us access into the building and maybe to some food and drink inside it, but no—she was only there to wedge an envelope between the front door and the doorframe. With the note delivered and her business done, she turned on her heel and headed back to her car.

"Excuse me, do you work here?" I limped over to her and asked.

"No," she replied, going on to explain that she knew the owner and was only dropping by to leave a written message for her.

"Edna is the lady who owns this place. We've been friends for years and years. She ain't deaf or nothing, but when that cell phone of hers rings, she's a real Helen Keller, I can tell you that. I had to drop this note off myself to make sure she'll get it when she comes back tomorrow."

I overlooked her nonsensical Helen Keller comment—HK couldn't hear a cell phone ring (she was deaf), she could not find a cell phone (she was blind), and she couldn't work a cell phone (she lived before cell phones). And, again, so she couldn't hear the voice on the other end of the line because she was deaf. Oh, and if you sent Helen Keller a text, she couldn't read it because She. Was. Blind.

I cut right to the chase and introduced Dave and myself as Mr. Thirsty and Mr. Famished, two bike travellers in rather urgent need of replenishing our food and water supplies. When she learned of our situation, she calmly told us "not to fret" because there happened to be hot dogs and burgers available until two o'clock that very afternoon "just up the hill at the old church."

I couldn't believe it. Lunch was being served at a Sunday social just north of us off Route 20—nowhere in sight, of course, as the church was hidden behind a hill, but food and drink were a short three miles away. The Trail Angels strike again! That random lady was probably the only person to stop at that store all day and we just happened to arrive ten minutes before she did.

It boggled the mind. Her timing was uncanny. Our timing was uncanny. We were delighted she stopped by to drop off that note and tell us where the food was.

Her tidbit of information saved the day. Without that stranger's help, we would've been stranded and up against thirty particularly tough miles that included Wauconda Pass. The next thirty miles had no services whatsoever. We never would have found the food and drink for sale outside an old church on a hill without her. So we thanked her and mounted up, and found ourselves about twenty minutes later, on a lawn outside an old church with a sweeping view of the valley.

A member of the congregation and the man to see if they bring back burning witches at the stake was the volunteer grill chef that day. He openly admitted to me that he "didn't like things rare." He sold us his last four burgers that tasted like they had been cut from a pair of old construction boots and left on a hot grill for a week. No matter: fuel was fuel at that point. We drank our fill of water from a church spigot and topped off our water bottles with it as well. With food in my belly and water in my canteens, I felt a whole lot more confident about pedaling the road ahead.

Dave and I ended up chatting with a few of the churchgoers and answering questions about our trip and our direction of travel. Just like many other people, some members of the God Squad bore us some unsolicited advice. For a moment Dave and I thought we were on to something when one of them suggested we consider an alternate route and take Boulder Pass instead of Wauconda Pass, as Boulder Pass had less traffic, less vertical, and was a little longer by "only ten miles or so." It sure sounded like a dream go-round option that we'd be crazy not to consider. Our maps showed no Boulder Pass route, so we had nothing else to go on but that guy's word and whatever road signage there was out there.

Thankfully, a woman nearby overheard the advice we were getting and interrupted the guy in the middle of his sales pitch.

The woman insisted she'd just driven the Boulder Pass route and claimed it was "thirty-five miles out of the way if it was an inch."

I looked at my watch. It was two thirty in the afternoon at that point, and I, for one, though very tempted with the concept of "less vertical," didn't have an extra thirty-five miles in me. After seesawing on the issue for less than a minute, Dave and I decided to stick to our planned and previously agreed upon route that would lead us up and over Wauconda Pass (4,310 feet).

The Buddy System works well when you have a buddy like Dave. He was not as tempted to go off-route as I was. Boulder Pass sounded good to me at first blush—anything to avoid another climb on a hurt leg. But the woman was right and the guy was wrong about the additional mileage numbers. It turned out all he was doing was giving out bum steers. It would have been foolish to heed him.

One thing of note and yet another piece of irony: the only time I had anything stolen from me was on that Sunday at that church social, surrounded by church goin' folk. I had a triangular orange nylon flag on a fiberglass pole maybe four feet long attached to the back of my bike when I stopped in, and no flag when returned to my bike an hour or so later. Some sinner grabbed it while I wasn't looking: he probably needed it for his upcoming ride on the highway to Hell.

So we loaded up and took a wonda toward, and then saunta ova, Wauconda. It only took the rest of the day with my tranny in granny. Forty-one uphill miles logged and all I wanted by the end of it was a cold beer and a comfortable bed. I'd spent most of the day just cranking along, trying my best to get to where I was going. An orange flag wasn't the only thing I lost that day: the honeymoon phase of the trip was over and the romance of bicycle touring that I'd been so smitten with prior to leaving on the trip was gone. I missed my family. As much as I was looking forward to seeing the rest of this great country of ours, I was looking forward to seeing them again even more. I also missed my mom and even my dad a little, but I knew they were nowhere to be found no matter how far I pedaled.

Thank God we stuck to our route. We arrived exhausted in Republic, Washington, much later than we expected, but we were still delighted about being on the other side of Wauconda Pass. We dismounted and shared a high five once we were off our bikes at day's end. Both of us were plumb tuckered. I didn't have one pedal turn left in me after I reached the motel. Had we had followed the advice of that stranger and gone the way he'd told us, I believe we would have been in real trouble. There were no services available on either route, but the Boulder Pass route was almost twice the distance. Beautiful landscape be damned: longer distance was too high a price to pay to avoid a climb.

"Directions are like candy, Fahey," said Dave. "Don't take either one from a stranger—especially if you have a damn map."

Chapter Ten

The Bacon Beast Serves It Up, Suzy's On The Road To Nowhere

I woke up on May 25th looking forward to breakfast. It wasn't going to be just any breakfast; we heard rumors the night before about a breakfast buffet hosted by the local volunteer Fire Department that was said to be a not-to-be-missed affair.

We checked it out and were served up a delicious mix of hot pancakes, two eggs, and—the best part—two slabs of Canadian bacon. Second helpings were enjoyed as well. I got a couple of extra pancakes put on my plate by a lady who told me I needed "more meat on my bones."

Serving up the bacon was the biggest, strongest man I had ever seen in my life. He was cartoonish huge and easily dwarfed everyone around him. The Bacon Beast stood six feet ten inches tall and had more muscles on him than all the guys on my high school swim team put together. A volunteer firefighter, he was standing on the same floor I was, but I would have needed the use of a stepladder in order to look him straight in the face. How in the world he had made it that far in life without someone handing him a football and making him sign on with some— ANY—NFL team was beyond me. I thought the Bacon Beast was big, but then his brother "Little John" showed up and somehow managed to cast an even larger shadow.

Before I get to all of the bike-citement that happened over the course of the rest of the day, I wanted to answer a question a kid had asked me during one of our stops.

"What's the fastest you've ever gone on that bike?" he asked. His mom held his hand while he pointed to my bike with his other arm fully extended and his index finger about one foot away from my front tire so I wouldn't be at all unsure of which bike he was talking about.

I told him forty-one miles per hour, and at that rate, it felt like I was piloting an open-cockpit biplane going at light speed. Don't try this at home, folks. Leave riding fast to the professionals. The shimmying issue I'd wrestled with at the start of the trip had been fully resolved by lightening my load and shifting the weight around. The problem was both too much weight on the bike (I shipped some stuff home and that helped), and poorly distributed weight. I was beginning to feel more confident about the bike itself, but I wasn't fully there yet. No biggie: I wouldn't be riding very fast up Sherman Pass or any other future hills for that matter, and I knew enough about the dangers of falling at speed to keep my speed down on the descents. The mountains out west grow just as big as the Bacon Beasts and are worthy of the same amount of respect and caution.

I ate breakfast in the land of the giants and climbed five thousand feet for dessert.

Dave and I spent that entire day getting closer to heaven with every turn of the pedal. We had nowhere to go but up. After another climb up a wall made of asphalt, Sherman Pass was summited, and then we were in the full embrace of some well-deserved downhill love.

The sun was shining, it was warm, the sky was crystal clear, and it was full-on bike touring terrific. I was minding my own business rolling down a long, straight stretch of recently paved black ribbon and was enjoying every second of it. The feel of the wind in my face without having to pedal even once for miles at a time was a special level of sheer fantastic—especially when I'd climbed for hours pre-paying for it.

It was right around then, during that glorious descent through a heavily wooded area on a car free, two-lane smooth-as-silk road, that I saw something crossing the road a few hundred yards ahead of me. I had a pareidolia moment. Everyone has one of those once in a while. It is when your brain thinks you are seeing something that it's not.

"Huh, I wonder what that is," I thought to myself, still rolling downhill at a pretty good clip right toward it. "That looks like a pretty big dog." I thought.

"Nah, can't be a dog. There are no dogs around here. There are no houses in a national forest and no parked cars as far as the eye could see. Couldn't be a dog. A wolf? A deer? Maybe it's a deer," I reckoned, continuing along with the process of elimination.

"Nah, can't be a deer either. Deer have skinny getaway sticks. A moose? Nah, legs are too short. Holy shit!" I finally realized, "THAT'S A BEAR!"

I screeched to a halt. Coming across a bear in the wild was one of my biggest fears, but even so, standing there in fear, I was awestruck by the size and power of that bear. It had huge shoulder muscles that shifted on its back with each step. It looked like about three hundred pounds of my very own personal nightmare was walking across the road ahead of me. I was hoping it would not see me. The bear paused halfway across the road, its front paws on one side of the double yellow line, its rear paws on the other side of the yellow line.

It swung its huge bear head my way and took a step towards me. It sniffed the air with its nose pointed skyward in the effort. I was dead as a doornail if that bear decided to investigate any further. Eighty yards separated me from the grave, but in terms of time, I had maybe ten seconds left on my Life Clock if that bear decided to dash uphill for some tasty two-footed white meat.

Why didn't I listen to Rambo for No Reason and bring a nine to cover my six?

Here's a little-known fact I heard somewhere along the way: the grizzly bear, or *Ursus horribilis* (translation: "terrifying bear"), has the largest adrenalin glands of any mammal. Well, that might be a little-known fact because it's probably not true, but I've heard that bears can get mighty mad mighty quick, so they can go from pacifist vegetarian to murdering carnivore in no time flat. And another little factoid worth mentioning that will delve you into another, perhaps deeper sense of sheer terror that you can share with me as you read these pages of bicycling adventure; grizzlies have *no sense of guilt whatsoever* about eating other things *while they are still alive.* Even though the only things we humans eat alive are oysters and littleneck clams, somehow I am totally fine with that because those little bastards are delicious and they probably had it coming anyway. Think about it: we don't gnaw on bovines when they are still mooing or much on manatees while they swim. We have some sense of humanity.

Not so with grizzlies. They will not hesitate to crunch into anything with a brain stem, dead or alive. They might swing by for a light lunch and simply pull your arm right out of its socket or taste your leg while you scream in agony during your last moments. They might take a bite from your thigh and decide that you taste funny like a circus clown and move on. Or, they might tear you to shreds and eat you whole hog. Who would want to go like that?

In contrast, the American black bear or *Ursus americanus* will rarely eat a human, however, when they do, they at least have the decency to kill *before* they eat. So with the black bear, you are dead before they tuck their napkin under their chin and start in. Personally, I would prefer, if given the choice, to be consumed by a black bear instead of a grizzly.

For these reasons and a handful of others, I say, "Respect the grizzly."

I was defenseless against that grizzly; I was unarmed, slower, weaker, and, though I was licensed to drive a car and carry a concealed weapon in thirty-eight states and although I had a worked nights and weekends to get a post-graduate education, it didn't matter to that bear one bit. (By the way, "MBA" does not stand for "Mr. Bad Ass"). I did not have any modern day advantage over said bear. That bear was the heavyweight and I the bantamweight. If we were on a seesaw, I'd be the guy up in the air.

So there I was, just looking at that bear, and there was that bear just looking back at me. Our eyes locked, my heart stopped.

Fortunately for me, the bear behaved just like Elle McPherson the supermodel had when she met me way back in 1985 at a Sports Illustrated swimsuit model party that I'd crashed. She swung her head my way, nodded hello, and looked away again, completely uninterested.

Just as Elle had done, that bear moved on.

Once that bear went into the woods, I started breathing again (just as I had done after Elle left).

Not ten seconds after that bear disappeared, Dave pulled up and asked what was the hell was wrong with me and why I'd stopped in the middle of the road on such a glorious downhill run.

"Dude, why you yuckin' all this downhill yum?"

"I just saw a *bear*." I answered.

"Where?" He looked all around him, nonplused, and saw nothing but trees and road. "You sure it was a bear?"

"Fuck yeah, it was a bear! I've seen bears." I was still pretty pumped up about my near brush with Death. "It was unequivocally a bear. Wasn't a dog, a deer, a rat, a 'coon, a moose, a fox, or a man. It was a bear, down the road, maybe eighty yards."

I was a little insulted that Mr. Outside doubted my ability to accurately identify a goddamn grizzly bear in the wild. Ok, I get it: I might not know my ash from my willow tree elbow (to mix sayings), but when it comes to identifying apex predators, I was one for one, the undefeated champ.

Regardless of all that, I still couldn't believe Dave's next move.

He looked skyward and *sniffed the air*, and then he said, "Well, the good thing is we're downwind from where you saw him. If he'd gotten a whiff of that jar of peanut butter you're carrying in that rear left saddlebag of yours, I'd probably be digging a hole for you right now."

"Dave, did you just *smell* the peanut butter in my pannier from where you're standing? And how in the hell do you know I was downwind? What are you, Cyrano de Bergerac or some kind of Aeolus or something?"

"Who the hell is Aeolus?"

"Was, man, was. Aeolus was the Greek god of the winds. And Cyrano de Bergerac was the dude with the huge sniffer."

"Yeah, I caught that. No, man, I am not the Greek god of the winds, but thank you for your vote of confidence." He laughed. "And I wasn't smelling your fucking food, Fahey."

He laughed harder.

"Classic. I was going to sneeze, but it passed. That's why I stuck my nose high. And I *know* you have peanut butter because we had some for lunch, dumbass. And what, did you live your whole life in an office environment, Cubical Man? Look at those branches over there," he said, pointing to a tree on the side of the road. "They are bending in the wind, the wind that comes from that direction, putting us both *downwind* from said bear. Don't worry, Cubical Man. That bear probably didn't even see you from that distance. Bears are notoriously weak in the eyes. You said he went into the woods?"

"Yeah, on the right, by that stand of trees down there."

"Guess we gotta go past where you saw him."

We did. I pedaled like I was going for the all-time Tour de France time-trial record and posted a 41 mph speed again for a second or two. My ass pinched a pretty good-sized crease in my Brooks B17 leather saddle as I zipped past the point where the bear had stood looking at me. It took the better part of a week for that crease to lie back down, but not before someone noticed it and asked me, "So, is that your bike with a crease pinched into the saddle? When did you see the bear?"

How was I to know the bear wasn't lurking on the side of the road, ready to ambush us as we rode by? Man, we shot past that point and kept riding downhill fast for a good couple of miles. The only time I ever want to see a grizzly bear again is when I have a receipt for a zoo admission somewhere on my person and there is a set of steel bars between it and me. More familiar with bears after coming across at least three during his five and a half month walk of the Appalachian Trail, Dave tossed an asterisk onto my "grizzly" sighting, downgrading it to a "most likely brown or cinnamon" bear sighting, and, in so doing, reduced the drama significantly.

Such bullshit. I know that on that day I'd looked near certain death in the face and lived to tell about it. That adult male grizzly was at the top of his game. I was an innocent onlooker. We locked eyes—and my archenemy, *Ursus horribilis*, stood down and ducked into the woods in ignoble retreat, and, yes, dare I say it, ignoble defeat.

I saw a grizzly bear out in the wild, and no one, *no one*, not even Dave, Mr. Outdoors, can take that away from me.

Question: What color is a grizzly bear? Oh, brown or cinnamon, you say? Boom! Case closed. My heart rate slowed with every mile of distance I added between that bear and me.

The forty-seven miles we pedaled that day led to a place I would not have been motivated to get to, so I'm glad I didn't have any prior knowledge of it at our start. We ended up in a shithole RV Park for fifteen bucks a night. What does fifteen dollars buy you? Not much these days, I can assure you that. More specifically it buys a rocky patch of uncut grass and scraggily weeds between two rusted RVs with a grand total of three wheels between both of them. The grass and weeds had the RVs surrounded. The one on the left had the word "Dreamweaver" still legible on the back above the filthy dirty rear window and the other one had the word "Weekend Adventurer" in scripted text with little birds flying out of the "r" in Adventurer along the side panel. Both former vehicles looked like they'd been abandoned sometime during the Nixon administration. So, to answer the question, fifteen bucks buys you a plot in the RV Park where dream weavers and weekend adventurers go to die.

I swear there is no rest for the weary.

Yet even in the place where dreams go to die, even in that place of disenchantment, there was someone there offering another way to look at things.

Suzy Bee was the RV Park Manager, and as depressing as I found the place to be, you could not wipe the smile off her face. She winked and big waved me up into her RV home/office with her whole arm. Her old broken down RV camper was called "The Explorer" and it, too, had silhouettes of little birds flying out of the last "r" in the word Explorer.

I stepped up one stair to give her the cash for one night's lodging. She sat in the driver's seat *with her hands on the wheel* like the Explorer was actually exploring. Judging by the grass growing up between the floorboards at her feet, I could see that the RV had not been living up to its "Explorer" name for at least five or six years.

But did Suzy care? Hell no! Old Suzy appeared to have everything she wanted.

While she was looking for her cash box to get me some change, she asked me where I came from and how many miles I'd ridden on my bike that day. I told her "About fifty." I'd rounded up from forty-seven or so.

"Fifty? Is that all you got?" she asked. It was an odd question coming from a woman who probably hadn't walked much more than fifty miles in the past year.

"We had a guy stay here one night who had ridden one hundred twenty-one and a half miles. He was a skinny little fella just like you, but determined."

As I stood waiting for my change, I wondered what determination looked like. Should I clench my teeth and puff out my chest? Maybe get a facial tattoo? Wear slimming clothes? I wanted to look determined, but didn't have a clue how to do it.

I took a gander around the inside of her business office and started to feel better about my "fifty miles is that all you got?" self. There were empty pizza boxes strewn everywhere and a couch buried under dirty towels. Everything was dirty inside that vehicle, including the dingy windows and, somehow, the roof lining. How does that even happen? Had water leaked from above and stained it? I wasn't sure. Way in back I spotted the handlebars of an old exercise bike drowning in pool of old clothing and storage boxes with papers falling out of them.

I was startled by a sharp knock on the door behind me.

"Hey, Suzy. Nine bucks."

"Hey, Tony. Change a twenty?"

"Sure."

Suzy leaned from the driver's seat and steadied herself with one hand on the steering wheel as she reached past me and handed Tony the same twenty bucks that had spent the day with me riding my "is that all you got?" fifty miles.

"Here you go," said Tony as he gave her the pizza. "And here you go again," he said as he handed her the change.

Suzy plucked the ten out of his hand.

"That last one's for you, so keep it Tony, thanks."

"Thanks," replied Tony, putting the dollar tip in his pocket. "And don't forget; we close early tonight, so call before seven thirty if you want another one."

Suzy turned to me as she placed the pizza box on the dash. "I call Tony the Pizza Priest because every day, sometimes twice a day—right, Tony? Every day he comes by and gets me closer to my one and only true love besides Brad Pitt. Tony brings me my pepperoni pizza. I swear I'd kill for a slice of that goddamn pepperoni heaven."

Tony pointed to the box. "No need to kill anyone, Suzy. You got the pizza right there and I'm just a phone call and three minutes away. See yah Suzy." Tony turned to me, "Bye, mister."

"So long," I said.

Suzy gave me my five dollars of change, popped open the box, and dug into her first slice, taking a bite of that "goddamn pepperoni heaven." She was already into her second bite by the time I stepped onto the dirt and closed the screen door behind me. I didn't see her chewing, but—unfortunately—I heard her taste bud orgasm. It came out in a high-pitched wail of pleasure that I would very much like to un-hear, but I can't.

Life lesson: even though she was sitting in the driver's seat going nowhere fast in an RV propped up by a pile of firewood and cinder blocks, Suzy seemed happy going nowhere. While others fought the good fight in an attempt to make their way in the world, Suzy had already arrived at her destination. It goes to show you that sometimes all you really need is a good slice of pizza, a comfortable seat to take in your worldview, and a sense of perspective to make you realize how good you got it.

"Hey, nobody's shooting at me and I can get a pizza any time I damn well please."

Five minutes after paying for the opportunity to sleep on another patch of weedy gravel, I slid six quarters into a coin box and stood butt naked under a dead spigot waiting for the shower to come on. It took a while, but clean warm water came my way for a good ten minutes. Fortunately, that was enough time to wash the road off me and get rinsed off before another financial payment was required. Nothing says you have made it in life more than having to use a coin-operated shower.

Before Dave and I headed out to dinner, I made a few calls. It was great to talk to my wife and son and it was also nice to catch up with my brothers and sisters. I missed seeing them, too. The calls left me a little homesick for the rest of the evening. I say this tongue in cheek, but somehow, life back home had continued on without me: my siblings had gotten together that evening for drinks and dinner and raised a toast to our dearly departed mom. I learned that my wife and son were happy and a little tired after a full day of summer fun in Maine.

All was well on the home front.

I slapped mosquitoes in the fading light and felt a world away from the sunny beaches and sunset toasts. I told myself that I'd be back home and would take another swing at that life after the trip was over. Bike trips don't last forever.

I couldn't pinpoint why I was feeling blue; maybe it was the pain in my legs and my lower back, maybe something else had me feeling down in the dumps. My mom had died less than two months before and I think the calendar was also pretty close to landing on the one year, two month anniversary of my dad's death, too. It might have been a combination of things, but, for whatever the reason, I was feeling pretty blah.

On the bright side, however, my friend Mr. Warren Buffett himself could not have spent his money any more wisely than I had: that shower got me as clean as a whistle and smelling fresh as a daisy once again. To boot, I took comfort in the fact that I had stared down a grizzly bear in the wild and had lived to tell about it. Not a lot of guys can say that.

"Yeah, including you," Dave would say.

The next day we were up and out by mid-morning and had another forty miles under our belts by day's end. We stayed at Lake Thomas campsite, inside or outside some small town further east in Washington. It was tough for me to tell what constituted a town out there sometimes. Regardless, where we were sure was beautiful and filled with my two very favorite things: peace and quiet. By the sunset hour, Dave was down by the lake being an artist, and I was up at a campsite picnic table being a writer. How strange that two near complete strangers could end up sharing a great bike trip like the one we were on. Just like the weather conditions, our riding camaraderie was working out well; we were both enjoying the trip.

Dinner that night was burgers at Beaver Camp, co-owned by a former long-haul trucker named Danny and his wife, Peggy, a part-timer at the US Post Office. They had a gift shop that had T-shirts that posed the question, GOT BEAVER? Nice, huh? Yeah, I really wanted one. It was so hilarious the way they replaced the word 'milk' with 'beaver'. It was super-classy and clever. It didn't take a nanosecond for me to decide to forgo the purchase and deny myself the chance to be a misogynistic dolt who would insult more than half the world's population by wearing the question '*Got Beaver?*' blazed across their chest. I suspected if the guys who wore those shirts honestly answered the question posed on their t-shirt, they would have to answer, "No man. I don't got beaver."

T-shirts like that put the 'ass' in class, yet they continue to sell. Well, they sell to big people: a sign in the store read: "We are all out of size XXL."

The bugs were having at me, and the sun was going down, so I called it a day, a day that had been the best riding day yet in a string of truly spectacular days in the saddle. We'd rolled through gorgeous scenery that could not have possibly shown any better. It was like rolling through an Albert Bierstadt painting. I stopped on a bridge to take a picture I called "Three Roads," as it shows a railway track, a river, and a dirt road with a mountain and a beautiful sky complete with white, puffy clouds above. It was beautiful out there on the road.

Get on a bike and go see it for yourself. It's worth it.

By the end of the next day, our tenth day of riding, saddle worn Dave and I decided we'd hoof it to dinner to give our legs a little respite from the pedaling. It was only a mile or so to the restaurant, so we walked on the very legs that had gotten us that far from the Pacific.

"Wow," said Dave, looking at me walk across the street. "You look like that third to last guy on the right on the human evolution chart. You know that chart, with all the guys walking in a line that show the various stages of human development?"

"Yeah, I'm familiar with that chart and you look just like the guy walking behind me, dragging your knuckles."

We made it to the so-so dinner place walking under a sky aglow with the sunset light bouncing off the leaden storm clouds that were approaching from the west.

The bar restaurant was dimly lit inside and came complete with red pleather booths and maroon carpeting. Johnny Cash was coming at us low and slow: Ring of Fire was being whispered through hidden speakers. The acoustics were spectacular. If I hadn't known Johnny Cash was dead, I'd have sworn he was singing in the next room. A party of eight was leaving just as we arrived which left us with the only other customer in the place, an amicable guy named Wes who was talking to the wait staff a few decibels higher than was necessary. Wes insisted on buying us a beer when he found out we were riding the Northern Tier.

Normally, I'd happily engage in conversation with just about anyone—as I am sure you have figured out by now—but I have never been a big fan of chatting up intoxicated people. Like the weather, their demeanors can change quickly and without warning. So it was with some reluctance that we gave in to Wes's demand to have a "Beer on me, goddammit."

Our dinners arrived. I had the chicken Alfredo, and Dave had a burger. The meal was as pedestrian as we had been walking over to it. After buying Wes a payback round from each of us and thus putting a smile on his face, we left the place and immediately noticed the storm clouds we'd spied earlier had changed mood and were now a more threatening dreary lead-gray front that was working its way toward us and casting a pale gloom onto everything below. A hard rain was coming so we picked up our walking pace to insure we'd make it back before the clouds threw a thunderous crying tantrum.

Ah, bike travel just keeps on giving. There I was, still wincing from a rather stubborn case of loneliness, residue from my recent chats with wife, son, brothers and sisters. Not even the distraction of a beautiful day's ride could shake me free of The Lonely. We made it back to camp just as dry as we had been at dinner, so we shot the shit until the rain hit, and ducked into our respective tents. I tried my best to make myself comfortable on the ground. Leg pain and dreary weather stoked a rather dour outlook. Big, gray drops of rain splashed onto my tent, spit from shroud suspended three thousand feet in the sky above. Even though it was a half hour past sunset, the battleship gray clouds remained aglow by the light pollution spewing from behind a nearby ridge.

And yet, through all that graying pall came an unexpected and rather uplifting ray of light, a gift delivered to me by the pure magic of sound that neither rain nor gloom nor dark of night could intercept. I coaxed sleep while the rain fell. I felt sad and alone in the world (SFX: weeping violins), even though logic said I wasn't. As the night settled in, the soundscape shifted gears. Commuter traffic and camper conversations waned while the raindrops began to hit my tent cover with more regularity. My concerns about rain pooling nearby and seeping up into my tent distracted me from other, more emotional thoughts. I poked my head out for a second for a check on the nearby drainage and everything looked ok. I was on level ground and the rain wasn't pooling…yet. A few minutes later I heard a hoot owl hoot and a train click-clack by. Another train, much further away, whistled a long lonely note that echoed off distant rocky cliffs.

People say the best time to listen to blues music is when you're feeling a little down, or a little "blue" yourself. Misery loves company, I guess. Well, if anyone was ready to hear the blues that night, it was I. Quite surprisingly, the lonely toot tooting wail of a train whistle sounded to me like a rousing blues performance put on by an anonymous conductor whose hand pulled a whistle lanyard miles away. Knowing someone else was out there and awake on that dreary, rainy night was somehow heartening to me.

The sound of the train's whistle drifted slowly away, it's note faded and blended into the background. The rain pattering on my tent took center stage. I listened harder for that lonely whistle, but it hid behind other sounds and was gone. That whistle lulled me towards the sweet, dark deliciousness of a good night's sleep. The whistle of a train was my blues lullaby and one of the last sounds I remember hearing that night.

The next morning I was happy to report that my tent performed just as well as the salesman had promised—it passed its first rain trial with flying colors. I awoke dry as a bone and warm as toast, but everything outside looked like it had spent a chilly night in a rolling mist. With the morning sun low in the sky, my bike looked like it was draped in sunlit diamonds. A blink of the eyes and a better focus revealed the truth. Those weren't diamonds—they were raindrops: my bike was soaking wet.

I got my lazy butt up and out of the tent and started the drying off and bivouac routine in the fresh air. I was no longer blue, and was psyched for another day on the road. The previous night's long stretch of sound sleep was just what the doctor ordered. Maybe I'd only have one Aleve with my morning cup of freeze-dried coffee. I was feeling more myself, more op-*Tim*-istic.

At eight o'clock that morning a factory whistle sounded somewhere off in the distance, behind the ridge, and I caught myself wondering if they ever stopped working on whatever they were working on. I'd heard that factory whistle sporadically throughout the night. Three shifts a day is a lot of production. I hoped they weren't making land mines. We have too much of those already.

Dave got up a little later. He stuck his hairy head out of his tent and took a look around.

"Dude, you catch that rain last night? Pussies and poodles, man, pussies and poodles."

"Don't you mean it was raining cats and dogs?"

"Conformist," he replied, then ducked his head back into his tent.

We made our way to a gas station convenience store in desperate need of a makeover. After tasting the coffee, we realized it also needed a coffee brewer, and after tasting the breakfast sandwiches, we realized it needed a cook. That particular convenience store was selling diarrhea in a cup and shit on a plate.

Both were just awful. How a dump like that could have any re-peat customers was beyond me.

Not a heck of a lot happened that day after we ate those sand-wiches. I saw a turtle on the road. Yeah, that was way cool. My thoughts upon seeing the turtle were as follows: road, road, stick, rock, road, road, road, road, turtle, road, road, road, road…wait, was that a ginormous red-and-yellow-clawed, green-shelled box turtle?

I turned around and helped the turtle across the road and twice prevented it from being hit by oncoming traffic. My tenure as a turtle traffic cop ended once said turtle entered the muck on the other side of the road. I figure saving an ancient multicolored box turtle from becoming a road kill pancake had earned me spe-cial reward points at the First Karma Bank of Effing Awesome.

Oh, and while I'm on the subject of animals, heretofore unmentioned is my observation that there was a tremendous amount of road kill all along the Northern Tier and probably along every roadway in the world. It is impossible to miss see-ing the roadside carnage at bicycle speeds. Every animal you can imagine besides man—deer, snakes, birds, cats, dogs, tur-tles, squirrels, opossums, moles, rats, frogs, fox, and raccoon to name a few—was seen firsthand in varying stages of decay by your author. I never saw a dead bat, though, and found it ironic that the blind flyers managed to dodge things even the flying sighted didn't. I saw a turkey and a hawk carcass, too.

We rode sixty-seven unspectacular miles that day: bike for sale.

We stayed at the Newport Motel that night. That's Newport, Washington, folks, a far cry from the Rhode Island seaside play-ground of the 1920s social elite. The Wi-Fi password was "mud-bay28," which beat the Wi-Fi password from another motel from the previous week, "bigbark2014," which was handed to me, fit-tingly, by a woman of stature.

Biking is great and all, but sometimes I found myself thinking that all I wanted to do was sit on my ass and twist on the gas. I had a perfectly good 2007 BMW R1200 GS motorcycle at home in my garage, identical to the one that passed me by during that day's ride. It was the same make, model, and color as mine. Why hadn't I brought a motor with me on this trip? What the hell was I thinking? Boy, it looked like that motorcyclist was having fun, twisting his wrist and logging the miles at a rate somewhere north of the speed limit. Why was I pedaling a bike again? Can someone remind me? Oh, yeah—on a bike I get to meet people like Kettle's owner and Suzy Bee and the Canadian from Penticton who used the word *foodstuffs*.

So worth it.

My odometer went just past the marijuana mile (420) when we stopped for the night. Most of the steep stuff was behind us and I was very happy about that. Better yet, I had much more confidence in my bike now that I had asked it to carry less weight and had learned how to pack better. In fact, because I had reached the decision to keep the bike, it was time to give it a name. I had been considering *The Flash* or *Red Lightning* or the *Tim-In-A-Tor* (say it aloud in an Austrian accent). Granted, earlier in the trip, I would have called it *Bike-Ageddon-Me-Nowhere* or *The Wobbler* or *Timmy's Shimmy*, but in the end, I decided to go with the *Fun Mover*. Not the *Bun Mover* (although that might also work), but the *Fun Mover*. The name was not wholly original: Dave had seen an RV trailer named *Fun Mover* and told me about it later. The name stuck in my head, and that was it. The Fun Mover moves the fun.

We were almost through the state of Washington. Up next: the state of Idaho. I saw a T-shirt once that read, "I-da-hoe? No, you da hoe!"

I love classy wordplay, don't you?

Ever hear the question made up of some state names? It goes like this: "If Mississippi gave Missouri a New Jersey, what would Delaware? Idaho, Alaska!"

My dad's friend Jack McCall taught me that a long time ago, and I still remember.

Damn, he's gone, too.

Chapter Eleven

A New State, A New Grad, An Old
Resort, A Trucker's Invite

We crossed over our very first state line and landed in Sandpoint, Idaho for the night. Tempted as I was to visit my cousin and her family in Boise, I dismissed the idea almost immediately as it was too far off route to be practical: at that point in my ride I would not go seven hundred miles out of my way to see anybody. Instead, Dave and I stayed put in Sandpoint. We'd been riding for ten days straight during which time we had covered 462 miles, gone over Rainy

Pass, Washington Pass, Loup Loup Pass, Wauconda Pass, and Sherman Pass, said goodbye to the Rockies, and weathered the changing moods of bicycle touring. We both needed a break from the road.

Stepping inside out of the cold and knowing we could stay for a while was a fantastic. Our motel room was not anything special in and of itself, but it wasn't a sidewalk or a tent site, so it certainly made the grade. Everything about the room was as expected: bad art, twin beds, maroon carpeting, polyester curtains, TV, mini fridge, and bathroom with politically correct notes on how to save the planet. 'Leave your dirty towels on the floor, hang towels you can use again on hooks so housekeeping knows what to take and what to leave,' that sort of thing. Yes, it was similar to every other motel room I have ever checked into, but man oh man, that night I really appreciated the climate controlled, bug-free environment.

A warm shower, a change of clothes, and a shave washed all of the road off of me and I felt like a human once again. One big load of laundry and everything would be right with the world. I shot down to the local Wash 'N Dry while Dave hung out in the room in front of the TV.

During the rinse cycle I met a grandmother of nine. By the time my clothes were out of the drier we were besties. We had covered a lot of topics while the clothing got cleaned. The economy, the trouble with children these days, the sorry state of government affairs, and the dearth of positive male role models in today's society had all been addressed.

"Where is the Steve McQueen type for my grandkids to look up to?" she asked me.

I had no answer for her.

When I was folding one of my last items, she told me I had her vote. I told her I was not a candidate for any office.

"Run anyway," she said, dismissively. "I'm worried about my grandkids and you seem like a good sort."

My name is Tim Fahey and I approve this message...

Too bad I don't have the stomach for politics: I killed it in Sandpoint. I had a lock on the Laundromat Ladies voting block.

As we put clean clothes into our laundry baskets, grandma and I agreed that the world is going to hell in a hand basket. We shook hands and parted company, but by working together we did something a lot of politicians have not done in years: grandma and I cleaned up Washing them, DC (Dirty Clothes).

That night we took grandma's restaurant suggestion and dined at Arlo's, an Italian restaurant owned and operated by a woman born and raised in Greenwich Village, New York. She was the real deal for the Italian meal, having grown up at the feet of her Italian mother and grandmother, both of whom were born in Italy and had spent a lot of time in kitchens on two continents. Her time in the kitchen had been time well spent: our meals were stupendous.

The next morning Dave and I reached a game time decision and declared it was to be a Zero Day. That's right— zero miles forecast. The mighty had fallen, but after ten days of nothing but straight biking, our break was well deserved. Besides, I got tired of kicking' *butt*, so I thought I'd try kicking' *back* for a bit. Just resting for an extra day in Sandpoint was the right call as there were no bears, dogs, or bugs inside the hotel. And with no legs to speak of, I had no real choice in the matter.

The day flew by. After a few hours of lazing around, I started to ponder taking a rest *week*—rest-day hours passed quickly and one day didn't seem long enough to fully recover from all those continuous days of riding, riding that included going over the Rocky Mountain range.

Our delicious dinner the previous night was followed up by a scrumptious breakfast at Connie's Restaurant right there in downtown Sandpoint. Good food is difficult to find on the road, so we really appreciated the two good meals in a row thing. Eggs,

bacon, coffee, orange juice, then more eggs and some more coffee and some whole wheat toast, hold the hash browns. It seemed
a shame to eat that much food and not put it to immediate use
as fuel for a long ride, but it did serve as energy for my return
trip to bed for a four hour nap. I don't know what Dave did on
that zero day, but I didn't see him much until late that afternoon
when we decided that dinner was to be a return engagement at
Arlo's Restaurant. That place was like the mafia: you try to leave,
but they just keep dragging you back...we sat at the same table
for a second night in a row. I ended the evening with a big bear
hug from our hostess on the way out. She was a nice lady and a
great cook.

The next morning brought the end of the month (May 31st)
and a new beginning. My legs felt better after spending a full day
off the pedals. A second straight good night's rest, a morning
with a bright sun and a cloudless sky, a cup of good coffee, and
warmer temperatures made for a huge difference in my mental
outlook. The previous day's zero was worth every second of rest
we'd gotten from it, but Dave threw in a caveat.

"Beware, man. Zeros can mess with your head."

We saddled up and pedaled long enough to cover a marathon distance (26.2 miles) and cross another state line before
calling it quits.

We'd traversed northern Idaho in less than three days and
just after getting into Montana we set up camp. Unfortunately,
we'd left comfort, good food, and warmth behind us when we'd
said goodbye to Idaho.

God, it was cold that first night in Montana. The temperature flirted with and then married the upper twenties. It was not
a two-in-a-bag situation, but by the following morning I better
understood the reasons behind such desperate survival moves.
Even though I had every single piece of clothing I had with me
on (again!), I was still cold and didn't remember getting much
sleep that night.

At first light I got out of my tent and joined Dave by the fire he'd lit about a half hour earlier. I took an action photo of him making oatmeal. Cool, right? That picture shows you the reality of the write and roll tour I was on. Don't believe the bike touring hype, folks: it ain't all unicorns and rainbows, I can tell you that. Bike touring is getting up on a freezing cold morning and mixing water, oats, and propane together for breakfast.

Curious to see how far it was to the next state line, I sorted through a pile of bike maps for a look. Yikes, I was still a full one thousand miles away from even getting to North Dakota. As I sat there shivering by the fire, in one had I had the one map section that was being used to get me across the state I was in, and in the other hand I had the other *eleven* map sections that I would need to navigate the rest of my way back home. Comparing the sheer number of map sections I'd used already (one) to the number I had to use to get home (10) showed me just how far I still had to go. My body, manufactured in 1961, was going to be tested. Five hundred miles into this venture felt more like five thousand.

Ah, but that morning's campfire warmed the cockles of my heart and soul and the coffee I drank got my blood circulating fast enough to warm my fingers and toes. Sure, I could see my breath and, sure, I had frost on the outside of my tent (again), but I had the campfire for warmth. It had been a cold dash from my sleeping bag to the fire, but the fire's warmth was worth it.

Alas, the coffee was not. A word of advice to the reader: when selecting sleeves of instant coffee, do yourself a big, fat favor: avoid Folgers. It is not "the best part of waking up." It couldn't be because if "The best part of waking up was Folgers in your cup", everyone on the planet would remain abed. How could selling freeze-dried coffee that tastes so terrible be a thing? I understand the convenience, but argh, that taste.

So after a night spent shivering in my sleeping bag and after a breakfast of instant black coffee, I reluctantly mounted up and headed out. I could tell I was running on fumes, even after the zero we took in Sandpoint. That day's short, sub-thirty mile ride was the straw that broke the camel's back. By the time we arrived at Koocanusa Lake and Resort I felt like all the energy in my body had been bled out of me. My batteries were depleted. Something seemed wrong: being tired after a day's thirty-mile ride is one thing, but reaching the point where you are a little dizzy and completely fagged is another.

Maybe it was the poor night's sleep that did it, or it was the cold temperatures of the past few days that wore me down, or maybe it was the culmination of my Rocky Mountain efforts that caught up to me. I had no idea why I felt so sapped. All I knew is that I needed to get off my bike and rest. That afternoon the temperature had bounced back, so that was good, but I still felt like I was eighty years old.

Just as soon as we'd turned down the driveway to the "resort," it was abundantly clear that the Koocanusa Lake Resort and Marina had seen better days. The lake was drying up to the point where any bather looking to get wet would indeed have to take a long walk off a short pier in order to do so, as all the docks ended far short of the water. Abandoned and decaying boats tied to moorings lay sideways like so many dead bloated fish rotting high and dry on land that had once been submerged. Someone had pulled the plug on the dirty bathtub and a bathtub ring one hundred yards wide collared the whole lake, staining the land with the water's retreat.

I wondered what the place must have looked like fifty years before when the lake was more likely full, when there were half as many people on the planet, and when no computers or cell phones clouded the minds of lakeside tourists just out to have a good time. It must have been nice back then when the American Dream was young, full of promise, and everyone still believed the hype. Wish I'd been there to enjoy it.

Today? Don't let the words *resort* and *marina* fool you by suggesting it was "nice" and/or "tasteful." The "Under New Management" sign was itself covered in dust and hung askew on a wall in the office.

"What happened to the old management?" I asked a kid looking out onto the water at a guy wearing a wife beater T-shirt that asked, "GOT BEAVER?" The guy was impressive: he was smoking a cigar *while waterskiing*. Now I knew where one of those XXL sizes had gone… Though the cigar smoking water skier would never in a million years been mistaken for a vacationing aristocrat or a fashionista out for a thrill, the guy looked like he was having a shit ton of fun out there. Tired as I was, I wanted to join him on the water. Give me the towrope and the stogie. Hell, gimmie the wife beater T-shirt in the XXL, too.

The place was just like the French Riviera, but without the French.

Or the Riviera.

The kid answered my question. "Oh, I don't exactly know when the new management arrived, but I heard it was a seamless transition of power officiated and overseen by a bankruptcy judge. I do know a little something about the old management, though. I heard the previous owner was not a good guy. He used to beat his children before he died in a drunk-driving accident." The kid did the air quotes thing with his fingers when he said, "drunk driving accident."

"The guy died under questionable circumstances. The new people don't have any kids, so…"

Usually when people end a sentence with a lingering "so…" they assume that the listener is able to patch together the rest of the point.

I was as unable to reach his point just as the resort docks were unable to reach the water.

The kid continued to fill me in on the old management backstory. It was not made clear to me if the previous owner of the resort had lived long enough to see his sons grow up to shoot one another in a drunken rage. All I knew is that one of the "Old Management" sons died from a single gunshot wound to the chest, and the other son, the shooter, went to jail for it. Two violent deaths, one incarceration, one totaled car; it sounded like the final score of an illegal gladiator match, not the final line of a family story, but there it was.

"New management" came in the form of a sixty-eight year old general manager named Theo. He wasn't really "new" or "management," but was more like a reluctant social worker assigned to oversee the case of a forlorn, ignored, and dying marina resort. From the looks of it, the patient was not long for this world. The place should have had a "Do Not Resuscitate" order stapled to the deed. Ironically, the lake was drying up, but it would still drown…in red ink.

With the season still a few weeks off, the Koocanusa Lake Marina and Resort was empty, which gave Dave and I the run of the place. We had first dibs on any and all accommodations. I was very interested in creating the perfect environment for the best night's sleep possible, so I decided to head out on a short housing inspection tour before I reached a final decision on where to lay my head for the evening.

Theo picked me up in a golf cart and we sped off along a pitted dirt road, our inspection tour underway. We were off to see the Cabin, the Apartment, and the Annex. Sitting in that golf cart with the wind in my face was great. It was like riding a bike downhill, but I was sitting down on the soft vinyl of the golf cart's passenger seat and speeding along quite nicely over level ground. It had been less than two weeks since I'd been in a four-wheeled motorized vehicle, but my appreciation for them had grown considerably.

Our first stop in the tour of housing hell: the Cabin. Oh, my good Lord. Little did the new management know—I would have paid five bucks *not* to see the inside of that shithole. It was worth nowhere near the nightly rate of eighty bucks my boy Theo was asking for it. On the outside, the Cabin looked like it was losing the war of atrophy: shingles were dropping off of it and it badly needed a paintjob. On the inside it was cold, dank, dark, damp and dumpy. It wasn't a cabin as much as it was a little wooden one-story aperture in the dirt where Depression and Decrepitude hung out. No one in his or her right mind would want to stay there. Worse yet, it smelled more than slightly of urine, a urine which I'd hoped was from some squirrel or feral cat that had somehow gained access inside. With no clear signs of a forced entry, the evidence suggested the stink was more likely leftover from a previous human occupant.

Ew.

Cabin? Hell no.

Next?

I climbed back into the golf cart, and off we went to inspect the "Apartment" accommodation, which had "its own private toilets with flushing action." (Be still my beating heart.) The Apartment was not located above some gourmet bakery or modern art gallery or tucked neatly into some cool old boat-house—it was just another shithole that sat sagging in the dirt right next to a big brown building with a broken window that housed the resort's common shower and restroom facilities.

Theo announced, "This is the Apartment" when we got there and repeated, "This is the Apartment" when he unlocked and opened the door. He stepped back. I peeked in and turned away almost immediately, repulsed. The Apartment's architect and the interior designer had conspired to erect a building that would never live up to the seventy-five-dollar-a-night rate. The best way to describe the place was "late 1970s decomposing disaster." It had a brown shag carpet and a simply exhausted crushed red velvet couch with more miles on it than a highway map. If the ugly ass couch and all the rest of the furniture from that hellhole was dragged to the curb and offered for "Free", there'd be no takers.

I know I'd seen the place before, though. I think I saw it on TV once, maybe on an episode of C.O.P.S. when they busted those drug dealing meth cooks.

"Thanks, but I'll pass on this too, Theo." It appeared to me that he couldn't have cared less either way.

"Well, we are all the way out here, do you want to see the Anus?" he asked me.

"Excuse me?" I asked, hoping he had mispronounced that last word he'd spoken.

"Do you want to see the Anus? You can stay there if you want, you and your friend. I'll give you a discount rate of fifty bucks. Interested?"

I looked at him sideways. I was pretty sure he meant to say 'annex' instead of...you know, what he actually said, but I imagined they were, in the end, pretty much the same thing if the Cabin and the Apartment served as any indication.

"Nah," I responded, adding, "Hey, can we go back to Dave now?"

I could only imagine what the "Anus" of the Koocanusa Lake Resort and Marina looked like. I had seen enough of the place already: the Cabin and Apartment alone made my tent seem like the Waldorf Astoria. I was looking forward to setting it up immediately and blocking out the past half hour just as effectively as I had blocked out memories from my awkward years in junior high.

And high school.

And college, for that matter.

Theo didn't care what I chose. The "Anus," the Crappy Cabin, and the Abysmal Apartment were all deplorable offerings. I was comfortable with my decision to sleep in the tent I came with.

So, for thirty bucks, I went with tent site number one, which was just another cleared patch of ground next to a dirt parking lot. There was no cell service in the Koocanusa Lake Resort and Marina, but there were a few bright spots. We were in Montana, after all, and you would have to try pretty hard to make that state look bad. Also, I got the chance to spend some quality time with my boy Theo, who was rockin' the old-man party mullet—reading glasses up front, bald spot and a gray haired rat tail in the back. Theo told me he used to play music loud because he liked it. Now he played music loud because he wanted to hear it. Ah, the rock 'n roll circle of life.

While I waited for Theo to return with my change from somewhere inside the manager's office, I sat down on the only seat available outside the building, a parked quad. There I struck up a conversation with a kid who was leaning against a door that said "Employees Only." She was on a smoke break from the kitchen. I asked her how long she'd been a smoker.

"Two years. I started smoking cigarettes at sixteen and I wish I never did. I'm hooked now and trying to stop. Where are you from?" she asked.

Stacy seemed impressed that Dave and I had ridden as far as we had and that we'd flown "All the way from the east coast, jeez." She confessed she'd never flown in an airplane and the farthest west she'd been was Portland, Oregon, "So I got to see the 'waters of the Pacific' as my dad called them, which is cool," she said.

She had driven the whole way there and back with her dad.

The farthest east she'd ever gone in her "whole entire life" was Eureka, IL. I thought it was funny that someone would go all the way to a place called 'Eureka' only to turn around and go home once you got there. To me, Eureka means, "Holy shit! I've discovered something. This is a moment of epiphany for me! Eureka! Let's discover more things!" For Stacy's dad it was more like, "Eureka, look at the time. Get back in the car, Stacy. You will never go further east with me than right here."

I learned all the men in Stacy's family had worked in the local asbestos mines before the mines closed a while back. Stacy told me about the time when her dad took her to visit the gravesites of all her uncles who she "barely remembered." All of them got cancer and died before reaching the ripe old age of fifty.

"My momma told me that if you inhale airborne carcinogens every day, you are going to die early, and they all did. Workers said sometimes it looked like it was snowing inside the mines and none of them had no masks." Stacy lit a second cigarette and looked at her watch. "There they were, all my uncles, lined up and dead in the graveyard, killed by the cancer that the corporations exposed them to, and none of them got no money for their troubles."

Stacy took a drag of her cigarette. I don't think she saw the irony of the last thing she ever said to me.

Our chat came to an abrupt close when Theo returned from the manager's office with my change. He rounded the corner and looked up from counting the dollar bills in his hands and stopped dead in his tracks.

"What the hell do you think you're doing?" he asked.

"Waiting for you to get back with my change," I replied, "Ten bucks back from forty, right?" (The tent-site fees were actually twenty dollars per site, but even though we only took up one site, Theo charged me a total of thirty dollars—twenty for the site, and ten extra dollars out of the goodness in his heart "because there's two of yah, plus taxes.")

"Never, ever sit on another man's quad!" he yelled.

"Sorry," I said, as I scrambled off of it.

"Damn! Where'd you say you were from, boy? Don't you know that sitting on another man's quad without his specific permission is like dry humping his wife when he's not around? You could get shot."

I took my ten bucks and high-tailed it back to tent site one. There I assembled my tent, and, after a quick dinner, brushed my teeth, zippered my tent shut, and called it a day. Sitting on that quad sure didn't feel like dry humping another man's wife, but I guess I had to go with the local knowledge: if taking a seat on a quad was the equivalent of a heavy petting session in Montana, it was no wonder the state had a dwindling population.

I went to sleep seconds after my hand finished zippering up the tent. I did not touch that zipper for thirteen hours straight. Yes fans, I spent thirteen hours in my tent (six thirty to bed with a seven thirty wake up) after attacking a bison burger at the Koocanusa Lake Resort dining room.

I woke up a new man.

When I say I woke up a new man, I mean I woke up a new man: my tent gave birth to an entirely new *being*. Nearly everything in my body worked well. I suffered no back pain, my leg felt a whole lot better, I lost weight, and my beard was longer. I'm telling you, something happened. My body had shut down and rebuilt itself overnight. Thirteen hours? Straight? I have not slept like that since I was a teenager. And mind you, I was sleeping on the ground, not in a comfortable bed. I felt *younger*. It was strange. That morning there was no need for Aleve, my body was well on its way to being fully repaired. Thanks bicycle.

My new lease on life notwithstanding, the climbs weren't over just yet. Even though there were no named passes to summit for a few more days, the unnamed inclines up ahead still wouldn't be easy.

After some freeze dried instant coffee and some packing, we put the K Lake Resort and Marina permanently behind us sometime before nine o'clock that morning. The wizened lake with the ring of stain around still ranks as the biggest bathtub ring I've ever seen. The whole place grew smaller and smaller in my rear view mirror before it disappeared altogether.

A few hours of riding later, Dave and I rolled into a gas station in East Glacier and took out the map to get some idea of where the closest campsite to our location might be. While we were stooped over our maps, a Hawaiian guy pulled up in his F-350, got out, and walked over.

"You guys thinking of camping tonight? It is going to rain you know."

He saw an opportunity, and made us an offer we couldn't refuse. He told us he'd just completed a renovation of an apartment he owned nearby, and he offered us a night's stay there for $120. I talked him down to $80, and the second we shook on the price I knew I could have gone lower. My guess was he would have taken twenty bucks for it.

Dave and I made our way into East Glacier Village to the address he'd provided and we found the key in the mailbox just like he said. It turned out to be a nice place, a second-floor walk-up with showers and three bedrooms and a nice view of a setting sun over downtown. At that point in the trip, though, I wasn't interested in the views, I was interested in comfort of the bed and the amount of sleep I could squeeze out of it.

The following day we woke up to clouds and rain and the second I stepped out into a chilly fine mist I was super thankful for the good, warm, dry night's sleep I'd had in a bed. Being inside was always preferable to outside when the air is cold and the sky is crying. How fitting it was that the sun did not shine that morning, the second-month anniversary of my mom's death.

Ah the highs and lows of bike travel. I had the memory of my mom's death on the one hand, and the Continental Divide I'd be facing the following day on the other.

The world-famous, vista-filled, Going-to-the-Sun Road, the only road in Glacier National Park that passed through Logan Pass (elevation 6,664 ft.) was a mere sixty five miles or so from where we stood in East Glacier. The Going-to-the-Sun Road was the only road in Glacier National Park that crossed the Continental Divide and if you were on a bike, it was a bear. Famous for its beautiful scenery and infamous for its snow, it is one of the most difficult roads in North America to snowplow in the spring. I'd heard that up to 80 feet of snow could be found on top of Logan Pass, and even more snow could be found downwind and just east of the summit where the deepest snowfields have long been referred to as the Big Drift. Get this: it takes ten weeks (that's two and a half months) to plow on average each year, even with snow removal equipment that can move 4,000 tons of snow *in an hour*. The guys use dynamite and front loaders and work 24/7 to get the job done.

We were planning to make it to Whitefish Montana together that night and share our last few miles of riding together the next day before we hit that fork in the road that would send me one way and Dave the other. You see, Dave, knew full well that the Going-to-the-Sun Road was closed, but he still planned on rolling out of bed in Whitefish the following morning and riding as much of that fifty-two mile long scenic highway as he could before the clearing crews and the massive snowdrifts turned him back. I planned to ride the go 'round option and head over Marias Pass (5,236 ft.) and make it to the other side of the Continental Divide that way.

Yes, biking fans, Dave was to leave my wonderful company the following day. He'd originally planned on heading down towards Yellowstone, but his summer bicycle ride and his land-scape research trip were to be cut short for good reason. A mere three days into our trip, his schedule changed after one of his Yale professors called to inform him that he'd won a summer residency at the Royal Drawing School at Dumfries House in East Ayrshire, Scotland for the whole month of July. So Yellowstone would have to wait. Dave would be in Scotland on July 1st.

God only knew where I'd be on July 1st.

Our last full day of riding together was an ugly fifty-six mile long slog from Eureka to Whitefish. We followed Highway 93 pretty much the whole way and our eyes didn't like what they saw the whole time. The road was narrow, and the posted speed limit was a scary fifty-five miles per hour. The road shoulder was no wider than my handlebars in some places and no wider than my thumb in others. The landscape on either side of the road was nothing much to look at either—not that it mattered as I was concentrating on keeping clear of cars and trucks whizzing us by at speeds of up to seventy-five miles per hour. It was dangerous going and a real white-knuckle affair for miles on end. Add a twenty-five-knot headwind and a spitting rain to the mix, and you will get an understanding of what it was like to make slow head-way in slippery conditions next to speeding cars. I was in granny gear on the flats and even then I was posting a measly five miles an hour. It was all I could do to not get mauled by a minivan or tossed by a truck.

After an ugly fifty-six, we arrived in Whitefish, Montana and stopped for an ice cold IPA at Quickee's, a beer-and-sandwich shop. That beer tasted like victory. Sebastian and his wife were only one month at the helm after buying Quickee's on May 5th and they were doing a bang-up job at quenching thirsts and sating appetites. The place was sparkling clean, open, and airy, with no road dust anywhere to be seen. The Koocanusa man-agement team could have taken some pointers from Quickie's new owners. I had the fish and chips (how can you say no to

Alaskan cod?) and the fish tacos (again, how can you say no to…). The beer was named Going-to-the-Sun IPA, so I had to have it.

We found a hostel in downtown Whitefish, owned and operated by two sisters that worked their way into my heart by doing my laundry for six bucks. I know it may sound like I did my laundry all the time, but, with only two pairs of bike shorts, three shirts, one pair of pants, a couple of pairs of socks, and with me sweating like the proverbial pig, things got dirty quickly. And dirty clothes stunk everything up fast when they are stored in watertight vinyl saddlebags. Put some sweaty stuff in those babies and everything in the bags starts smelling like sweaty me. I prefer to have my clothes smell like just-out-of-the-shower me versus just out of the dumpster me, so I launder like a madman.

That night I had the rare opportunity to share a room with six strangers. There were a couple of seasonal workers, some French dude, a guy named Eddie from Queens, a drunk, and a kid on break from Purdue University travelling the States in a busted up Subaru. You could not get a more assorted mix of people if you tried. Well, maybe if you enlisted in the army. But, even with such diversity under one roof, we all shared a common goal of a good night's sleep and we all succeeded. Go team!

Whitefish had a topnotch bike shop that came in handy as Dave's bike rack popped a screw and needed some immediate attention. I bought a new rear view mirror for my bike, one just like Dave's, which offered a better view of the approaching vehicular traffic—a huge improvement on what I had been using. I could now see things behind me more clearly, which was key to my safety, especially since I'd be riding alone for the next few thousand miles. I switched out my pedals and replaced my bike cleats. Good riddance.

Graduation day, June 4th. We spent our last morning riding toward a roadside restaurant, the scene of our last lunch just before we reached the fork in the road that would set us going separate ways. I paid, as usual and as was the deal.

After I'd finished eating, I sat back from the table and said, "Well, Dave, I'll be glad to finally have your sorry ass off the payroll. This is the last mooch meal you will ever get from me."

He looked up to a waitress that wasn't there and asked, "Waitress, can I have three meals to go, please?"

We laughed.

"I must have been crazy desperate to have you along, because I have found your camping skills to be lacking at best. Dude, I was as proficient as you will ever be after hanging one bear bag and setting up my tent the first time. I'm all caught up with you and your fancy camping skills. I was Appalachian ready in, like, ten minutes. You suck."

"*You* suck."

"I'd hit you with a frying pan right now if I had one."

"Motel pussy."

We both laughed again. We'd traveled over 550 Rocky Mountain miles together and our shared experiences forged a lifelong friendship. I will be the first to admit that I could not have covered as much ground as I had without Dave's help and company. It had been great having him along for the ride and I had lucked out when he had decided to join me. I remain forever thankful he was along for the start of my trip.

Bike trips sure are a great way to lengthen one's list of lifelong friends.

"So, this is it, huh, the end of the Odd Couple?"

"Looks that way," he said.

"Well, let's step outside and document history once again."

We stepped out into glorious sunshine and our waitress, fittingly a woman named Gloria took the photo. All three of us would be gone from that place by summer's end: Gloria said she also would be heading out of Montana to move back in with her family in Seattle at the end of tourist season. She wished us luck, gave me back my phone, and returned inside. After a big bear hug and one last fade away fist punch, Dave took off, too. He rode northeast to the Going-to-the-Sun Road and I rolled east into "Great Bear Territory" (that was literally what it said on the map) to climb the Continental Divide. By day's end Dave would be back in Whitefish for another night of shared sleeping space with a whole new cast of complete strangers at the hostel. He'd ship his bike home the next day and end his biking segment of the summer with a train trip to the nearest airport. In contrast, my biking adventure was one-seventh complete and I had no idea where I'd be sleeping that night or any other night from Montana to Maine.

Without big Dave along, I was now a one-man show on two wheels, and just as scared of bears and crystal meth addicts as I was when I'd started. But thanks to Dave, I had a much better idea of what I was in for, and thanks to those Rockies, I had my legs with me now.

The first couple of miles traveling alone were brand new to me. It felt weird being without a buddy. No one knew where I was, so, if something happened, I'd find myself in a real tough spot. When I considered the additional risks involved in solo travel, I realized that I had to be more careful about having enough water and food. I had no backup, no buddy, and although Trail Angels may be out there, it would be foolish and irresponsible to rely on them showing up to help out. The world doesn't owe anybody anything, so be prepared for everything.

Thankfully, the weather and road conditions cooperated with me that day, so I had an easy go at first. It was sunny, the road I rode had a generous shoulder, and there was very little traffic. What a difference a day makes. I even got a text from Eileen. She reported in that she was out to dinner with the girls, and George was in a tent somewhere at an end-of-the-year school camping trip. I sure hoped he had some bear spray with him, just in case.

Well, after about twenty miles of pedaling through God's country and after a while of being truly alone on a bike in the middle of nowhere for the first time, I stopped in for an ice cream served up by a guy named Gene at the Stanton Lodge along Highway 2. I sat outside and enjoyed some afternoon sun while I devoured a heaping cup of vanilla ice cream. When I'd finished, I went back inside the lodge and asked Gene for some local lodging suggestions.

He used the G word on me. That's right. *Grizzly!* A grizzly had been spotted two short weeks before, walking through a neighbor's yard not two miles from where I'd been enjoying my ice cream on the side of the road...with my back facing the woods. I could have been blindsided. Had I known that, I would have opted to eat inside sitting in the seat farthest from the front door. Gene came up with two lodging suggestions for me, both of which included him some-how. He offered free camping behind his restaurant or, for $80 a night, access to a cabin on his property. I declined both with thanks, as I still had a few miles left in my legs and I took it as an omen the guy's name rhymed with the word "scene", as in "grizzly bear attack scene." Instead, I opted to stay at the Izaak Walton Hotel off Route 2 a few miles down. That historic hotel offered a grizzly-free zone, so I was all in.

Izaak Walton wrote a book on angling (fly fishing) way back when, and no one I spoke with knew why the place that once housed sixty train workers employed to keep snow off the train tracks all winter was named after a Brit who died in 1683. I wasn't overly concerned about the name of the place as long as it could deliver the environment I was after. It did. I looked forward to not camping, to not having to suspend my food in a bear bag fifteen feet off the ground, and to not having to use a bear box (a bear proof container) if one was around. Although they have "that crazy Wi-Fi thingy" at the hotel, it was "broke," and the hotel management delivered its sincere apologies.

In addition, there was no, repeat *no,* cellular phone service at the hotel, but, strangely, there was a payphone in the lobby entrance, so I used that. The wife and kid were not home, so I left a message.

Right after I hung up I heard a sound I hadn't heard in nearly a quarter century: coins dropping into a payphone coin box. I had to think far back in time to the last time I'd used coins to make a call. My best guess was sometime in the early 1990's in New York's Grand Central Station. Back then I didn't have a mobile phone (hardly anyone I knew did), so I'd made it a practice to call ahead to let my parents know which train I'd be on so they could met me at the Rye train station for the lift home. If someone told me back then that a quarter century would pass before I dropped my next quarter into a public payphone, I'd have told them they were nuts.

When was the last time you made a call from a payphone? Who'd you call? Are they still around? Those are great questions to ask someone sitting next to you at a dinner party when the conversation lulls. Try it.

Much like the payphone in the front entrance, the Izaak Walton Hotel seemed a little stuck in the past. The front desk clerk spouted some local lore while checking me in. An Amtrak train derailed on February 27, 1981, just five miles from the top of Marias Pass and the Continental Divide. Framed and fading news articles about the disaster hung stained and yellowed but still prominently featured on hotel lobby walls. Not too much had happened in the area since the derailment which seemed like good news to me; the place was fine just the way it was with its oak paneling, cozy rooms, and welcoming restaurant.

It was late by the time I took a seat for dinner. My presence brought the restaurant customer population up from absolute zero to one. With things so slow, my waiter, a thirty-five year old man, was looking to kill some time before his shift ended. He saddled up at the table next to mine and waxed his tale of woe.

I did not ask him to, but I guess I have that kind of "tell me any-thing" face.

After dating his "hot, blond girlfriend from ages seventeen to twenty," he found out she had screwed around on him "every chance she got," which included while on "a girl trip to Mexico that turned out to be anything but a girl trip, if you know what I mean, Tim," he said. Not only had he had his heart broken, the remaining pieces had evidentially turned to stone, rendering him "only capable of a relationshit."

"Of a what?" I asked.

"Of a relationshit. That's all I've had since then. A relation-*shit* starts off with relations, then goes to shit. Get it?"

"Yeah."

He boasted of "dumping chicks left and right" and "leaving bitches" in his wake. Fifteen years had passed since the big break-up and he spoke of the wound as if still fresh. In my humble opinion there isn't anyone on the planet alive or dead that was worth that much hate, pain, and lament. I managed to keep my big mouth shut on the matter, so he never got my opinion. Look, at some point or another everyone alive dines from the old shit plate. You just have to get over it and get on with it. You have to just keep pedaling, as it were.

With his shift ended, he stood up to go "do some slaying at a singles bar one town over." He thanked me for chatting, and I thanked him for the new word.

"Relationshit." Twelve letters say so much.

The next morning my room was a coffee cup of fresh brewed sunshine filled right to brim. Warm light poured through the windows and cozied the whole room up nicely in a soft glow. Starlings were singing and darting about outside while I lay com-fortably under the covers and out of reach from the morning chill. Seriously. Starlings. I flirted with the idea of taking a zero and spending the entire day in the Heaven I awoke to: why not? Who would ever want to leave a place like that? But my stomach had woken up, too, and it had something to say on the matter. It voted on the Stay In Bed referendum and I lost. With breakfast service ending at nine o'clock, I reluctantly got my ass out of bed and headed downstairs before they closed the doors until noon.

After three eggs easy over, OJ, whole-wheat toast, bacon, and some coffee, I returned to my room and the idea of a zero at that point seemed foolish: I was already up and the Sandman had left the building. It was time to go, so I got dressed, packed my bags, and said my credit card goodbyes to the Izaak Walton Hotel. The Fun Mover was exactly where I'd left it the night before and I was happy to see it. My bike was like a loyal mule I didn't have to feed. I loaded my saddlebags onto that steel steed and took the reins (well, the handlebars really), and told myself to giddy the hell up.

I rolled down the driveway, hung a right, and merged back onto Route 2. Holy shit. I slipped into an invisible river of cold air blowing west that I did not expect. It must have been a twenty-five degree difference from the bedroom temperature I enjoyed early. The freezing air that slipped down from the snowfields above the tree line fueled the wind. I'd see a penguin before I'd see a Starling in weather like that. I pedaled twenty-nine miles that day in something like three and a half or four hours, and every one of those miles was terrible: cold, slow, and hard earned.

Sometimes I just want four doors, a windshield, a radio, car heat, and an accelerator.

At one point I was going downhill and I got blown off my bike. Yep. A nasty side wind came out of nowhere and took me down—well, forced me to set foot on the ground in order to prevent a flesh splat. I cursed the Gods, but they weren't listening. They never do. I shook my head in frustration and pushed on against the incessant thirty-knot headwind the whole day. Oh, and to all you weather fans, it snowed on me for about a minute. Why wouldn't it? Even though the temperature was five or ten degrees above freezing, the air mass was raw and cold and carrying flakes from who knows where. I had planned on making it to Browning, Montana by the end of the day, but I pulled up way short of that target destination and tossed in the towel in Glacier. I was forced to as the wind chill made it feel like twenty-five outside. My body was at the shivering stage of hypo by the time I got to the Glacier diner. Dave had left only recently, but his wise words stuck with me: "Hypothermia is best prevented 'cause it's a bitch to fix."

I stepped into the still air and warmth of the diner, it's air effused with the smell of the soup da jour and morning bacon on the grill, nose orgasm material to the road weary cyclist. I ordered a cup of hot tea and a big ol'bowl of the chicken soup. My waitress asked me how far I was going, and when I told her, she replied, "Browning? Why would you want to stop there? Browning's a dump, and there is nowhere to stay in town. You know there's a hostel attached to a bakery less than a mile from here, right?"

"No," I told her. "I did not know that." I looked through the drops of rain on the window to the gray sky, the wet road, and the bleak scene. "But guess what? That's where I'm staying tonight."

"Smart man. Want more soup?"

Originally I had stopped in to thaw my hands and feet and grab a cup of something warm, but as soon as I sat down at that counter and began thawing out, I knew that day's ride was in the books. After some more of that soup and some chitchat with the pretty waitress and her short-order cook boyfriend who turned out to be a very disturbing young man and a writer of short horror stories and teleplays that left me uneasy about him after the telling, I rode the cold mile to the bakery/hostel and checked in.

I was given the choice of either a "dorm-room setting with four men" for twenty bucks a night or "your own room for twenty-nine."

Every decision in Life should be so easy: I spent the extra nine bucks.

"Man, I'd splurge the extra nine bucks on a private room, too," said Zack, the twenty-four year old baker/hotelier.

"Why?" I asked.

"I just wouldn't want to sleep anywhere near them dudes."

I never laid eyes on "them dudes," and for nine bucks, it was nice to know that I wouldn't have to.

Good-looking Zack from South Dakota had worked as a carpenter the previous summer, but then "lucked out and scored the bakery-hostel gig" because his buddy's dad owned the place. "I like both doughnuts and women, but not in that order, so this place is the bomb."

What great lines you get from people if you keep your ears open and your mouth shut.

I went up and found my room. To those of you unfamiliar with hostel accommodation, upon payment, you may get handed a set of sheets with which to make your own bed. I noticed the set I'd been handed didn't match, not that I gave a shit. It was to the degree they didn't match that bothered me. The top sheet they gave me was a gaudy, floral, pink number, and the bottom sheet was sky blue with a big bloodstain on the lower right corner.

Ew.

Again: Ew.

It was only after the bottom sheet was on the mattress that I saw the bloodstain. I am not crazy about sleeping on sheets that had probably been used as Exhibit A in a murder trial, so I went downstairs and exchanged both sheets for some new ones and set back to making the same bed a second time. Once the clean, non-bloodstained sheets were wrapped around the old mattress, I collapsed onto it. That day's twenty-nine miles burned more calories than triple the distance ridden in more temperate conditions would have. What got me was the cold more than the distance.

On the seventieth anniversary of D-Day, I was up and out after a conveniently located fresh cup of coffee and a Danish to die for. The cold front that had kicked my ass the day before had grown tired of waiting for me, so it left the area sometime during the night. A bright, big, beautiful blue sky full of warm windless air sat right outside my window, waiting for me to knife through it with my two wheeled cutter. I crushed that morning ride and arrived in Cut Bank a few hours later. It was nice to cover some ground for once without having to push against an invisible force of Nature. The land was opening up to prairie and the mountains were grouping up behind me in a snow capped receding line. Adieu, Rockies, adieu.

That day had an extra special bonus for me: I got the rare chance to check another item off my bucket list.

During the stop in Cut Bank, I decided to get a haircut from a young woman named Betty who, by law, had to hang her barber's school diploma up on the wall in full view of paying customers. "See that diploma? Yeah, I got that after I passed my final exam. Had to pass a shaving test."

Betty claimed that she was good at wielding a single edge blade and "gathering hair off of skin surfaces." I confessed to her that I'd always wanted to lie back in a chair and have warm towels put over my face while a barber whipped up the shaving cream and sharpened the single-edged razor on a strip of leather like they did in the old cowboy movies.

"Yeah I remember those movies. They used to cook bacon in frying pans over the fire."

I looked at her like she had two heads, and then looked around for Dave.

No, it couldn't be: she didn't know about the frying pan thing. She could not possibly have been included in the frying pan joke. It was just a coincidence.

"Hey, I've always wanted to do that. Can you give me a shave?" I asked Betty.

A little while later, a steaming hot towel covered my face and my big smile. That towel softened the scruff on my cheeks, chin and neck enough to point where I was ready to have a woman I had never met before come at me with a large, sharp knife and put it to my throat.

It was a bad idea for me to allow that to happen. The knife was duller than a bowling ball, so young Betty had to get a little aggressive with her dragging of the blade across my sweet tender baby face in order to get the needed purchase of my facial hair against the knife's edge. It was like shaving a baby's ass with a dull hatchet. In addition to that, she was unsteady with her stroke. Man, I got diced more than a Vegas craps table. I don't know how she managed it, but the hair on top of my head was cut shorter in spots than the hair on my face. I opened one eye and took a closer look at the diploma on the wall: I think she got her diploma off the Internet.

As I handed her payment for the haircut and shave from Colonial times, she apologized profusely and admitted it was the first time in her life she'd ever "shaved a man in the face."

"I shaved my own legs to pass the single edge test," she admitted.

"Oh," I said and started bleeding from my face again. A piece of tissue fell from my mug when I formed the "oh" with my lips. Betty gave me a couple more tissues to take with me. With a cut up scalp and face, I stepped back outside into the sunlight. There was nothing to keep me in the town of Cut Bank, so I left. Cut Bank? Ha! More like Blood Bank. I was outta there.

With the sun still high in the sky and my legs still open to the idea of moving more, I decided to push on to Shelby, Montana. After another afternoon of riding, I checked into the Crossroads Inn and then ate my dinner alone at a truck stop.

Or almost alone. I chatted up a husband-and-wife trucker team from Canada who sat in the abutting booth. The wife turned my way and threw an elbow over the backrest and shared some stories from the road.

Did you know that in Illinois the police force truckers to slow down when they go through construction sites? Did you know that if you hit a construction worker with your truck, it's a mandatory $15,000 fine no matter what happens to the guy you hit *and* fifteen years in jail? I didn't know that until I met Nancy, the long-haul trucker. She and her husband, Jim, told me a story about another trucker they knew who had picked up the serial killer Aileen Wuornos and lived to tell the tale.

Jim didn't say one word the whole time. He just nodded when Nancy made an important point.

"What happened was this: the guy, let's call him Ted, picked up Aileen at one truck stop and headed out. She was going in the same direction as he was, so he did her a solid and gave her a ride. A few hours later, they pulled into another truck stop for some shuteye. Ted's rig had sleeping accommodation. Well, old Aileen the psycho killer had other plans for Ted the Trucker. She tried to join him in the truck's bunk bed for some roughie stuffy..."

Aside: I had never heard the term "roughie stuffy" before, but when Nancy said it, she put her right index finger through the hole she made with her left thumb and index finger, the international grade school hand signal for sexual intercourse. She took her finger out then put her finger back in several times before the hand show with pumping action was over. Her obscene sign language drove the point home (no pun intended with her being a trucker and all). I will forever now know what "roughie stuffy" means: it was trucker-speak for sexual intercourse. Nancy was skilled in non-verbal communication: can you imagine how good she was at charades?

"...Roughie stuffy, but the truck driver declined all of her sexual advances. He told her that it wasn't like that. Ted just wanted to get some sleep and help her out by giving her a ride to Alabama, just like she'd ask him to. So he turned her down."

"Well, when Teddy woke up a few hours later, Aileen W., the serial killer, was gone. She'd left him some money and a nice note of thanks for showing her what she called 'respect'."

"When Ted stepped out of his truck for his morning piss," Nancy continued, this time without using any sign language, "a state cop stuck a gun in Ted's face and told him to 'Hold it right there, mister!' (Nancy was pointing her mock gun at me. She was back using sign language. I don't think she could help herself.)

"The cops were investigating a murder in the truck right next to his at that truck stop and everyone was a witness until being proven guilty."

Another aside: Man, you just gotta love The Nancy. She was a talking mime who spun trucker tales and non-stop yarns about respect, murder, and, as we'll find out soon, money.

"I guess what happened was that Aileen W., the psychiatric (sic) killer, got out of one man's truck, and talked her way into another man's truck. Trouble was, she also put her knife in to the other man's throat right there at the same stop. That other guy musta been horny enough to say yes to her advances. And Tim," she paused, waiting for me to catch her drift, "by 'advances', I mean her sexual advances."

"Thank you for making that clear, Nancy," I reassured her as she thrust her index finger back and forth, again and again, through the circle she'd made with her thumb and other index finger. I was all caught up.

"Well, you are welcome there, Tim." She turned to her husband Jim and asked, "Did I tell that story just the way it happened?"

Jim nodded yes and The Nancy turned back my way.

"Well, the cop holstered his gun once our friend Ted passed muster. Although he had transported a known fugitive, he hadn't done so intentionally, so the cops let him go after taking his name and license number. Ted told the cops about the note Aileen W. had left, and they confiscated that, of course. And by confiscate, I mean they took that note with them. But Ted's no fool. He did not tell the cops about the money Aileen had left along with the note. Ted kept that to himself and made a dollar or two in the bargain."

Nancy looked outside the window at a truck that was leaving the parking lot and let the sound of its engine fade away before delivering the moral of the story.

"I guess crime does pay sometimes. I mean, Teddy made a buck, right?"

I shrugged my shoulders and said, "Yeah, I guess he did at that."

Nancy turned to me and asked, "Can you imagine coming that close to a serial killer and living to tell about it?"

Then she added, "Hey, where are you heading, anyway? Need a ride?"

Chapter Twelve

With the wind at my back most, if not all, of the following day, I averaged over seventeen miles per hour for the forty-three mile long trip from Blah Blah, Montana, to Blah Blah, Montana. God knows all the towns out there looked pretty much the same to me, so I was beginning to call them all 'Blah Blah.' I liked a lot of the towns I rode through, but I was too busy moving through them to see much of a difference among them. After pedaling all morning, I found myself standing in a spot of the Western Plains that looked pretty much exactly like the spot I'd started from forty-three miles earlier. I was in a blah-blah mood, so Blah-Blah it was.

Spud's Café was still serving lunch, so I ducked in and met the lovely Daisy, the eighteen-year-old high school graduate who was working the lunch shift. Daisy carried a knife, a can of mace, and a pink cell phone with her at all times, "primarily for self-defense." Blah Blah, MT, had a total population of nine hundred when ten people visited, so how bad could it be, I wondered.

"Pretty darn bad. Some kid got stabbed a couple towns over a few years ago," Daisy said. She worked three jobs and had been living on her own since the previous October, when she'd left home, something she'd been wanting to do since she was fifteen. One of her three jobs was a housekeeping gig over at the MX Motel. She suggested I stay there "because you have to. It's the only place, and the rooms are super clean. My friend Betsy and me are the housekeepers and we make sure we do our job right. We might over bleach a little bit, but we are after making sure that nothing else besides people stay overnight in those rooms."

I told Daisy that was welcome news. If the rooms were clean, I'd call them home for the night. Again, not that I had a real choice; not only was the MX Motel the only game in town, there was not way my tent was coming out of its sleeve if it didn't have to.

Daisy was an interesting young woman who was being stalked by a creepy guy (not me). Said creepy guy regularly traveled fifty miles each way to "stop in to see her" at different times of the day at all of her different job locations. He knew where she worked, and he knew where she lived. Local authorities had been informed of the situation and told Daisy she was not the first person to complain about the creepy guy. The sheriff suggested she "go on ahead and file an official complaint and fill out an application for a restraining order just like the other girl done did."

Daisy did not ask my opinion, but I told her it might make sense to do what the police officer suggested. Daisy replied with a shrug, ending any further discussion on the matter.

After a pregnant pause, she said that while I was in town, I should check out the nearby sect of religious crazies who lived mostly by the book of Job. She'd forgotten the sect's name, but Daisy told me they were a lot like the Amish: "Some are nice, and others are not, but they generally stick to themselves. All the kids got bad haircuts and wear weird clothes. They all dress like they are living fifty years ago." Daisy nailed it. Children of cults always look a little off with their period piece clothing and their North Korea inspired hairstyles.

I asked Daisy how she'd come to live in Chester, Montana (a.k.a. "Blah-Blah"), a small town in what I considered to be the middle of nowhere. To me, she seemed more of a fit for a Paris catwalk or a college campus: she was a bright, attractive young woman who I thought might be interested in seeing more of the world.

She explained that three years prior, her family was living in Michigan in search of two things: a cheap rent and a way out of Michigan. Her mom had found a good rent on Craigslist and took the place, *sight unseen*, with no idea where Chester, Montana was. By the time they arrived in Blah Blah, it was too late to turn back. So they stayed—and had been there ever since.

Somewhere along the line, our Miss Daisy managed to find a tattoo artist and a hairstylist with revenge issues. Try as both her stylist and tattoo artist might, neither could take away from the statuesque beauty Daisy had been born with. Bleached pink hair and a green and yellow rose with a running unicorn coming from the inside of it were not my idea of a fetching combination, but hell, some guy was driving fifty miles each way to see them, so I was open to the idea that I could have been wrong about that.

Before paying for my chicken-salad sandwich, I asked Daisy about the nightlife in town and what there was to do around Chester. She said everyone went to the same place every night, the only bar in town. Great. I wouldn't have hung out alone in a bar back in the day, so there was no chance I was going to that night.

Desperate for some entertainment, I asked Daisy if there was anything at all else going on in town. She mentioned a library, but she said it was closed.

"Anything else to do in Chester besides go to a bar and visit a library?" I asked.

"That's the problem with this town and most of the towns within a hundred miles of here. There's nothing for kids to do, so they drink, smoke, trip, and snort."

"'Drink, smoke, trip, and snort' sounds like a track-and-field event at the Ruin-Your-Life Olympics," I replied.

"Yeah, Olympics where everybody loses everything. Will that be all?"

I went over to the MX Motel and checked in at the Quik Stop convenience store that also served as the motel lobby. I wasn't exactly sure what Daisy meant by "super clean" until I keyed into Room Eleven and opened the door.

I took a knee immediately after inhaling a lungful of weapons grade chlorine gas. My training took over: I tucked and rolled out of there, and somehow managed to kick the door the rest of the way open to let the gusting winds air out the place. Through tearing eyes, I witnessed the death of a half dozen innocent brown sparrows caught in the gaseous fallout, their bodies fell from flight and landed with sad, soft thuds in the parking lot up to fifty feet downwind.

Daisy did not kid around when she cleaned. Over bleaches "a little bit?" Yeah, I'd say.

After the oxygen levels in the room had returned to normal, I had a nice nap and woke up at dinnertime. Being a creature of habit, I returned to Spud's Café for a quick dinner and hit the sack early; I was planning on riding sixty-one miles the following day, and my legs weren't getting any younger.

My room came with a bedside lamp. I reached over to turn it on and got no Edison. I looked: there wasn't even a light bulb in the socket. The previous renter must have been suffering some pretty hard times to think to swipe a light bulb.

I went back and got a bulb from the high school kid at the Quik Stop/ MX Motel lobby. Then I went into the bathroom and flicked the light on. This time the bulb was there but, alas, it was dead.

I ventured back to the Quick Stop.

It was as if the kid had never seen me before. Scary.

"Huh? You looking for what? A light bulb? I gotta call my manager to see if we have any."

"Why don't you try under that sink next to you? There were a bunch of them there seven minutes ago."

"Huh? How'd you know that? Oh yeah, you're the guy who was just in here, weren't you?"

"Yes, I am." I decided right there that if he ever became a bank teller, I'd rob him. Hell, I wouldn't even bother to wear a mask.

"Ok, here is another light bulb. I'll remember you the next time."

Yikes. That kid must have medaled at the Ruin Your Life Games. I returned to my room and put the bulb in the bathroom. Room Eleven was alit and its occupant was clean as a whistle by nightfall. Oh, and if you ever need the WIFI password in Blah Blah its freddie08.

Here's a little extra bonus to all you readers who are still with me. I enjoy a running competition with my buddy Dom to see who can find the corniest hair salon name on the planet. Past contenders include *A Cut Above, Hair Today Gone Tomorrow, Hair Apparent, A Breath of Fresh Hair, Hair with Flare, Mane Attraction, Shear Delight* and so on. We're both convinced there must be a hairstyle shop somewhere named *Scalp-Tacular* or *Blow You Away* or *Scissors for the Sistas* and we won't stop until we find it.

Well, right next to Spud's Café was another one for the hair-salon files: *Shear Happiness*. Ironically, it was closed. That was a sheer shame, and sheer ignorance on my part not to have known about the place beforehand and called ahead first for an appointment so I could experience Shear Happiness for myself. You have no idea how long I've been searching... People search for sheer happiness their whole lives and there I was, standing on its doorstep, the door locked.

I was *this* close, man. *This* close.

Sixty-five miles of pedaling occurred the next day. You know the drill. I felt like I was back in spin class on a mount that didn't move when you pedaled it. The western plains scenery moved in slow motion at best while I cranked away. I felt like they looped the landscape and I was pedaling through an endless hour of the same slow moving scene.

I pulled into to Harve, Montana, looking for a place to stay and thought I'd try something a little different. Instead of staying at a campsite or a motel, I tried Warm Showers for the first time. Warm Showers is an online portal linking cycling tourists and local hosts willing to put up with each other for one night. Think of it as couch surfing exclusively for cyclists.

Wished I hadn't. Don't get me wrong: it was very kind of the young woman who hosted me to board me for the night, but I got the distinct feeling she didn't want me there t'all, and I realized soon enough it might have been better if I'd just checked in to a local motel.

Her place was "not on the GPS map for some reason" so I ended up climbing the hill that lead to her driveway like three times before I found her place. That sucked. The first thing she said when I finally got there at five thirty in the afternoon was that she was leaving for the evening to go on a hike with two of her friends. An invitation to join her was tepidly extended and tepidly accepted. Although I was tired after riding sixty-five miles, I did not feel comfortable spending time alone in a complete stranger's home. I barely knew the woman and she had a cat. The cat, incidentally, was not mentioned in the online accommodation description. If it had been, she wouldn't have made the cut. I'm not allergic to cats or anything: I just can't stand them. I'm a dog guy.

Not only did she have a cat, everything in her house smelled like she had a cat. She had a boyfriend, too, who happened to be away for a week. I could smell him as well. The guest bedroom seconded as a repository for dirty clothing, sports equipment, and used towels. It was a staging area for what looked like two weeks of workout laundry that desperately needed to spend some time in the spin cycle. Extra bonus? My room was the very same room where the cat shat.

Litter boxes are one of the things every person with an inside cat needs to have because cats tend to crap indoors and can't flush a toilet. If you aren't up to speed on cats, know this: Cats defecate in little boxes of sand or clay that are supposed to suppress the stench. They don't, really. Litter boxes often come up far short of the mark. Also, when your cat shits craps the size of a human forearm, you really should do something about it sooner than later. Fetch the pitchfork and carry the baby arm outside somewhere and throw it into a dumpster. Cat litter boxes are like little shit farms that generate a daily yield of crop (crap?). Most cat owners don't seem to have what it takes to keep a cat in and the smell out. My hostess was not very attentive or concerned about the shit farm: the litter box in her guest room (where I slept) was a diorama of tire irons lying on a beach.

We left her place and drove forty minutes to a place called Beaver Creek Park and hiked it until past nightfall, then returned to town for a pizza dinner at Pizza Hut as all the other restaurants were closed at that point. I had not been inside a car in nearly three weeks and her high speed driving along a twisty road with ditches on both sides had me white knuckling it the whole time. I didn't want to die in a car accident on a bicycle trip, but, reluctantly, I could see the irony in doing so. I finally got my warm shower around midnight and swore I'd never contact Warm Showers again.

I was very upset with myself: why had I put myself through that hike to nowhere, the lousy Pizza Hut dinner, the leftover asparagus she offered me in the frying pan on the stove when I got there? I should have bailed the second I walked in and saw that cat. What was I thinking? All the signs were there: it was a bad trade, but I still made it. Worse yet, I barely slept a wink that night, as every time I drifted off, I'd roll over and that damn cat would be there, staring at me, weighing the options, figuring how best to attack.

Did you know that if any housecat grew to weigh over a hundred pounds, it would eat its owner? Notice I did not say, "could eat its owner," I said, "would eat its owner." And notice I did say, "any housecat." This might be my first time writing a book, but I make every attempt at choosing my words carefully.

Take a just moment to ponder that little feline factoid. Now be honest: envision your cute little "Fluffy" or "Mr. Snuggles" tipping in at around a buck thirty and measuring five feet long from tip to tail. Picture Fluffy as hungry and just a little pissed off about being caged up in the house all day. It's a Friday, you arrive home, all beat up from a long week at work, with a nice long weekend ahead. You walk over to the fridge, pop yourself open a cold beer, and sprawl out on the couch and flick the TV on to see what's doing.

Well, I hope you enjoy your last moment alive because the supersized version of you little Mr. Snookems is going to get after it and take you out. That cat, *your* cat, every single cat in the world in fact, is a miniature Grim Reaper that, if super sized up, would not hesitate to end you.

Now don't say, "Oh, but Tim, my cat is different. My cat is like a dog. My cat loves me."

I've got two words to say to that: Bull. Shit. Cats are known to kill small birds and mice in huge numbers—animals that are smaller than they are. They taunt and play with their victims. Cats are cruel, selfish beings on four paws. (I know, right? There go most of my book sales right out the window.) But I have a News Flash: your precious little Peaches is a born killer and would see you as little more than a two-legged mouse if it could look you in the eye from a standing position. Go ahead; find some way to scale up your precious feline and come tell me you aren't looking at your last day on Earth. Guess who's coming for dinner? Yeah, that's right, it's you, you're coming to dinner and Peaches is sitting at the table with a knife and fork looking for the person whose been serving him food out of a can its whole life and making him fall for the laser pointer trick over and over again.

That following morning after a night of keeping one eye open, I got the hell out of there the moment my hostess declined my obligatory breakfast invitation, an invitation I felt I needed to extend as she had, after all, allowed me to crash in her guest room for the evening. I left the bed in better shape than I'd found it. Sure, it was still dirty and covered with disgusting black cat hair, but at least it was made, which is more than I could say about the way I found it.

But that litter box on the floor at the end of the bed I slept in? Yeah, I didn't go anywhere near that nose horror. I could see and smell that it was full of newly issued cat logs the size and shape of a newborn baby's leg or of an overfed pet gerbil and it stunk to high hell. It was a rectangular box of visual and olfactory pain that I instinctively sidestepped on my way out the door.

Again, why would anyone own an animal that defecates *inside the house?* I see zero upside to cat ownership. Again I am so sorry to all you cat lovers out there, but I told y'all straight off: I'm a dog person. When it wasn't giving me the creeps staring at me through the night, I guess that cat was opening up its own drive-thru Shat In The Box franchise.

Before I left, I let slip a nickname I'd created for her cat. Its real name was 'Sam' I think, but I called it "the Sphinx" which delighted my hostess and threw her into a flock of giggles when she heard me say it.

"Oh that's so sweet. You think Sam is like the Great Sphinx of Giza."

Wrong. "The Sphinx" moniker I'd come up with was actually short for "sphincter," a word that came to mind after I'd seen the amount of feces her "wonderful cat" had generated over the course of twelve short hours.

Happy to be back on the bike, back on the road, and putting distance between the Sphinx, the litter box, the bed, and me, I rolled downhill a few chilly miles and found a coffee shop in Harve on Main Street.

"Ah, back to civilization," I said to myself as I pulled the glass door open and stepped inside. My kind waitress spotted my iPad and said, "If you want a good shot at Wi-Fi, you'd better take the booth near the window. Lots of my customers say it's the only spot that gets reception."

So I ate breakfast sitting in a sunny booth while mooching the Wi-Fi of the Town House Inn that was located across the street from the coffee shop, the place I should have stayed the night before. My waitress suggested I sit as close to the window as possible for the best signal strength. Well, winner, winner, chicken dinner; I was online and in contact with my wife in no time flat, making her howl about the cat. She knows I can't stand them.

I took time over breakfast to study the map for get a better idea of what was in store for that day's ride. Even after a poor night's rest I was going to attempt my all-time longest day of eighty-eight miles over what appeared to be relatively flat terrain. I needed a clear view of the landmarks and the route: getting lost just meant riding unwanted extra miles. Spending time with maps was another thing I learned to do under Dave's tutelage. If you are going to get where you are going, you must get to *how to get there* first.

Finished with my meal, I dug out my wallet and caught the attention of the attentive waitress with a wave and a signing-the-check hand signal to her from across the diner. Nancy the Trucker would have been impressed with my miming skills at that point.

My waitress came over to me and just stood there like a stone tower.

"Delicious breakfast. May I please have the check?" I asked.

Her response blew me away: "Your breakfast has already been paid for by an anonymous customer here who thanks you for your service."

I was a bit confused—until I realized my bike jersey said "US Army" on it and I was sporting the brand new buzz cut I'd picked up from Betty the Butcher back in Blood Bank. Someone at the coffee shop mistook me for an actual soldier, and that someone had very kindly—but errantly—paid for my breakfast.

What was I to do? I tried to insist on paying, but my waitress was tougher than a Drill Sargent. She was as steadfast and defiant as Stonewall Jackson, holding a BUNN coffeepot in one hand with the other on her hip.

"No chance honey," she said. "It is my customer's wish to remain anonymous and that's the way it's gonna be." She took a step closer to me and advised in a soft tone, "Mister, just let the person do a good thing for you. It won't hurt a bit."

She was right. I graciously accepted the meal and the kind gesture from the anonymous patron, and secretly promised myself to pay it forward the first chance I got. I did not feel at all comfortable being mistaken for a real live soldier, someone I deeply respect, but I considered it more courteous to accept the misplaced generosity and let the well-intended gesture be.

My business was not complete, though. Before I left the coffee shop I still wanted to thank the person who paid for my meal. The problem was I had no idea who to thank, so I figured I'd give a shout out to the whole place and bolt.

That was the plan, anyway.

I stood up and said, "Your attention, please."

To my complete surprise, it was as if I hit the pause button on the whole world. I was thinking Whiskey Tango Foxtrot to myself: forty or so people froze in place when I stood up and called for attention. It was as if God Himself came down from Heaven with fresh news and a ten more commandments. Maybe the whole place was aware that someone had paid for my meal. Man, soldiers sure got the attention and respect they deserved in Harve. Everyone, I mean *everyone,* went ten-hut on me and was waiting to hear what the Big Voice was going to say next: the cook came out of the kitchen, some kid stopped drinking his breakfast soda, and the guy halfway through the men's room door turned around and *returned to his seat.* The patrons went all wax museum on me.

I cleared my throat. *What the hell was I going to say?* Now I had to avoid being an Oxygen Thief. I cleared my throat a second time and gave it my best shot:

"I don't know who you are 'cause you ain't wearing your tough guy suit, but Tango Mike to the person who got my six in this DFAC."

Rambo for No Reason had rubbed off on me: I spoke Scuttlebutt fluently.

No one there seemed to know what I said exactly, but I'll translate: "Thank you to whoever it was who bought me breakfast in this dining facility."

I thought about leaving at that point, but my audience just sat there, so I thought I'd toss in something we could all understand and agree on. All I added was, "God bless America."

Not so bad, right?

Well, right after I said it, there was a pregnant pause during which time no one moved or spoke. Time stood still and I thought I'd made a soup sandwich of the whole thing.

Then...three, two, one...

Their standing ovation hit me with all the force of an oncoming train: all at once the forty or so hard working folks in that coffee shop stood up, hooted and hollered and clapped their palms raw. It was a deafening outpour of love and support for a soldier that wasn't me.

I waved a goodbye to them, grabbed my stuff, and un-assed it the hell outta there before someone asked me any details of my service history like where I'd served, or what a fifty sounds like close up, or how to field strip a HK VP 9 pistol or to demonstrate takedown and reassembly of the AR 15 with extractor removal. I figured the breakfast bill I never even saw was, with tip, right around ten, maybe fifteen bucks.

(Fifteen hundred miles later I paid my bill back to All Who Serve in full, and then some. Here's how it went: I was sitting at the counter in an ice-cream store in northern New York State when a guy walked in and ordered five gallons of ice cream for his brother's welcome-home party.

The soda jerk who obviously knew the guy asked, "Is Phil back from Afghanistan already? Man, time flies."

"Yeah, so do bullets. Phil got shot, but he's OK," replied Phil's brother.

Phil's brother went to use the men's room while the ice cream was being pulled out of the freezer. I jumped at the chance I'd been looking for. I darted over to the front counter and paid the cost of all the ice cream at the welcome home party for the Purple Heart recipient. No Army Ranger or Special Forces Team member could have executed a stealth mission any better than I did that day: I was back in my seat and the ice cream was bought and paid for by the time Phil's brother emerged from the men's room. Mission accomplished.)

Back to the Harve coffee shop. The sounds of the standing ovation followed me out the door. I was embarrassed about the whole mix up and rode Army Strong all day.

About fifty miles in to a ninety-three mile day (longest to date), I stopped in Harlem, MT for a break. I sat in the shade under a bright sun and a clear sky for about an hour and heard parts of some humorous conversations people were having.

"See you Saturday. What can I bring?"

"Ice and worms."

"Worms are for the fish, right Joe?"

"No, they're for your wife. I hear she's hooked on them."

I laughed. I was looking out over land so flat that if your dog ran away you could see it run for three days. There was no water in sight for miles and miles and I'd just heard a terrible fish joke.

Another exchange I overheard was two guys stepping out of a pickup truck en route to the convenience store I'd just left:

"Hey, Bob, ready for a shit sandwich?"

"Sure am, Fred. You buying?"

I nursed my chocolate milk while my ears scooped up all the dropped bits and pieces of conversation that happened my way. I said hello to some people and most said hello back. I felt lonely just sitting there and it became evident to me that I was in need of some company to share the road with. Sitting alone at a picnic table and laughing to yourself about overheard fish jokes is no way to spend your time. You come across to others as crazy and sitting doesn't get you any closer to home.

But who could blame me for feeling a bit out of sorts? Since Dave's departure I'd spent majority of my time alone and I wasn't having any of it. I had tried (and failed) to recruit friends to join me: nothing doing. I was an unpredictable moving target as any bicycle tourist is and last minute plane tickets and rental car fees were too dear for my friends to pay. I was on my own and was going to be on my own for the next few weeks.

Another look at my maps reminded me how much ground I had a to cover before I'd see another familiar face.

"Fuck it," I said to myself and shrugged my shoulders. I folded the maps and tucked them into my handlebar bag and tried not to think too much of how much cycling distance they represented. I had to stop looking at the sections of maps and just concentrate on one panel at a time. (Each panel represented about 30 to 50 miles; each section was made up of twelve to fifteen panels.)

I left that picnic table and just kept pedaling until I arrived in Malta, Montana. My ninety-three mile personal best record that day was awesome, but relative. On my way out of Chester,

MT a day or two earlier, I'd run across a sixty-five-year-old Brit named Graham who had begun a cross country journey of his own in Boston, Massachusetts twenty-eight days' prior. Not only had Graham taken *no zeros* by the time we met, he had ridden a hundred miles or more *every day* for twenty-eight *straight* days and had maintained a seventeen-mile per hour average speed. Just the fact that Graham kept track of his overall trip mile per hour average was proof positive to me he was more racing than touring.

Regardless, he was a flat out *man*imal. In addition to his long distance riding stats, Graham was hauling thirty pounds' worth of gear. And he was riding against the prevailing winds. Wow. That was something. Granted, he only stayed at hotels, so he was on more of a credit card tourist then an unsupported bike tourist like myself, but so what? He wasn't bogged down with much camping equipment but did admit to having "emergency housing" with him in case he got stuck somewhere.

Graham's approach to navigation was radically different from mine. He rode without a map and preferred to get his following day's riding assignments phoned in from his kids back in jolly old London who pored over maps of the American Midwest. Graham was also on a different riding schedule. In order to avoid headwinds, he would set off at three o'clock each morning to ride through the still night air. By doing so, he'd managed to get the majority of his riding miles in under his belt before the sun came up and the wind started blowing hard against him. We crossed paths at a coffee shop just outside of Chester at 9:30 in the morning. I was one mile into my riding day heading east with a favoring wind, and he was finishing up his day with a 116 new miles on his odometer.

Even though sixty-five year old Graham rode over three thousand miles in just twenty-eight days, my ninety-three mile long ride that day was still one for the history books and still something I could crow about. Ninety-three miles is a long ride on a bike, I can assure you that. After learning about Graham's headwind avoidance strategy and early morning riding schedule, I was tempted to adopt his approach in order to avoid some of the headwinds myself. But after further consideration, I decided to stick to my own schedule and concentrate on just enjoying the ride, focusing on the people and the scenery instead of on my watch and overall average speed.

After a night of near comatose rest following my record-breaking ride, I ate two breakfasts the following morning in Malta. The Fun Mover and I got going at the crack of noon after sleeping straight through the night (*yes!*) and waking up at seven thirty. A casual breakfast of oatmeal, raisins, brown sugar, milk, whole-wheat toast, and coffee was followed by a return to bed and, later, followed up with a return to the table: two hours after breakfast, I ate a BLT, a burger, and a cup of something-something soup that tasted like liquid chicken. With the sun high up in the sky, my fuel tank was full, my eyes were finally open, and I was ready to face the world.

While I was surrendering my key and signing the bill at the front desk, the owner-operator made some chitchat while my credit card was being assaulted. He asked me which way I was headed.

"East on 2," I replied, trying to keep it short and sweet. As many who are acquainted with me know, I have a bit of a gift of gab, but I figure sometimes it's best to keep my big mouth shut. Sometimes when I ask open-ended questions, I learn things I'd rather not. I did not mean to be curt, but it was getting past noon and I had to roll.

All the guy asked me was, "Got bug spray?"

"No," I replied.

"OK, then. You should think about bug spray. Mosquitoes are pretty bad 'round here. It's not so much that they're plentiful; what surprises most folks is the sheer size of 'em."

I told him I'd spent time in Maine and that the 'skeeters were bad there, too. Every local everywhere claims to have the worst mosquitoes, black flies, no-see-ums, etc. in the world. The tendency for people to boast about things like that was familiar to me.

I ignored his warning about the flying bloodsuckers.

That was that, but before leaving town, I had to buy another t-shirt because the one I had been wearing had either shrunk in the wash or had been too small to fit me properly in the first place. For whatever reason, my shirt was tighter than a Speedo on a fat guy. I wasn't going for that look, so my too tight shirt highlighting my love of beer and my need to do more pushups required immediate replacement.

The cashier at the T-shirt store asked me which way I was heading.

"East on 2," I replied.

"Do you have bug spray? You should get some bug spray."

I'll spare you the third conversation I had with the guy at the convenience store before I departed Malta, but suffice it to say a third person warned me for a third time that morning about the mosquitoes east on Rt. 2. Three hundred people live in Malta, so 1% of the town's population had tried to sell me bug spray before I left. Was everyone there on commission, or were those 'skeeters that bad? I did not buy bug spray: to me the stuff is too grimy, sticky, and slimy to consider applying to my skin. Besides, I would be riding for most of the day. I ride faster than bugs can fly, right?

I mounted up and headed east on Route 2 without a chemical defense screen.

Twenty miles into my ride, I stopped to read an historical marker about some sacred Indian rocks that look like a herd of sleeping buffalo. It was one o'clock in the afternoon, I was standing in direct sunlight, the wind was blowing ten to fifteen knots, and my legs still got covered with blood sucking mosquitoes. I shook them off and got the hell outta there. Holy shit, everyone had been right to warn me: those little bastards were big and there sure were plenty of 'em.

I definitely should have purchased some bug spray. The mosquitoes east of Malta were the worse I had ever come across before or since. Now if I hear others brag about how bad the mosquitoes are in their area, I tell them whatever they have ain't nothin' in comparison than the flying Volkswagen bugs east of Malta. Coordinated swarm attacks are unheard of in the insect world, but I experienced them first hand. Individual squadrons dropped from the sky with rhythmic precision. I was pedaling against a fifteen-knot wind and still, those damn things found a way to stick me. I think they hovered in my draft and then flew in for the kill, the bastards.

But here's the rub. Literally. Earlier that morning I'd been distracted by the need to secure a new t-shirt and had forgotten to apply Chamois Butt'r, a.k.a. Butt Butt'r. I never looked forward to applying that cold, clammy goo to my nether regions every morning, but it served a purpose; Butt Butt'r had kept my taint mute and my ass saddle sore free thus far, so if the show had to go on, the Butt Butt'r had to go on first. The daily application of it was a necessary evil.

(I'll save this story for my grandkids around a campfire someday and I'm sure they will find it riveting: "There I was kids, deep in 'skeeter country with no bug juice on hand and no Butt Butt'r on the buns. At some point, I knew I'd have to stop and grease the parts or face an Eternity in saddle sore hell, forced to listen to a barking taint for more miles than I cared to even imagine…")

I faced a problem that morning, several of them, actually. My roadside lube application deep in mosquito country demanded all the speed and coordination of a well-practiced NASCAR pit stop and I hadn't a clue where the goddamn tube of Butt Butt'r was. I knew I'd have to stop and sort through my stuff in order to find it, apply it, put it back in the saddlebag, and get rolling again before the 'skeeters sucked me dry. In addition, I had to time my stop correctly so as to avoid horrifying the innocent occupants of passing cars.

In the end—no bun, I mean pun intended—I went for it. I looked both ways up and down the road to made sure there wasn't a car in sight from either direction before I stopped, got off the bike, and searched for the big purple tube of lube. It turned out (of course!) that the Chamois Butt'r was in the fourth bag I searched and, by the time I found it, I was jumping up and down to shake the mosquitoes off my legs, arms, and neck. I dropped trou and quickly slopped on a handful of said lube to areas that didn't normally see any sun. I figured the worst damage I could do at that point was blind nearby cows with my blazing white ass as it reflected the sunlight into the heifer's retinas.

With my business completed, I tucked the two largest muscles I had back into the protective cover of my bike shorts just before some creepy dude in a busted-up minivan took a slow roll past me and asked, "Need any help?"

Yeah, right. Ten bucks says that if I'd accepted his help, by nightfall I'd be at the bottom of a dry well in his basement listening to instruct me to "put the lotion in the basket."

No thanks. I'm not into any *Silence of the LambSilence of the LambSilence of the Lamb* role-play shenanigans.

I cleared my throat and told the creepy dude, "No, I'm good," hoping he would not see the mist from my mouth and detect the slight falsetto tone in my voice. Nothing makes the berries cold like Butt Butt'r. I was back on the bike in a flash, and I didn't get off again for the next thirty miles. Operation Lube Job had been a success. The cost? Oh, I'd say it cost me a half a pint of O positive.

Farmers in those parts were calling for a dry summer in 2014. (They were correct in their prediction.) There had been some early snow the previous winter, but precious little since, so the abnormally thin snow cover in the mountains meant there was not a lot of stored moisture to be found in the hills. Sure, a bit of spring runoff from the early snowmelt was enjoyed, but it had been weeks since that happened and farmers were thinking that was going to be about it for rain. Though the crops themselves were thirsty, the area I happened to ride by had thousands of gallons of standing water by the roadside, gallons that provided an excellent environment for mosquito breeding. I'm sure my blood donations helped feed the next generation of those needle-nosed pests.

I thought I had sixty-one miles in front of me that day. I was wrong. It turned out to be more like seventy-two. Eleven additional miles might not sound like much to someone driving in a car, but when you are riding a bike and counting on a finish line to be somewhere and it moves farther into the distance, it can mess with your head. As a result, guesstimating arrival time on a bike is more of an art than a science and the rider has to be flexible and willing to go the extra mile (or miles) at any time. Many factors including wind, weather, traffic, leg stamina, and road conditions can play a role in increasing or reducing the rate of forward progress.

My wireless bike computer, which activated only after I started rolling, reported a saddle time that day of seven hours. That was seven hours pushing, pedaling, and cursing against an undying wind in my face. If there were ever a device that could count the number of times I cursed that day, the needle would be pegged in the red zone. Teeth clenched against the headwind, I uttered words that would make the Devil himself blush like cherub in a whorehouse.

I finally rolled into a hotel parking lot and was greeted by a female desk clerk in a sequined top with a compassioned look. She told me she'd seen me working against the wind for the last few hundred yards and had decided if I pulled in, she'd give me her last room. True to her word, she gave me her last room, the one that had just been canceled an hour or so prior to my arrival. Wouldn't you know it? My room was at the end of a very long hallway on the third floor.

"It's the farthest room from the front desk, so I am sorry about that. Looks like you have had yourself a full day already," she said.

I shrugged my shoulders. "Well, I've come this far, what's a little more?"

The "little more" wasn't much: there was no elevator in the place, so I had to carry my bike up the stairs. No surprise there. I reached the second floor, got back on my bike, and rode to my room door. It was strange to ride indoors and have no wind blowing against me while I rolled on a whisper soft, butter smooth carpet. I was happy to be in a room at the end of a long hallway and at the end of such a long day. The view from my window was lacking, but not for those who liked Case tractors.

On June 12th I was up and out of the room early, with only breakfast on my mind. When I walked the bike and all my saddlebags down to the lobby and out to the sidewalk, my legs felt like rubber, or, if I was to say that in my Boston accent, my legs felt like "rubba." I hoped against hope that I was not in for another long day of pushing against my invisible foe. It's a problem when your legs don't wake up at around the same time you do. If your legs are still tired after a night's sleep, your riding range will be greatly reduced. "Leg burn in the morning, cyclist take warning." Just the effort of bringing my bike back downstairs from room 262 in Glasgow gave my legs the chance to start complaining about how tired they already were. They were chanting, "We want a zero! We want a zero!" at me, but I wasn't listening.

Well, wouldn't you know it? The day brought more wind, more near misses with trucks, and a bunch of views that all looked pretty much the same. I figured that particular stretch of ugly was going to be the most tedious and grueling part of the ride.

After fifty miles of effort riding east on the Lewis and Clark Trail, I arrived at Wolf Point in the early afternoon and in one piece.

"Glad that's over," I thought to myself. Given the fact that I had been tired from the start, I was proud of myself for pushing my way through the miles and getting closer to the North Dakota state line—and thus, closer to home.

At that point in the trip, I had abandoned any real thoughts of camping. Instead, I embraced my Motel Pussy-ness and opted for cheap motels every chance I got. Dave could call me a Motel Pussy all he wanted, but the decision to stay under a roof that was not made of rip stop nylon was a sound one as my cross-country ride was a demanding physical effort that required me to hammer out the miles nearly every day. A night's stay in a motel tended to leave me better rested than a night's sleep in a tent lying on terra firma.

As I mentioned earlier, rain was sorely needed in the area, and the lack of rainfall was the number-one topic of conversation at kitchen and café counters across the state. Montana's May rainfall totals were 25 percent of normal and had turned local-area farmers into amateur astronomers. Nervous about their crops, they looked skyward for any sign of moisture.

I stopped in Oswego for something to drink and was told some of the locals had done a rain dance earlier in the day. Word was there would be some rain coming in that night as a result.

For the sake of the crops and the economy, I hoped they were right.

The place I'd stopped at was typical for the area: it was a low-slung building with a couple of dusty pickup trucks parked outside. Inside was a barmaid watching TV. She took my dollar for the 12 oz. pressurized can of sugar and caffeine that I was longing for, the two things I was in need of, without taking her eyes off the screen. The only other customer in the place was an off-duty emergency dispatch operator. She was the one who told me about the rain dance. She'd just gotten off work; her four-days-on, four-days-off work schedule allowed for some morning cocktailing. She said she was not looking forward to returning to answering 911 calls later on that week.

"Work is a bitch. I need to wind down," she said, and raised her drink skyward.

Between sips of her whiskey sour she told me Montana was the worst state in the country for drunk-driving convictions and deaths. "More times than I like to admit I'm the DJ at a party gone bad. I coordinate the cavalry and get everybody dancing in step in order to save lives. Sometimes they get there in time, sometimes they don't, and ex setter rah, ex setter rah," she said. She took another sip of her drink.

That summer there was big money being made in the oil fracking business and the thirsty dispatcher didn't like it one bit.

"People come out here from all over the country to make fast money in the Bakken oil fields just east of here," she said, pointing due west with a lit cigarette leaning out of her mouth. "The jails in Wolf Point are full with overflow from Bakken oil-field lockups. I'm telling you, it ain't good. The people who make it here to work got no work where they're from. So we end up taking your poor, your tired, your annoyed and your unemployed and ex setter rah."

The oil-field jobs had attracted many workers in a short time, which made the area east of Wolf Point the fastest-growing place in the country. Boomtowns are law-enforcement challenges: hotels were at overcapacity, people were making do by sleeping in their trucks, and human frailties had to be fed. "Man camps" were rows and rows of RVs, trailers and campers that had popped up all over like mushrooms after a spring rain. The off-duty 911 operator warned me to stay clear of the Bakken area because the truckers were reckless drivers who were known to drive smaller vehicles like Ford F-150's off the road altogether. Pimps were shipping in hookers and pushers were trafficking in drugs. The Northern Tier route used to run straight through the Bakken area, but an alternate route had been concocted and adapted by the thoughtful Adventure Cycling cartographers in 2012, saving traveling cyclists like myself from all sorts of trouble.

I downed my soda pop and hit the road. I stopped a few hours later at another place, this time an ice cream store that had a pickup truck loaded with rocks. Two dogs were standing on the rocks. I wandered in and asked the owner of the truck why he had his dogs ride in the back, on rocks.

"Oh, I got my two grandsons with me, so dogs gotta go in back," he said.

It turned out the guy was on an ice cream cone run after doing some hunting with his grandsons. He said he was also trying to teach them about hard work, so, after he took them hunting, he made them load a bunch of rocks into the back of his pickup. I saw his grandkids—two wiry mute fifteen-year-old boys slouched in a booth, bone tired and focused on shoveling ice cream into their mouths by the spoonful.

I supposed their grandfather was teaching them about completely unnecessary lower back pain as well.

Chapter Thirteen

MY 1ST CENTURY, A CHIMICHANGA, PLANE TICKET FOR A STRANGER

June 13th was a day that started early and ended late. The long ride was seasoned with a few characters that made all the effort of riding against the wind worth it. Though my day began with a hiccup, it ended with a broad smile and included a new distance record and a moment of epiphany.

It was a banner day, indeed.

My best-laid plans for an early start were dashed because an alarm clock ten miles away from me didn't sound off. I was up and out of bed by six o'clock, all dressed and ready to roll and heading over to the motel dining room for some breakfast. The hiccup? A hastily written sign outside the closed restaurant's doors read, "Kitchen Open at 8:00 a.m. today. Chef Running Late."

I went to the front desk to ask about other breakfast options.

"Nah, no food close by here other than our place," the woman behind the counter said. "I just spoke to the chef over the phone. Tommy's alarm clock didn't go off this morning. He lives about ten miles south of here. Now his day is all messed up because now he's gotta drop his kid off at his mom's place, which is fifteen miles the *other way*. Yeah, so he won't be in to cook the eggs until at least eight. Motel management sends its sincere regrets."

Just knowing that motel management cared enough to send me sincere regrets that early in the morning made me feel all special and warm and fuzzy inside and much better about the whole situation.

What do you do when plans are dashed? Just keep pedaling and initiate Plan B.

My day got a second start with the rollout of an improvised Plan B, which ended up working out just fine. Hell, I figured I still had my camp stove, fuel, and instant oatmeal with me, so why not head out to the parking lot and fire up some breakfast of my own?

That's exactly what I ended up doing: I went outside, found an empty parking slot, and fired my badass Jet Boil stove right up with the water I got from my room. As the sun climbed into the sky, I sat there thinking about how it, too, had to climb out of bed every morning to get the day started just like everyone else.

The water had just begun to bubble alive when a busted-up beige van drove slowly by me and parked a few spaces over. A disheveled man got out and, with both his hands pressed against the faded paint on the driver's side door, he gave a shove. With a big squeak, the driver's side door lurched shut. The guy stood up from his effort and wiped both hands off on the front of his dirty, dusty shirt. He stood between the sun and me. I could see the dust billow off his shirt when he wiped his patted and wiped hands on his chest.

He walked directly towards me.

"Here we go," I thought, "Looks like Crazy gets up early out here." (It must: I was up, wasn't I?)

The guy said hello as if he knew me already. I said hello back.

"Going fur?" he asked.

"Uh...yeah. Heading to Maine."

"Walking the whole way?"

"No. I have a bicycle inside."

"Cool. Nice stove. I'm here to pick up a friend from Germany. Now *that's* fur!" He told me his German buddy had flown seventeen hours in "from Germany!" the previous day.

I opened the packet of oatmeal and dumped it into the mini caldron of churning water. I stirred slowly with my spork, and kept him in the corner of my eye. I was hoping he'd just mosey along.

He didn't.

I didn't ask, but it turned out the guy was a Native American who played the role of spiritual host and leader to the jet lagged German. Every year the German made the trip along with up to seventy other people from "all over this great wide land floating in the space of eternity."

As my parking-lot buddy talked, I noticed his left eye was frozen in a squint. It was only when he stressed a point, like he did when he emphasized "from Germany!" or "seventeen hours!" that he would push his head forward like he was sticking his face through a head-in-the-hole cutout you might see at a country fair. When he did that, the hair on his forehead would push back and both eyes would open wide as saucers and he'd hold that pose for a moment, standing stalk still like he was waiting to have his picture taken.

He seemed to be a nice enough guy, but honestly, I wanted to eat and roll; I was shooting for a hundred-mile day and had little time to chat.

He continued talking. He knew cooking stoves, that was for sure, and he claimed to have done a lot of hiking in his day and to have spent a great deal of time in the "backcountry, under the glory of her nighttime sky."

"Whose sky?"

"The Great Her."

"Who is she?" I asked.

"Mother Earth and Sister Sky."

"Wouldn't that be the Great 'Them'?" I stupidly asked.

He stood as still as a store mannequin as he processed my question. A full five seconds passed and I was worried the guy had just died standing up, but then he broke out into a long laugh.

"You are a funny man, Biking Bear."

'Biking Bear'? I liked my new Native American name, *Biking Bear*. It sounded noble. It was certainly better than the Native American name I was given as a young single man on the scene in New York City. My difficulty to get a second date with any woman alive earned me the nickname *Chick-A-Way*.

I attempted to wrap up the conversation with, "Ok, nice to meet you."

No luck.

The van man's one good eye continued to look at me with an intensity I was uncomfortable with. The rest of him was an unruly head of Einstein hair, a homeless beard, a halfway tucked in shirt, a pair of pants that screamed, "Wash me," and a pair of sandals that neither fit nor matched. He'd been close to but no cigar when it came to matching his shoes. Yes, both were Teva sandals, sure, but they were two different sizes and styles. I know because

I was sitting on the ground and got a good look at them out of the corner of my eye as I stirred my breakfast. His hammertoes and yellowed toenails almost cancelled my breakfast plans.

"Hey," he said, "I am meeting my German friend to go up to my small ranch in the backcountry to celebrate the New Year. We call it the Lodge of Love and Peace. You can put your bike in the back of my van and join us for some prayer and some peace-pipe offerings that the US government gave us religious freedoms for in 1972. We will stay at the Lodge. It is a New Year's celebration for us. I am inviting you to come with us and pray. I am inviting you to the Lodge of Peace. It is only with my invitation that you can join us. So come on, brother. Let's pray together."

I sighed and pondered his kind offer to take me into the woods in the middle of nowhere so his German buddy and he could cut me into small, bite-sized pieces. I extinguished my stove and pulled the oatmeal off.

"That sounds tempting, and thank you for your kind invitation, but I can't make it. I'm meeting a friend of mine later today."

Here is a little bit of free, unsolicited life advice from yours truly, folks: it is never, under any circumstances, a good idea to accept a ride from a disheveled guy who drives a rusty beige van, especially if that guy openly admits he intends to bring you to an isolated, wooded area loosely known as the "backcountry" to "pray." Little did my new parking-lot buddy know that if I was stupid enough to join him on a venture into the woods, my praying would start right after his van door closed and he threw it into Drive. My praying would continue as he headed out of the motel parking lot with his German buddy, probably Ernst Kaltenbrunner, Jr., and me on what would most likely be my one and only beige van ride to the boonies.

Biking Bear wasn't interested in taking his Forever Dirt Nap just yet.

In one last-ditch effort to close the deal, Chief Hammertoe promised he'd have me back to the hotel by Sunday. Right. I'm sure giving Biker Bear a lift back to civilization after a three day weekend bender would be priority one for him come Sunday morn.

"Three days provide barely enough time to dance and share food with all the other Lodge visitors. They will be your new friends for the rest of your life. Pray with me now, brother."

Yeah.

No.

Crazy as it seems, I declined his kind offer to drive me away and get me stoned on peyote for three days straight. I told him I was busy, but of course the real reason I declined his kind offer was that I wanted to live.

So, instead of chillin' with Drug Geronimo at the Lodge of Love and Peace, a visit that would most likely end with me being tied to a tree and bleeding from self-defense wounds, I ate my parking lot oatmeal, jumped on the Fun Mover, and headed east and then south for most of the day.

Twenty miles in, I stopped at the post office in Vida, Montana, just because I loved the name and needed to shoot the shit with someone more normal than the last guy I'd spoken with. It is nice to chat on a break from the road. I was "Livin' la Vida, loca in MT" in Big Sky Country, or "Viva Vida, Montana!" as I like to say.

I met the Vida postmaster, a very nice woman who had lived there her whole life. She said that when she was a kid more post-office boxes were rented, but times had changed since then. By the time I rolled up, two hundred and eighty-three of the three hundred post-office boxes available for rent stood empty, which left only seventeen boxes enjoying a daily diet of junk mail and bills.

Now pregnant with her fourth child, the postmaster worked from eight in the morning until twelve thirty in the afternoon, and had the rest of the day off to spend with her three girls. Her fourth—yes, it was a girl—was due to arrive that August.

She had an interesting tale to tell and time to tell it: no one was in the place except for us, so she grabbed a chair behind the brass bars under the word STAMPS and told me a story. A few years back she found out where her estranged, crank-addicted older brother was living and turned him in to the cops for some much-needed jail time and drug rehab. By doing so she'd saved his life. He was now thirty-one with no friends and no chance of ever seeing his two daughters again.

"His parole officer is the only person he sees on a regular basis, and that's only because he doesn't want to go back to jail. I'm telling you, my big brother's life is one great big hot mess."

After he went to jail, his baby momma dropped him like a hot rock and married someone else. "Not *remarried,* but married," the postmaster made clear. "The whole time that skank was with my brother and had those two kids, she never officially married him, thank God."

The good news was his two little girls were "smart as hell and doing real well."

"Crystal meth is a big problem out here," she reassured me. "The people who do it are dumb. Here's a story for you, Bike Man: I went to the gun range one morning to put holes in paper only to discover some crank heads had brought their trash down there and set it on fire. The dummies left some unburned envelopes with their names and street addresses in the trash pile, so I called the cops, and they all got arrested."

Of all the people in the world to find partially burned envelopes, the postmaster! Cranks got no luck.

That postmaster was an ass kicker. One last thing she told me before I headed out: her oldest girl was ten years old and could field dress a deer "better than any man alive" and routinely came home covered from head to toe in deer blood after a hunt. How freaking Vida (loca), Montana, cool is that?

"I'm raising all my girls to be independent so they won't never need a man." She looked down and spoke to her swelling abdomen as she rubbed it with open palms. "You hear me, Tiffany? You grow up to be like your older sister. You get good with hunting and dressing, and you will never need a man in your life to put food on the table."

I'll spare you the drama of the rest of a very difficult and long day of riding, but I'll tell you of an epiphany I had that made a big difference in my attitude toward headwinds in specific, and adversity in general.

The first few hours of biking dead straight into that day's fifteen-to-twenty-knot wind were tough. I was pedaling as hard as I could, but was making very little headway. After five or six hours of slogging against steady headwinds, I will admit they got under my skin. Wind plays with your head. (I think that might be one reason they call them *head*winds…)

Anyway, after several hours of pushing and getting nowhere fast, I began cursing at the unflagging force I was up against. No kidding. I was riding alone in the middle of nowhere, yelling words that begin with the letter f, g, and d at the top of my lungs. I was losing it; the wind was driving me mad. It blew, gusted, dropped, freshened, howled, lashed, ruffled and veered, but it did not stop. Not once.

Winds can test the resolve and sometimes break a biker's will to continue. Some people, mostly westbound riders, end up throwing in the towel right around North Dakota. I was beginning to understand why.

As I fought and pushed, shouted and screamed, it suddenly came to me. I thought of something that made all the difference in the world, a simple realization that saved the day once I accepted it. The moment I accepted the headwind *as part of the landscape*, all of its destructive power vanished. The wind was the same; *I* had changed. I broke through to a new understanding by fully embracing the suck. Instead of wasting my time wishing for a lull that never came like a petulant child screams for, say, another ice cream cone that isn't coming, I accepted both the wind's intensity and its duration as just part of my riding day. I stopped kidding myself and stopped hoping for a lull. I sort of grew up a little and recognized the obvious, I guess.

After all, wind blows, right? And headwinds really blow. They really suck, too. (Confused? Go ride a bike outside Vida for a few hours straight and you'll get my drift…)

So instead of bitching about the things I could do nothing about like the undying wind, I focused on something I could do something about, as small as it was: I focused on moving my bike forward, one pedal turn at a time. The moment I started to do that, all the anguish I'd been suffering from and all the dashed hopes I had experienced while waiting for the wind to stop disappeared instantly. They were gone with the wind, as it were.

Turning that corner mentally worked like a charm. I continued to push on against the wind for the next *eight hours* or so, progressing agonizingly slowly against an invisible force over an unchanging, unremarkable landscape.

Speaking of landscape, there is a reason they call the plains the *Plains*. They are *not* called the *Incredibles* or the *Awesomes* or the *Unbelievably Interestings* or the *Fantastics*. No, they are referred to only as "the plains", or as the oxymoron, the *Great Plains*. That's because they are just that: plain. I took pictures every twenty miles that day and looked at them later. Things look all the same, same, same on the plain, plain, plain. The mental game of biking requires the cyclist to believe that he or she is getting somewhere, making progress against a wind, along a road, through a landscape. It can be difficult when the pedaling effort is put in, but the landscape seems to stand still.

So, after over a hundred miles of embracing the suck, I discovered that my home for the evening, the Yellowstone River Inn, was located atop a hill. What a cruel twist and torturous last jab of the day. There I was, having ridden all day in the sunshine against a powerful unrelenting wind over roads that were flat as pancakes. I had not seen so much as one hill ALL DAY, yet the Yellowstone Inn sat atop one.

Which brings us to the subject of the last jab of the day ("LJOD"). They are the polar opposite of trail angels. Instead of someone coming out of nowhere with their just-in-time help to save the day, last jabs pop up as unanticipated obstacles that make matters seem, or make matters actually get, worse. LJODs take many forms: your motel being on top of a hill, for example, or getting a flat tire a mile from your campsite, or learning about a water main break that closes your only campsite option for thirty miles. Jabs can happen any time, day or night, but Last Jabs of the Day come at or near the end of a long effort.

I understand Last Jabs very well because my patience had already been tested by so many: freezing cold on my way to Klipchuck Campground, rumble strips as wide as the shoulder itself, getting lost a mere mile from finding a campsite, missing a turn and going down a long steep hill, only to have to backtrack up it to get back on course. And the thing about jabs is you don't know when the actual last jab of the day will happen. As my friend Yogi Berra once said, "It ain't over till it's over." I am always on the lookout for another jab, as too often I have hoodwinked into believing there are no more jabs left in a day. I have thought, "Oh, hey look, they put the motel I am staying at tonight on the only hill in five hundred fucking square miles. Huh. Weird. Now I have to climb said hill on a loaded bike to get there after I've just ridden over level ground for thirteen and a half hours straight against a fifteen-knot wind. Wow. Huh. That sucks. Soooo weird. That must be the last jab of the day. Well, here's to that, anyway."

Ha! Wrong again. The hilltop location was not my last jab of the day that day.

I checked into the inn only to find out the only room left was on the second floor.

Hotel management communicated its sincere regrets, but there was no elevator on the premises. Even though I was flat out bushed, I had to carry my bike up two of flights of stairs to get to my room on the second floor. Someone should teach architects to count. Honestly.

On the bright side, my being forced to lug my bike up two flights was, indeed, my last jab for that day.

As arduous as the day's ride was, it was also my personal best: it took me thirteen plus hours, but I managed to ride 104.5 miles and make it all the way to Glendive, MT.

My first impression of the town left me thinking the people who incorporated Glendive should have left the "Glen" part out of the name.

Little known fact: the Yellowstone Inn is the sole sponsor of the Miss Montana Scholarship and State Finals Pageant. Right there in the lobby was the official gallery complete with some of the past winner's pictures on the wall.

"There it is," the guy said, "The official gallery of past winners."

I took a look and asked, "What year did the elk win?"

The desk clerk looked at the wall and then at me. He didn't think that was funny. "Elks can't enter beauty pageants," he said. "What's the matter with you?"

Some people just don't get my sense of humor.

I carried my loaded bike up the stairs. I was plumb tuckered out and knew enough about long-distance cycling to know I had maybe an hour of consciousness left in my day before my eyes closed shut for at least eight straight hours. After a shower, I was off downstairs in search of a quick meal.

Thankfully, the Yellowstone Inn had a restaurant, so I did not have to venture far to fill my stomach. The Yellowstone Inn & Restaurant quickly became a favorite of mine as they served up a stellar IPA and they had very comfortable, sturdy wooden chairs with strong backs, which I melted into like warm butter melts into all the nooks and crannies of an English muffin. After a century ride, a comfortable chair and a cold beer are about as close to Heaven as anyone can get without being dead first.

Sitting behind me and to my right was a young waitress who was busy wrapping and rolling knives, forks, and spoons in cotton napkins. From the looks of it, she was about halfway through her task. I turned around to her and said hello.

"You look different than most of the other sales guys that travel through here," she said. "You're thinner."

I told her I wasn't a sales guy. I was checking an item off my Bucket List.

She said she had a bucket list once, but she'd lost it, which made me laugh—until I realized she probably didn't understand the concept behind the bucket list (you can't lose a bucket list). I certainly didn't blame her for not knowing. Why in the hell would she know what a bucket list was? She was young, beautiful, and probability-wise, very likely far from Death. She had a ton of time on her side and a lot to look forward to before she'd ever even start to *think* about things like Bucket Lists. Bucket Lists tended to be authored by people with little time left, people who are closer to their end than they are to their beginning.

I explained, "A bucket list is a list of things you want to do before you die. Me? I'm riding a bike across the United States. How about you?" I inquired, "Is there something you always wanted to do?"

"Well, sure."

"I mean in life, something you want to be sure to get done before you go toes up out of here. Would you like to run a marathon, say, or drive the California coast in a classic convertible, or travel somewhere you've never been?"

"I don't know," she replied as she mulled it over with a napkin in one hand and a knife in the other. "I've only been to Disney World, and that was when I was five. Mickey Mouse's voice scared me. I remember that part. My mom said I hid behind her skirt and cried when he came up to talk. She still has the pictures she took of me on the teacup ride, but I don't remember anything much more about Disney World or Land or whatever you call it. I remember my mom holding the camera in front of her face when she took the picture, though. That's about it for my travel experience. No, wait. I went to Fargo once."

"How about now? Say you could go anywhere..."

The young woman's hands went still while she pondered an answer. She gazed out the window at the far end of the room to the closed bank building across the street.

"I guess I would like to travel to a country where they have real castles. I don't know countries real good, but there are places in this world where the castles are real, right? I'd go there, far away to a country with real castles, not make believe." She returned her attention to the project at hand: wrapping cutlery in cotton napkins.

For some reason, right then and there, I wanted to buy a complete stranger a plane ticket.

The waitress working my section cleared her throat. I turned back around to find her standing in front of me, waiting with a pad in hand. She told me about the special, the Hungry-Man Green-Chili Chimichanga with a side salad. Guess what? I rolled the dice by saying, "I'll have that, thank you" and came up a huge winner. Those chimichangas were delicious and filling. Top them both off with a great IPA, and my taste buds were dancing in the streets. Four minutes after I paid the check I was deep asleep, a world class slumber that only a hundred plus miles of riding can provide.

The next morning I cycled out of my R.E.M. sleep and joined the rest of humanity as it set about getting its day going. I activated the mini coffee brewer that came with the room and listened to it gurgle and drip the black stuff into a cup while I packed my bags. I made my way to the front desk on tired legs. Just after I checked out of the Yellowstone Inn, I learned I would miss the annual Miss Montana party at the EPEC (Eastern Plains Entertainment Center) held later that night. Attending that function might have put the "Glen" back in Glendive for me, but no: I chose to keep moving down the road.

Wish I hadn't. I should have stayed and taken a zero day in Glendive. Not only would I have enjoyed a recuperative day of napping, but also I would have stood a good chance at attending the Miss Montana party only because it was open to the public and I would have had not much else to do on that Saturday night.

The previous day's monumental effort to ride over one hundred miles against the wind had taken its toll. I was past the point where one night's sleep would be ample enough to provide a full recuperation. I didn't have a lot of gas in the tank when I headed out, so I knew my range would be limited.

Fifty miles into my day, with no energy left, I was rolling piece of human toast. I was fortunate that overnight accommodation presented itself just after my will to roll on disappeared. I looked up from my handlebars and saw a big sign, "Welcome to Beach,

North Dakota." Perfect timing. The next town down the road was another thirty or forty miles, so no thanks. After pedaling fifty-miles that day and a hundred plus miles the day before, my legs went on strike. Unlike the beach towns I was familiar with, Beach, *North Dakota* was beach less, which was kind of a "beetch" if you know what I mean. I would have loved to spend a day lounging on a real beach, but that was not to be. My hotel, the Buckboard Inn, was next to a truck stop, a Subway sandwich shop, and a visitor's center with no visitors. I dined at Subway (there are no subways in North Dakota), next to the visitor's center (that had no visitors; the null set has no center), and stayed in Beach (again, there are no beaches in North Dakota). There is irony in North Dakota if you look hard enough for it.

Father's Day was the very next day, a Sunday holiday brought to you by retailers and restaurant owners eager to sell greeting cards and food items off brunch and dinner menus. I thought long and hard of what to give myself for Daddy Day and decided to give myself the gift of a zero, coupled with an early Monday morning departure from Beach, North Dakota.

My hard earned Father's Day started early and ended poorly. I was awoken at 5:20 a.m. by the sound of a sharp bark followed by a whining howl. Night was still outside my window when I checked, so I couldn't understand what had awoken me when I first blinked awake. But then came another bark, another howl, followed by another and another. The repeated yapping eventually needled me reluctantly into a state of full consciousness. "Bark, bark, whooo!" "Bark, bark, whooo!" I was ready to strangle that little yapper. I like dogs, but I didn't like that one. All my efforts to return to sleep—including the classic pillow over the ears two hand squeeze—failed, so I finally threw something on and made my way to the front desk around seven o'clock. With eyes half open and with my tee shirt inside out and backwards, I shuffled up to the front desk and asked about a good place to stuff my face for breakfast.

Nancy, the octogenarian desk clerk, suggested a place and then offered to drive me there, as she was "about to head into town for a Sunday meeting'" anyway. As a policy, I only accept rides from folks I know I can beat in an arm-wrestling match, so I immediately took Nancy up on her kind offer.

It so happened that Nancy was the proud owner of Smokey, the fourteen-year-old yapper who'd been personally responsible for robbing me of my precious slumber. Nancy apologized "for Smokey talking so much" and turned to Smokey saying, "Smokey you keep it down now so decent people can get some sleep" to which Smokey replied, "Bark, bark, whooo!"

"I'm so sorry," Nancy repeated. "Smokey here can't hear or see very well."

If Smokey was mine, I would have named him *Go Play in Traffic, Time to Bury You,* or *J. P. Fugly,* but, happily, Smokey was not my dog and never would be. He had been my problem, however. I was weighing my options on what I could do about it when...

"Woof, woof, *woo!* Woof, woof, *woo!*" ...The damn thing went at it again.

He looked like a dirty gray hand towel that an auto mechanic might discard after a long day of changing motor and fixing flats. I couldn't stand the sight or sound of Smokey. Love must be as blind as that dog was because when I looked down at the little thing, I could not come up with even one redeeming quality. An ugly, stinking, yapping, dirty parcel of dog looked back up at me. Who in their right mind would want a deaf, blind, dirty, dusty yapper? To this day, I'd know Smokey's bark anywhere. Why not? I'd listened to the goddamn thing for nearly two hours.

Nancy left Smokey to run the front desk while we shared the mile and a half ride into town. She dropped me off for breakfast at a diner named, La Playa. I'll translate it for you, because sometimes I can: that's "the beach" in Spanish. I'm such a playa...

I had three eggs over easy, hash browns, whole-wheat toast, coffee, orange juice, water, and a twelve-ounce rib eye steak. I don't even know why I bother to say "medium rare" when I order a diner steak—they arrive well done every single freaking time. Steaks in diners are always about a half inch think—just a little thicker than a one subject spiral notebook maybe—and always, *always* cooked straight through. Maybe the next time a waitress asks me how I want my diner steak cooked, I'll quote Friedrich Nietzsche and say, "Faith means not wanting to know what is true. Medium rare please."

And when it does arrive in an overcooked state, I'll eat it as is, knowing the same result will occur no matter how many times I request a different outcome.

Regardless of the steak's condition, my plate had no calories left on it by the time I set my knife and fork down. I paid, tipped, and departed. Sometimes on bike trips, you get lucky. My trip to Beach was well timed: there was a town-wide Father's Day rummage sale going on. Twenty-one people had decided to fling open their garage doors to offer curios for sale to the general public. It was a tag sale on a grand scale. What else was I going to do that day? I wanted to stretch my legs after breakfast anyway, so I went for a walk. With so much tag sale activity going on, I had the rare chance to meet some Beach people who would normally ride out Father's Day on the couch watching TV. It looked like the whole town was outside on their front lawns selling something or on someone else's front lawns considering a purchase. Tag sales are awesome: I love how people put all the things they no longer want or need out on their front lawns, drive a "For Sale" sign in the dirt, and expect the world to come a-runnin' their way.

Tag sales should be called "Tell sales" only because they reveal so much about the seller. You can usually tell a lot about the people by the stuff they are selling and by what they chose to have purchased in the first place. Got some old toys and children's clothing for sale? That tells me your kids have grown up and probably moved away. Got some hand tools, saws, drill presses you are willing to let go for a song? Got some books, shoes, furniture, rusty bikes, bad art, ancient deflated footballs, and broken lava lamps? I can tell you are getting old and want to get rid of all the crap you can before you make the move to assisted living or to the apartment over you kid's garage, which is really the same thing as assisted living if you think about it.

The fifth tag sale I visited was over at Kay Smith's place on First Avenue. I saw tables and chairs, a carpet shampooer, a Tri-Star vacuum, Oreck floor buffer, weed eater, Bev's "real nice garden weasel," some throw pillows with a western theme, vinyl records, and, yes, some old tools for sale, including some gently-worn garden tools from the 1950s. Ah, the 1950's…when the Beach houses were new, freshly painted, and filled with young families. I tried to imagine Beach back in the day, with kids playing on a swing sets or running around shooting water pistols at each other on hot summer days, their parents laughing and saying stuff like, "Easy on that trigger, Champ!" or "Hey there, Sparky!"

The housing stock in Beach, North Dakota on the day I saw it looked a little worn out. Rusty swing sets stood idle and forgotten, plastic Big Wheels collected dust in the back of garages. The houses no longer sat up straight in their foundations, instead seemed to slump, tired from the endless cycle of hot summers and cold winters. And I noticed an absence of young people. I assumed most of the local kids moved away for better opportunities. Small towns in America tended to lack the draw they once enjoyed, so most small towns had dwindling populations. Beach was no different than some of the other rural towns I'd seen: some fixer uppers stood empty.

The people running the tag sales were all around Nancy's age and all of them used the same move to get up out of their lawn chairs: elbows out with both hands firmly placed on the arms of the chair, a lean back, then a violent lean forward with a push of the arms and then a moment of teetering as their legs kicked in the final effort to stand straight up. I know the move well: I'm sorry to say I've used it before myself with my bad back orchestrating the move.

While I was kicking around Kay's garden tool section in her one car garage, I happened by a nifty little item that immediately caught my fancy: a garden shovel. I spotted it leaning against a wall in her uninsulated garage, probably where Kay's now dearly departed husband had last left it. I plucked it off the ground and hefted it in one hand and then the other. It was a well-balanced little devil that I bet could cut through topsoil like a hot knife through butter. Turned-down edges atop the blade on both sides were perfect for planting your foot down on and stomping the blade deeper into the earth. That shovel was made way back when 'Merica was still cranking out good gardening tools, dag nabbit.

"One could certainly dig a hole in a hurry with this little beaut," I said to myself, and then checked quickly left and right to make sure I was out of earshot of any of the other shoppers. Things were coming together—a diabolical plan, rough as it was—was beginning to take shape in my sleep deprived brain.

"Yes, yes this would work nicely for the quick job I have in mind," I thought. I checked the asking price: three dollars.

Though I had ten bucks burning a hole in my pocket, I was confident I could negotiate with old Kay and settle on a price of two dollars, or maybe even less. I flirted with the purchase of my perfect single-use shovel, but in the end, I decided to let barking dogs lie. I put the shovel back in its final resting place, and moved on.

Smokey had no idea how close he had come to meeting his maker that day. Though I love dogs, I held a grudge against Smokey for waking me up so early on a Sunday morning, on Father's Day, no less.

I was glad I didn't buy the shovel, as I would have had to explain to Nancy why I'd purchased it. You see while I was walking back to the Buckboard Motel and Inn, out of nowhere came Nancy with another offer for a ride. Her arms hadn't gotten any stronger since I'd last seen her, so I didn't hesitate to take a second ride with my front desk clerk and chauffeur. I climbed into the front seat and shut the car door before I learned that Smokey, the nasty little barker, was in the car, too. He ambushed me from the backseat by jumping to the front and right onto my lap. I couldn't believe it: I was riding shotgun with Smokey the Barker. I never would have imagined that scenario a short few hours before. Life is funny.

Smokey looked up at me with cloudy bulbous eyes, and lopsided, completely ineffective ears. Smokey's eyes were milky— irony here again—a DOG had CATaracts. He shivered like a dirty gray squirrel on crystal meth, and he smelled like poop. Both ends of Smokey leaked odor, but, as I was a guest in Nancy's car, I had to follow social protocol and not toss the little bastard into the back seat and stick my head out of the car window for the rest of the short ride to the hotel. Looking down at Smokey I wondered how anyone could love the little howler, but to each his own. Smokey was Nancy's love, no doubt.

I think Smokey sensed my dislike of him. He looked up at me from my lap as if he had something to say. I could have sworn I saw him smiling. If Smokey could talk or if I was some sort of dog whisperer, our conversation might have gone like this:

"What? What is it, Smokey boy? What are you trying to say? Is the barn on fire?"

"Screw that Lassie shit. There ain't no barn on fire, dumbass. How about that wake-up call at five twenty this morning? Nice, huh? In dog parlance, me waking you up like that kinda made you my bitch, yes? Ha! You were made my 'beetch' in Beach, ND! How do you like them apples, Motel Pussy? That was all for you this morning. Woof, woof, woo!"

If I'd had that shovel, I'd have been tempted to put it to use at that point. I'd certainly have used it to bury that dog two minutes after Nancy came to a complete stop and return to bed for some guilt-free catch up sleep. Was mercy killing legal in North Dakota? God knows it should be; if ever there was a dog that needed to catch some shuteye under a quilt of topsoil, it was Smokey. Of course, then I'd probably have had to follow the age-old mafia "no witnesses" policy and bury Nancy as well. Then, of course, I'd have to get rid of the car by driving it to a remote spot and setting it on fire like they do in the movies. But how would I get back to the hotel? What if anyone could identify me as the person they saw driving Nancy's car?

Life gets awfully complicated when you try to solve all your problems with a shovel.

We returned to the Buckboard Inn with everyone's hearts still beating. After an afternoon full of napping and a late start (10:00 p.m.) to a night of sleeping, I ended my Beach vacation the following morning when I hit the road. Neither Nancy nor Smokey was there to check me out of the inn.

Oh, and the 'J. P.' in 'J. P. Fugly'? It stands for "Just Plain," as in "Just Plain Fugly."

Smokey was indeed that.

Chapter Fourteen

TIMBLEWEED KEEPS ROLLING

L ots of numbers on the June 16th ride:

- 64 miles traveled at 18.2 miles per hour on average
- Total time in saddle—three hours and twenty-eight minutes
- Top speed achieved—36.2 miles per hour
- One flat tire (back)
- Three horse heads poking out from a horse trailer in downtown Medora with each horse staring at me with

brown eyes the size of softballs and lashes long and thick
as 8-penny nails.

The *Tim*bleweed was back in action with a twenty- to twenty-
five-knot wind on my butt the whole day. What a difference a day
—or a couple of days and wind direction—can make. I overtook
tumbleweed rolling along the road, pushed along by a wind
that was going in the same direction I was. It was nice to fly
without wings.

Not much happened during that day's ride other than
pavement passing below my feet. Although my legs showed
up to work that morning, my head didn't get out of bed
until I was almost run over by a guy in a camper who came
within one inch of hitting me. That near miss sure got my blood
pumping and my head in the game: I was pissed off at the
driver's carelessness and found it especially frustrating that as a
rifleless cyclist, I had no recourse against the injustice of it all.
There was no way I could catch him on my bike, but plop me
in a car, and I would have given that pox filled wart toad a
piece of my mind. But all I could do at the time was lower my
index, ring and pinky fingers and flash the remaining digit
his way in hopes he'd check his rear view mirror to see it.

After the steam stopped shooting out of my ears, I remembered you have to take the good with the bad; I was riding along
on a beautiful day, I had the wind at my back, and I was on a bike
trip sharing thousands of miles of open road with really cool
folks, so things like near misses with cars were bound to happen
once in a while. I calmed down, but kept a more watchful
eye for upcoming traffic. I suppose that's how accidents
happen—people don't see or hear things coming.

I rolled into the Dakota Cyclery shop in Medora for supplies—a new inner tube or two, chain grease, and a pair of new
bike gloves. Five miles after I left the bike store, I suffered a flat.
I'd run over a carpentry staple, of all things, which my front tire
must have kicked up into kissing position just in time for my back

tire to roll on top of it and get fanged. I was in the process of putting the rear tire back on when a super nice couple, Dick and Marie from Scranton, Pennsylvania, pulled over and got out of their gold-colored minivan with an offer to help. They were like a trail angel pit crew, but their timing was off: the flat was fixed. All that was left to do was put the wheel back on.

It was too bad because Dick happened to have a van full of bike tools and the skills to put them to good use. An active biker for more than forty years, Dick seemed disappointed that the tire repair work was already completed. I think he wanted to show off his skills.

Dick jumped into action and attached the wheel and gave the rest of my bike's moving parts the once over to make sure all was up to snuff. He gave my brake pads a half turn to tighten them and checked the cables and the tire pressures. It was like having a heart surgeon apply a Band-Aid to a skinned knee. He could have trued a wheel or pulled cable or readjusted the de-railleurs in the time it would take me to find my tools. He did a bang-up job of re-inflating my back tire and affixing the wheel back onto the bike. What did I do? I was pulling some Vogue moves while Dick's wife Marie kept taking pictures of me. I think she mistook me for a celebrity. Ah, but fame is fleeting: as soon as they left, it was over. I was underway again, just another average Joe homeward bound on a bike.

I will repeat what Dave mentioned after our first zero: zero days mess with your head. There is no doubt about it. My legs were still tired from the century ride from a couple of days prior, sure, but my mental drive train was also showing signs of wear. I was still a little foggy in the attic and was having a tougher than usual time of getting my butt out of bed in the morning. You say goodbye to some momentum and hello to a little more inertia when you take a zero.

I pushed on.

The next day was a new day, June the seventeenth, or what I will always refer to as Devil Day. I had originally intended to cover the ninety-three miles it would take me to reach Bismarck, but I failed to cover even half that distance. What can I say? The flesh is weak. It all began with a big breakfast and a late start, so I guess Gluttony and Sloth, two of the seven deadly sins, were in the bag before I started rolling. A heavy breakfast coupled with a terrible night's sleep turned my legs into nothing more than a way for me to reach the pedals.

Devil Day was filled with biblical signs. Look at the evidence. The first thing I came across a convenience store called "Kum & Go." That is the Devil's work, no? I believe brothel instructions should not make the cut when looking what to name a convenience store. Worst yet, the Kum & Go store was not a one off: it was part of a large, multistate convenience store chain. Can you even imagine? Who is the CEO of Kum & Go, Beelzebub?

A mile or so down the road from the Kum & Go was the entrance to a sprawling Sacred Heart Monastery. Ah, the irony. Two multistate institutions right there next to each other. The Yin and Yang of it was not lost on me. One urged the passerby to Kum & Go, while the other urged travellers to Stay and Pray. One offered redemption at a nickel a can, the other offered redemption for eternal salvation. I shook my head and kept pedaling.

The rest of the day brought hellish headwinds, thunderous rains, tornadoes, pestilence, black cats (a sign of lost souls in some circles), and a soul train (OK, a *long* freight train) that prevented me from "crossing over" to the "other side" (of the tracks, in this case).

Some daylong rides require more breaks than others, but hardly any require a nap. At one point during that particular day's riding effort, I reached Richardson, North Dakota and stopped for a short break that stretched into a couple of hours, part of which had me sleeping in the streets.

Oddly, a garden supply store served smoothies, so I had one. After making loud gurgling noises with my straw in an attempt to get the last few drops from the bottom of my first one, I ordered a second huckleberry smoothie and wondered across the street and ducked into an unlocked foyer of a building for rent. It was greenhouse warm, out of the wind and cozy as hell. It wasn't Heaven exactly, but it served as Purgatory as it sheltered me from the hellish headwinds. I wasn't exactly inside and wasn't exactly outside; I was between worlds. So, Purgatory it was. I grew drowsy once out of the wind and sitting on the carpeted steps that lead to a locked interior entrance. With the glass door closed and with a napping temperature quickly reached, I went out like a light. The French call sleep *petit mort* or "small death." There you go: Devil Day was killing me. I died a small death by the roadside.

You haven't lived until you've power napped in a foyer. I woke up and had no idea who I was or where I was or what I was doing there. I had to re-boot the system. One look at my bike and it all came rushing back. "That's right," I thought, "I'm a middle-aged orphan on a bike trip. Great and fascinating at the same time."

I shook the rest of the dream dust out of my head and let out a huge sigh. I had to push on. I shoved the door open and stepped into the cold stream of wind I'd pedal against the rest of the day.

I was hoping for a break from the signs of the Apocalypse, but they just kept coming. By the time I saw a motel I was ready for it. I went up to the motel office and rang the bell. No one answered. Repeated door knocks and doorbell presses yielded no joy. I opened the screen door, cupped my hands to the side of my head and pressed my forehead against the glass for a look inside. The manager's office was dark, but I found a hand-written note that had slipped from its post and fallen between the doors. It read, "Call me if you want to check in." I dialed the number to summon the owner, who was off premises and busy herding cattle (For you sign watchers out there, cattle are "cloven-hooved beasts," much like the Devil Him/Herself).

While I waited for what seemed like 66.6 minutes for Debbie the manager to return from her hoof farm to check me into the place, the skies opened up, and a ferocious rain came down upon thee—I mean me. A tornado warning had been issued for Stark County, or 'Stark Reality', as I like to call it, and the sky was putting on a pretty good show. Green and purple clouds indicated the skies were cruising for a bruising. Hail followed by winds and drenching rains soaked both saints and sinners alike. Some dude named Noah floated by in a big boat, and he waved good-bye to me as he passed by. I yelled over to him.

"Permission to come aboard, sir."

"Not granted. Sorry, man. The Arc has a strict two-by-two policy. Already have two jackasses. Don't need a third."

The only other person I met in Stark besides Debbie the manager was a guy named Doug on an extended stay at the Ray Bern Hotel. He was an electrician who was staying a few doors down from mine at the otherwise empty motel. Doug was done with work for the day; so there he was, sitting on a white plastic chair outside his room, looking across the street past the parking lot over the fields and into the sky when I approached.

He confirmed Debbie was "the owner/operator of this fair establishment" and that she was gone but "would return after she got the cows in."

Doug was halfway through a six-pack of canned beer and a carton of Marlboro cigarettes. He must have liked working with his hands a lot because even during his time off his hands kept pretty busy with putting either a beer or a cigarette into his mouth. The only time either hand wasn't holding something was when he was reaching for something like another beer, a lighter, or another cigarette.

We sat outside his room on plastic chairs, shot the shit, and watched the clouds turn mean. He introduced himself and told me he had been living at the motel for four or five months straight. He was doing union work nearby and was being well paid for it. A divorced father of two, he had not seen his boys in over two years, although he tried to. He drove six hours home every weekend to be close to where his ex-wife and sons lived in the house that he'd "paid for with long hours at work and an Olympic pool of sweat." It didn't sound like Doug had it easy at work or in his personal life. I did not envy him for a minute. He told me he did the same four things every day: "work like a mule, sit like a Buddha, drink like a fish, and smoke like a chimney."

"Don't get me wrong. I haven't given up on Life; I've just given up on this one. Three and a half years I'm going to retire to North Carolina and play golf."

We just sat on those plastic chairs, me drinking water out of a thermos, him drinking beer out of a can, and both of us watching the winds kick ass and the clouds take names.

Even though he was sitting, Doug was standing in a three and a half yearlong line that ended on a first tee somewhere in North Carolina. I hoped things worked out for him. Hope he found some fairways in his retirement and managed to see some holiday weekends with his two boys beaming back at him from across a shared table filled with plates of food. I hope his life ended up like something Norman Rockwell would want to paint.

One last biblical note: the name of the motel was the Ray Bern Motel. Hey, there is the word "burn" in there somewhere, right? "Bern" in hell? It was a Devil Day, no doubt. I was glad to have had that long day over and done with. It seemed an eternity before it finally was over. The Devil him/herself could have stuck his/her pitchfork or forked tail into me by late afternoon: I was done.

Gotta keep pedaling...

For me the next day started at six thirty when I stepped out into an empty parking lot with Doug's car gone. He had obviously already started doing one of the four things he did everyday.

The previous night's storm had left me with one big beautiful morning on my hands: the sun was shining, the air was fresh, the road looked clean of dust and dirt as though all of the sins of Stark County had been washed away. Devil Day had ended with a baptismal rain that had given us all a fresh start to a new life. We were all born again after our "little death" of a night's sleep and I was hoping everything was right with the world and that the winds would be blowing my way.

Alas, no luck. I looked up to see an American flag flat snapping and pressed creaseless in a rock steady, wrong-way wind. About two miles down the road I saw a smokestack coughing up a stream of white, fluffy cancer-starter into a crystal clear early morning sky. Just as soon as that plume emerged from that active chimney, it got pushed flat by the wrong way wind. The plume blew arrow straight and west, parallel to the fields three stories below. That smokestack was a smoke windsock with very bad news for this bicycle pilot; I had another Bob Seger day in front of me where I'd be "riding against the wind, riding against the wind..."

Five hours and ten minutes in the saddle later, I had covered a measly forty-nine miles. Going less than ten miles per hour all day was a tough go, but that's what you get and you don't get upset. I even had to pedal when going *downhill*. The terrain was not a challenge in and of itself, but the wind limited me to a slow crawl at best. Bismarck was out there somewhere. I'd been trying to get there for two days with no luck. So far, it was Bismarck 2, Fahey 0.

Riding all day with the wind hard against. Now I know where the crude term *this fucking blows* comes from.

Two things of note: I suffered another flat tire, and this time there was no Dick and Marie from Scranton, PA around to help me out. I patched the tube as best I could and it seemed to hold air. I was hoping to reach Bismarck before the tire ran flat again. My first order of business once I reached Bismarck, then, would be a visit to a bike store for some new inner tubes.

The second thing of note was that I was now an hour closer to Eastern Standard Time. I'd crossed into Central Standard Time the second I left Stark County and had reset my watch to the new time zone. The bicycle computer clock on the Fun Mover remained on Pacific Standard Time—not because I was nostalgic, but because I just didn't know how to reset the damn thing. I still don't. To this day, my bike's computer, wherever it is, is set to PST.

Here's how that day's uneventful ride went: Pedal, pedal, pedal, pedal. I arrived in New Salem, North Dakota—probably named after Salem, Massachusetts, where they killed people for being witches, remember?

The first place that had water in New Salem was a diesel motor repair store just outside of town. A very helpful and informed woman named Colette pointed me in the direction of a faucet. After I topped my water bottles off, I assessed the weather. It looked like it was worsening as the sky was darkening in the east. Colette told me a storm with a tornado or two were forecasted for that afternoon, so that great news put my arrival into Bismarck, still thirty-five miles away, off for another day.

New Salem was going to have to be my home for the night. I don't do tornadoes.

Colette had some more bad news for me. Due to a water main break, the local camping/RV park was closed; I couldn't camp there even if I'd wanted to. Worse yet, the only hotelier in town would not rent to cyclists because "of what had happened the last time." Whatever the hell that was. So, I faced an age-old problem: where was I going to find a shower and get some sleep?

Desperate, I said, "Look. I need a shower today and a place to sleep tonight. Any suggestions?"

Long story short? It turned out that Colette was the mayor of New Salem, and her enthusiasm for her town and her sense of hospitality spilled over into an invitation to grab a shower at her house. She wasn't going home until after five o'clock that day so she suggested I hit the local coffee shop to kill some time. I'd meet her at her house after she got out of work, at about five fifteen. She said she had to go right home to mow her lawn and feed her wiener, "so, no problem." She seemed like a good sort, so I agreed even though I didn't understand the wiener reference exactly. I just assumed at that point she had a small low-lying elongated black pet dog. Besides, she was the mayor, for gosh sakes. She wasn't going to ruin a young and promising political career by murdering me in her shower stall. So, even though an agreement had been reached, I looked her over and pondered my chances in a fight to the death. I knew for sure that I would lose against her in an arm-wrestling match, but with her being a little slow in the shoes, I figured I'd have a better-than-average chance at survival if I could apply some of my fast-footedness to the situation and stay clear of dem guns.

I was in.

I headed off to a local coffee shop to kill an hour or two. The shop sold not only coffee, but also delicious smoothies. I had one and began to bend the ears of the three or four locals who were lingering around the coffee shop. In the course of blabbering on about something or other, I mentioned that I was a bit worried about pitching a tent during a tornado. As soon as the woman who ran the coffee shop heard I was going to shower at Colette's place, she excused herself to make a phone call. Before you knew it, I was being handed the telephone.

I thought to myself, "Who would be calling me on a land line in a coffee shop in New Salem, North Dakota?" Everyone I knew in the world didn't know where in the world I was.

Well, sure enough, it was Colette on the other end, inviting me to stay the night in her basement. She'd still be home at five fifteen to mow the lawn. I gratefully accepted her second offer. I think the coffeehouse owner shamed Colette into inviting me to stay the night. Regardless of her motivation, I was grateful for the invitation.

I learned the name of Colette's favorite bar in town (the Field), and dropped off a twenty-dollar bill to the barkeep for Colette to spend in any way, shape, or form she wanted.

By the time I pulled up to Colette's place, she was on her lawnmower and halfway done shaving green stripes into her backyard. I waved. She didn't see me. I whistled, and she looked up, threw me a chin, finished her row, and dismounted at the turn to show me the way to the shower and the basement. When she turned the lawn mower engine off, the whole town seemed to go quiet.

We went down into her basement, and it was immediately clear to me that she was a rabid Packers fan. Her basement was full of Packers paraphernalia and odds and ends from her past career as a softball player. I was happy to meet her little eight-year-old wiener dog named Uber or Hedrick or Spaten or some other German name that I forgot immediately after she told me. I concentrated on not telling wiener dog jokes and pointing out the irony of the fact that she lived with a wiener and yet was still single.

Perhaps I search for irony too much.

I showered up while Colette finished mowing her lawn and began mowing her ninety-three-year-old next-door neighbor's lawn. Colette had a heart of gold: I'd vote for her in the next election if I could have. Colette then gave me the keys to her truck and told me where to find a good place to eat. I took her pickup truck to the recommended restaurant and tried to top it off with gas, but it was full already. Another one of my twenty-dollar bills found its way to her driver's-side visor with all the

CDs stuffed up there. I tucked it up next to the soundtrack from *The Wizard of Oz*. Not sure which character she may have identified with, but my top guess was the person behind the curtain—Oz himself, as he, like Colette, was mayoral by nature. Colette was very generous and trusting to let me, a complete stranger, crash in her basement and borrow her truck.

I'd trusted her, too. She could have locked the basement door and decided not to feed me.

I awoke the next day at the feet of a life-sized custom cardboard cutout standee of Bret Favre throwing a football. It was like waking up at the foot of an alter in a church built for Saint Farve. But hey, I was alive, my pants were still on, and my throat wasn't slit, so I figured things were going my way—and I had not even started pedaling yet.

Not ten minutes later, dag nabbit, I was proven wrong again. I went out to the shed where the Fun Mover had snoozed the night away, only to discover that the tire I had so professionally patched the day before was flat again.

Even more bad news took my "this is going to be a good day" optimism down a couple more notches: the wind was blowing stronger than it had the day before.

Still against. And it was drizzling a cold rain.

Great.

After fixing my tire and saying my goodbyes to Colette, I rolled under a grey sky that spit rain at me as I made my way over to the warm and cozy cover of the Muddy River Coffee House. There I dillydallied over a scone and two cups of coffee as I dreaded having to face another day of wet, wind, and chill from my saddle again. While I procrastinated, the wind waned and died and the rain eased up. Not even the recent memory of a flat tire could dampen my lifting spirits at that point: I was going to ride in no wind! That made me very happy. Rain? Snow? Hail? Heat? Bring it, bitches: I'd take any and all of them over a fifteen-knot headwind any day. With only thirty-five windless miles to Bismarck, I made it in two hours and forty minutes with a couple of rest breaks along the way.

As soon as I landed in Bismarck, I found the best bike shop in town and emerged with a bunch of new gear and a small-world story. (I am fully aware there might be a bit of redundancy in saying I have a small-world story from the state of North Dakota, a small world unto itself.)

The bike mechanic who trued my wheels and sold me two new tires was very impressed with my New Salem street cred. It turned out he was from New Salem and the thirty plus miles I'd just pedaled that morning was his daily commute. He knew Colette, but not well enough to crash in her basement. He and his wife (no kids) had recently moved from Portland, Oregon, fleeing the traffic, the drugs, and the gangs. I could certainly understand the appeal of less traffic and fewer gang-bangers in my daily life, but you better *love* the small-town feel of things when you move to a town with eight hundred people—because there ain't much else.

Emerging from a bike shop with a brand-new set of tires and inner tubes and wheels recently trued made me feel like a man with a new lease on life. What a great, fresh feeling of confidence it was to know that my bike was mechanically sound. Brand new tires rolled smoothly, and newly trued wheels no longer rubbed against brake pads.

Alas, only one short mile later, I suffered the second flat of the morning. This one was a pinch flat. It had to be.

Tires will go flat from being punctured by a sharp object and then they either pop like a balloon or leak like a sieve. A pinch flat is different in that it goes flat from the inside out, the result of an improperly installed inner tube. If the inner tube is twisted or wrinkled at installation, it will "pinch" against the wheel rim when the tire is inflated. Put some weight on that wheel, and the rim will cut the inner tube like a knife. All inner tubes must be placed carefully onto the rim at installation in order to insure they lie flat against the rim to avoid pinching up against it.

So, there I was again, changing a tire for the second time that morning, only this time I was changing out a brand-new inner tube that should have lasted me one thousand miles, not one.

I changed the flat in the shadow of the state capital building, or what the locals called, "the Penis of the Prairie." It deserved the nickname: it is the only sixteen-story building in the entire state and thus was a phallic symbol of epic proportions. It was built with federal money, designed by architects with no sense of scale, and conceived by Washington, D. C. politicians, the "Penises of the Potomac" if you will, hell-bent on spending every-one's hard earned tax dollars. I thought the nickname "Penis of the Prairie" was fitting on many different levels.

I fixed the tire and left.

Throughout the day I made bad food choices…by not having any. All I had for breakfast were two cups of coffee and a scone at the Muddy River Coffee House. I'd skipped lunch. Skipping meals might work when clocking hours in a cubicle, but it comes up short if you ride a bike all day. Even by dinnertime I wasn't hungry, but I knew I had to eat. Unfortunately, a drenching rain-storm began just before I was about to head out for some dinner. That storm stunted my appetite for exploration; there was no way I was going to leave room 121 at Motel 6 and search the town for a good restaurant in the pouring rain.

So, instead of making the effort to find the best place in town to eat, I opted for the closest place. Ironically instead of eating well, I ate local. I splish-splashed across the motel parking lot in a drenching rain and ducked into a German diner conveniently located just next door. I ordered and ate only out of obligation, as I still wasn't hungry, but knew I would be at some later point after the restaurant closed. All that would be available to eat later would be the overpriced bags of peanut M&M's in the Motel 6 lobby vending machine that were long past their expiration dates. By the time I finished the *Käsespätzle* I felt uncomfortably full and knew a constitutional was necessary to get my digestion process started, that is, for me to get some of that Germany down into my lower colon. The rain had stopped, so I wandered a few blocks over shiny streets to a movie theater that was showing *Edge of Tomorrow,* a Tom Cruise sci-fi thriller. I enjoyed the movie. You gotta hand it to Tommy C.; his personal reputation notwithstanding, he was a successful entertainer. I perversely enjoyed watching his character die multiple times over the course of that film. Then, with nothing waiting for me but the inside of a Motel 6, I doubled down and watched *22 Jump Street,* which was terrible, absolutely awful. I ambled back to my room and shut the door behind me, closing the door on the day.

A cautionary note to the Motel 6 curious: don't do it. Staying at a Motel 6 is like spending a night in prison with the locks on the inside of the doors. You walk up to the front desk, check in with the warden—I mean the Motel 6 manager—and let him know your expected release date—I mean your checkout date—before you head to your cell—I mean your room. Flimsy doors with cheap locks provide only the illusion of security. Motel 6 room doors would, at best, only momentarily thwart an unwanted intruder. With walls and windows as thin as paper, sounds from nearby rooms drift easily in to irritate occupants like me who are more interested in experiencing R.E.M. sleep than listening to R.E.M. songs. Sounds from nearby rooms drifted in with almost no distortion or suppression. Someone was listening to "Everybody hurts" upstairs from me, another guy was listening to a baseball game. I heard Carl Yastrzemski's name being mentioned after a great play to the plate and was, for a moment there, under the impression that I was listening to quite possibly the greatest comeback in all of sports history. Alas, it was a re-run and why the guy was listening to it was beyond me. The rest of the soundscape of my night's stay included a family argument from next door and some roughie stuffie lovemaking from God only knew where.

Fortunately, my exhaustion won in the end, and I managed to get some shut-eye.

I was delighted to report that things went well for me the following morning with my Motel Sucks—I mean "6"—parole board. I stepped out of the place and into the sunshine a free man. I'd served my time, paid my debt to society. I could go where and do what I wanted, so I climbed on to my steel horse and rolled.

I was five weeks into the trip and, all in all, physical pain aside; it had been a good roll so far. I was beginning to shed a few pounds and see some things and meet some people I'd otherwise have missed. Pet peeve? I hate it when east and west coast folks use the term "fly over states" to describe the part of our country that lies between two oceans. There is a condescending smugness to the term that I find off-putting. Do me a favor: next time you hear someone use the term "fly over states," ask them if they've ever visited those states or met some of the people who call those states home. Ten bucks says they haven't, and a hundred bucks says they should.

After a full day of riding, I found a campsite in Napoleon, North Dakota, that would serve as my home for the evening. Unfortunately for me, the campground abutted the town pool, which, when I rolled in, had a static-ridden radio station blasting Top 40 Hits and advertising spots for local restaurants, bars, and farm supply stores. I had stumbled back into the media onslaught and I didn't like it at all. I guess I was getting addicted to peace and quiet and was becoming reluctant about enduring a soundscape I hadn't specifically requested.

There were maybe a dozen kids no older than twelve splashing around in the pool. Three local teenage girls served as the lifeguards on duty.

At the risk of sounding like a crusty, cranky old man, I wasn't a fan of the music being blasted. I know that Top 40 hits are Top 40 hits for a reason—people vote with their ears in the music industry. Yet just because it sells in quantity doesn't mean it is good in quality. Some of the songs played that evening were just horrible both in sound and in substance. Many of the songs I heard were about booty calls, sexual stamina, club and party lifestyles, and poppin' caps into people. I ask you: what is the advantage to subjecting today's twelve-year-old kids to such dribble?

One of the more memorable musical masterpieces being regurgitated from the boom box featured a particularly aggressive female singer who vociferously lamented of her lover's sexual shortcomings. In so many words and in so many ways he'd come up short. So unsatisfied was she with his bedroom performance that she openly challenged him in song to step up to the sexual plate (and to perhaps do so with a larger bat next time) and improve on his ability to bring her to a place called "climax with a 'k' hey, hey, hey, hey." The dirty diva made it abundantly clear to all of us listening what it would cost to "get on up in there":

You don't know what to do; you don't know how to handle me.
I ain't as simple as one, two, three; if you want to be whiff me,
Then get you self a Benz and take me out in da city.
It's only den I'll get whiff men, and get it going sexy

Wonderful, just wonderful. I'll bet her mother is quite proud.

That evening, under a beautiful setting sun, I was being ear raped by a boom box that was sound vomiting horrible, unimaginative song lyrics promoting stupidity, baby momma-ism, thug commercialism, frequent use of the *N* word in rap songs (bleeped on the radio, but everyone knows the word). It was "stereo"-typing at its worst. "Da pimp's life" was being glamorized and those kids and I were being subjected to it. There was no escape.

I'd bet the "musical artists" who belted out that rubbish were more concerned with how much money they made than the harm they were doing to people by glamorizing stupidity. Oh, and the biggest double standard of all: it seemed some people can use the *N* word anytime they please, as long as there is a thumping beat in the background and a dollar sign up front. Whoever drops the N bomb should be ashamed to do so. I know—maybe I *am* an old crusty man—but I can't help but be offended by meaning of the word when someone utters it. How can people end up *being paid* to use such a hateful term? How is any song or conversation improved by the use of that word? And don't try to convince me that the N word is a black on black term of endearment. I don't buy it.

It is a racist term no matter who says it.

Evening birdsong and crickets' chirps were drowned out. I say an early summer evening should be filled with the sounds of kids splashing around in a pool filled with water and the air filled with laughs, giggles, and chirping crickets, not haters hating.

Wow. Is this a bicycle book or some old guy's opportunity to rant? Sorry for that.

After setting up my tent and paying my camping fee, I headed out to get something to eat. Just my luck—once a month, the town got together to make burgers and raise money for park maintenance, and that night was the night. I enjoyed my first dinner of a chicken burger with a small vanilla-chocolate swirl in a cone at the White Maid on Main Street, and then stopped in for a second dinner at the fundraiser. I had a couple of burgers and some fries there, too.

Well, not much else was going on in the town of Napoleon that evening, so I headed back to the campground, took a shower (for free), and changed into clean clothing, one of the simple pleasures in life. I was all ready for bed, but the sun wasn't. It still hung stubbornly up in the sky and my watch indicated that it would be at least 9:30 before it winked asleep. I asked the girls what time the radio wave thrusting was turned off and they said nine o'clock. So, I went as far from the sound puke as I could and found a park bench to wait it out.

Just then a guy drove by me in a quad with a couple of kids and parked near a jungle gym that was part of the pool and recreational "complex." Yeah, it was more like a pool and recreational "simple": there was a jungle gym and a swing set with two swings. The kids jumped off the quad as soon as it stopped rolling and dashed over to the jungle gym. The driver, a guy familiar with cigarettes and sun, nodded a quiet hello and took a seat on an adjacent bench, the only other park bench there, and lit up. I could tell he was curious about what the heck I was typing on my computer, so when he asked me, I told him I was writing about my bike trip. He asked me how far I was biking. I told him.

"Guess your are not a smoker. I'd offer you one of mine if you were."

It turned out the guy was a granddad twice over and was a year younger than me. He'd just left his management job at a chemical seed company earlier that spring because he couldn't take having his boss "step all over on him anymore," so he quit.

"I was either going to quit that job, or kill some folks," he said.

"Oh," is all I said. I had never knowingly been so close to a human land mine before. I thought it best to change the subject, but he continued on. (Of all the days to be without my blast suit...)

He explained his work experience and long career in manufacturing management positioned him well for another job, but instead of "getting right back on the horse that threw him," he had decided to take the summer off and do some fishing with his grandkids and try to "really quit smoking this time." From my seat, it looked like he was doing OK with his two grandchildren, but not so well kicking his habit.

He continued talking between puffs, or "drags" I guess you call them, on his cigarette. He confessed that he was sad about all the many changes he'd seen happening in the world. His whole life he'd dealt with stand-up guys like farmers who did business with a handshake and stood by their word. Then the oil boom came along and invaded his region, bringing "all the crime and the goddamn drugs." He looked over at the two kids on the playground.

"Changes are ruining the state—changing the way things used to be," he said.

Even way out here, in the middle of the plain, plain, plains, things change, change, change.

He felt that he needed to do something about all the stress and anger he was feeling, so he smoked, but didn't drink. He'd lie awake most nights and "stare at my bedroom ceiling like the answers were up there somewhere. They ain't."

If he'd asked me for a solution to his problems (he didn't), I'd have suggested some two-wheeled therapy. It was working for me. I wonder what the world would be like if doctors gave out bicycle prescriptions: "Here you are, Tim. Ride two wheels and call me in the morning." I predict that someday doctors will eventually favor prescribing specific regular exercise over pills, but that will be long after the pharmaceutical companies decide to stop putting profit ahead of people.

So, that was it. The sun went down, Angry Man collected his grandkids and zoomed off, the girls closed the pool, the radio was turned off at 9:25 p.m., and I settled in to my tent as a solo camper in Napoleon, North Dakota. The good news was that for the first time in a few days, the tornado risk was low, and I had enough food for breakfast the next morning, so I was out of excuses. Wouldn't you know it? After not using my sleeping pad for a couple of weeks, I'd decided that very morning to ship it home, figuring my camping days were behind me. Bad idea. Mother Earth can be especially hard on the over fifty set.

Ouch. The next morning I crawled out of the tent as if I'd been shot in the lower back. I unzipped the tent and then groaned like a porn star for the full five minutes it took to get up and out of it. I smiled, thinking how the sound of a zipper unzipping followed by grunts and groans could have been misconstrued. Luckily there was no one else within earshot to get the wrong impression. I sure missed that sleeping pad, the one I'd mailed home on the very day I ended up needing one.

I decided to go to breakfast instead of sharing mine with a bunch of bugs, so I packed up and pedaled past the town swimming pool, now quiet and calm save for water bugs that zipped to and fro across it and leaving tiny wakes, the only evidence of their presence. Rolling the few blocks into town got my blood pumping and my eyes fully open. I came upon a place named Reuben's and took my time over a plate of eggs served by a waitress who dropped by every once in a while to pour more coffee and serve up something I didn't order: a fairly serious pair of bedroom eyes. Check, please. Maybe someone else would be interested in a little dessert with a stranger after a scrambled egg breakfast, but not me.

Sure seems like loneliness lives everywhere people do.

I'll be damned if I didn't run in to Marty for the second time that week when he walked into Reuben's Restaurant. I'd first ran into Marty way outside of Bismarck in the front lobby of a place called the Sleep Inn. Bike tourists usually greet each other as friends, not strangers, so that's how we met. At that time, his brother and sister-in-law were with him. They had joined Marty for a stretch, but left the day after, rendering him a solo rider once again. An easygoing sixty-three-year-old retired steelworker from

Portland, Oregon, Marty rode a recumbent bike and was slowly making his way to Bar Harbor, Maine, the official finish line of his go at the Northern Tier. Even though he struggled with "the dye-a-beat-ess," he continued to roll slow and go. He was really enjoying himself; every breath of air he took cross-country had to pass through his broad smile to get to his lungs.

Although he was traveling solo, Marty was by no means alone. You see, Marty had a Thomas the Train toy along for his ride, a toy that his three-year-old grandson had insisted he take with him the night before Marty had left for Anacortes, Washington. Initially reluctant to add even an ounce to his load, Marty had acquiesced and brought the toy with him at his grandson's insistence. What a treat. Thomas the Train turned out to be a bridge between a grandfather and grandson: Thomas was in every picture Marty sent home, much to the welcome delight of a very grateful grandchild, who would pepper his parents with questions about his grandfather's progress across the country, well, Thomas the Train's progress across the country, really. In his grandson's eyes, "Granddaddy was just there to take the pictures."

Yep. Marty had his grandson *and* Thomas the Train along for the ride. Lucky guy.

Marty and I decided to leave Reuben's together and start that day's ride, so we set out after breakfast.

The first thing I noticed was the squeak. Every time Marty cranked the pedals, there would be a *squeak*, then nothing, then *squeak*, then nothing. You get the idea. That bike squeaked louder than the wind blew, so I pulled him over, dug through my bags until I located the chain grease I'd picked up in the Dakota Cyclery Shop, and applied a little chain lube to the squeaky wheel—and bingo! Marty could now hear the prairie sans squeak. You should have seen the smile on his face.

"I got so used to that damn squeak, I didn't know it was there! Thank you, Tim!" he said. He was very appreciative. We parted ways with a thanks and a wave. I never saw Marty again, but I later learned that he had made it to Bar Harbor, Maine and had put his feet in the ocean. I am sure he had a smile on his face and doubly sure he had Thomas the Train right there with him at the finish.

A few miles later, I came across another small town that had a community gym, the first gym I'd seen on my trip. It had the best, most appropriate, name for any gym in the world: it was called "the False Hope Gym". It was open 24/7, and there were no membership fees. Just go in and work out and give yourself some false hope. Some guy named Honey Miller opened it up for the world to use. Maybe he was fighting obesity one gym at a time?

A score or so of miles later I hit Gackle, North Dakota, and took a shot of the Fun Mover outside the Tastee Freeze where I had a great lunch.

At that point I was thirty-five miles into my day, it was 2:20 p.m., and there were seventy-five miles of no services to speak of in the next leg. Bike wisdom told me to stay put in Gackle. But the wind was a-blowin' my way...

Right in the middle of hemming and hawing about whether I should push on or stay put, a trio of cyclists arrived. They came from the east, and had been pushing against a steady wind all day. They dismounted with wind war stories to tell to anyone who'd listen.

"It is blowing like hell," they said when I asked them how they were doing. One of the group didn't say anything much. He unclipped his foot from the pedal and put it on the ground as he rolled to a stop. He dropped an f bomb and said nothing else. His eyes were opened wide and unblinking. He'd been through something out there. He was suffering from PTWS (post traumatic wind syndrome).

For the first time in over two weeks, the wind was with me and it was picking up. So, there I was with the wind in my favor, some juice in my legs, food in my stomach, and some time on my hands before sunset. *Bam!* I shot outta there like a midget out of a circus canon and kept a twenty-five mile-per-hour average for more than an hour and forty-five minutes. Thanks to Mother Nature's push, I really flew.

While I was setting my own land speed record and enjoying a mighty push from a favoring wind, I'd managed to overtake a Spaniard on a heavily loaded bike going slower but in the same direction I was. I slowed down and chatted with him for a bit before continuing on. We were on a straight road under a bright sun, surrounded by fields as flat and as far as the eye could see. His name was Manuel. After he took the ear buds out of his ears and looked at me, I asked Manuel if he'd seen any other eastbound cyclists, and he nodded.

"Two girls from Martha's Vineyard a couple of days ago. They were as beautiful as the sun and they rode like the wind. My love for them was much stronger than my lungs and my legs. I let them fly away as I would a pair of pretty butterflies." He had turned down their kind invitation to join them for a few days on the road. He told them he was more of a fifty-mile-a-day guy, whereas they were more the seventy-five-to-a-hundred miles a day type. I couldn't blame Manuel for not joining the two cuties on a ride at that kind of pace. You gotta ride your ride, man. Pretty butterflies or not, ride your ride.

Manuel had a way with words and was clearly a poet of sorts, and I was sorry our conversation had to end, but the wind was at my back and I wanted to take advantage of it, so off I went. I waved goodbye and saw him cock is head to the left and then to the right as he put his ear buds back on and settled back into his riding zone, alone on a loaded bike, under a blazing sun and a big blue sky.

A while later, I stopped at the only convenience store I'd see that day and learned from a guy named Tom that the next motel was another twenty-five miles further east.

"Oh, ok, thanks."

"Don't you got a map there onboard that bike of yours? It is funny, you are the second bicyclist to ask me about the location of the nearest accommodation in less than twenty-four hours." Tom got to talking about a pair of bicyclists, two twenty some-thing girls, who had stopped by the day before.

"They were from Martha's Vineyard and they were real cute," he told me. "I mean Timmy, they were *real* cute."

"Ha!" I laughed. "I've heard of those two from another cyclist I passed by earlier today."

I told Tom about Manuel and about how fast they rode. Then I asked him a question. "Were they cute enough? Would you bike a hundred miles a day to be able to hang out with them?"

While considering his answer, Tom hiked his jeans up over his sizable beer belly with both hands in a twist-this-way-and-then-twist-that-way motion so that his brass belt buckle (which said "TOM" on it) was visible and in the middle of his belly for the moment. He leaned up against a counter, carefully weighing his answer. The brass belt buckle slowly slid right back down his beer belly and dropped completely out of sight under it. Only the floor could read his first name at that point. With his jeans settled back low on his hips, he scratched his chin.

"I'll tell you what," Tom said seriously, looking both ways and then back at me, his eyes bright with mischief. "I'm no biker, but I'd pedal a hundred *and twenty* miles a day to have dinner with either one of them. They were *real* cute."

"Go get 'em, Tommy!" I said, slapping him on the shoulder, and laughing at his reply. He smiled, blushed, and reached for his belt again.

"Well, maybe not today," he said with a chuckle. He pushed himself off his lean and stood up. With both hands and another twisting motion, he pulled up his pants over his belly to a place where the world could, once again, read his name.

I filled my water bottles with cool, clean H_2O from the utility sink and returned to my thoughts, my bike, and the wind that remained at my back.

By day's end, I was very proud of myself for pushing forward. I made it 114.5 miles—my all time personal best. I slept in Enderlin that night, having left Gackle and the three shell-shocked riders far behind.

Chapter Fifteen

SO FARGO, SO GOOD-OH, ADIEU, BEAUTIFUL BICYCLE BUTTERFLIES

O n June 21st I found myself in a convenience store in Kindred about forty-five miles into my day, with still Fargo nowhere in sight. Fargo was a "big city," but I'd grown to learn the plains are slow to reveal what's next. All they give you is what seems to be about seven, maybe ten miles of worldview before the earth curves away and puts things out of sight.

While I was pedaling, someone upstairs turned up the heat. That afternoon had turned into a scorcher. I could feel heat radiate in waves up from the pavement. The same sick bastard who turned up the heat had turned down the fan a couple of notches, too, so there was yours truly, pedaling along at fourteen to seventeen miles per hour, sweating buckets in seemingly still air and reluctant to stop at all for a rest because the black flies would find wet skin so quickly.

The welcome sign in Kindred informed visitors "Kindness is a way of <u>LIFE</u>! In Kindred!" with the word *life* capitalized, underlined, and exclamation pointed. Wow, so upbeat. Nothing bad could happen in a town like that, right? I sat inside that gas station convenience store and had a 7UP to match the <u>UP</u>beat nature of the town. In no rush to return to my spinning workout in the outdoor oven, I sat on a stool and refilled my cup of water and soda a couple of times, giving my bloodstream the chance to distribute the sugar and the hydration to the tissues in my legs that needed it most. I sat there for the better part of an hour and was witness to exactly zero acts of kindness. People didn't even hold the door open for one another in Kindred.

"Kindred, Schmindred," or so I thought.

I should have known better; you never know what's coming in life—or on a bike trip, for that matter. As I sat in a chair, tired and spacing out, reluctant to return outside and face heat, my phone pinged, signaling the receipt of a text message. It was from someone I hadn't communicated with since 1979. That someone had once been a special someone to me and had ranked pretty high in my puppy-love phase. I'd had a mad crush on Mariana back in high school and hadn't heard or seen her after my family moved to another state right after I graduated. Somehow she had gotten over me and gone on with her life: she'd graduated high school, went to college, got married, attended medical school, and became a doctor. While sitting on that seat plumb tuckered out and nursing a cold soda, I learned my old puppy love had settled in Dallas, TX to work and raise her family. I had no idea how she found out about my bike trip, but she wished me well and a safe return home. Turns out I was wrong about Kindred. Mariana's reaching out to me was an act of kindness, and if I remember correctly, kindness was a way of life for her, too.

Kindred, North Dakota, had lived up to its name after all.

Ah, the magical reach of social media.

Replenished with sugar and sugar sweet memories of unrequited puppy love, I mounted up and faced the road ahead, a road that shimmered in the summer heat and ended with mirage pools in the distance. That was one long hot afternoon spent in the saddle. Well, that's what you get sometimes. As mentioned before, it ain't all hot buttered popcorn, dancing unicorns and cheese dip on a bike trip, I can tell you that.

When I reached Fargo, ND, the first thing I saw was an A&W Root Beer/Long John Silver's restaurant and it beckoned me. I love root beer and I hadn't had an A&W Root Beer since a forever ago, so I popped in for one. In addition, a sign on the door said there was air conditioning inside and at that point in my day, any large square chamber with a roof on it that promised cool relief from the heat I'd been riding through was indeed a welcome sight. A small root beer went for $1.69, and it was mostly ice. In about a second I was sucking the root beer off the ice cubes, desperate for more sugary soda. Why do they put so much ice into the glass when the soda pop is refrigerated anyway? To save money, sure—I get that, but still. It was a complete rip-off and no way to run a business.

Long John Silver's offers a very bizarre variety of food, food that is sourced thousands of miles from where it is served up for sale. Long John Silver's offered hot dogs, fries, clams, floats, and fish. Yuck. For those of you out there with stock in Long John Silver's restaurants, *sell, sell, sell!* The service was nonexistent, everyone else in the place was at least eighty-five years old, they put too many ice cubes in their damn drinks, and the place looked as dead and worn out as the customers, me included. And the bathrooms? Put it this way: I had stayed in RV parks all across the

country, and there was no way I was going to stoop so low (literally) as to use the bathroom in that dump. *Wrong* John Silver's
was more like it.

About an hour later, I was after a place to stay and experienced
a little pushback from the man responsible for showing me the
way to one. I had a little bit of a hissy fit when a doorman treated
me like a second-class citizen because I was on a bicycle. He initially turned me away from the Radisson Hotel after he said, and I
quote, "We don't house you people, move along."

Huh? What?

I don't suffer fools gladly. The guy was dressed like a
Christmas nutcracker but he was really a ballbuster: he blocked
my entrance into his little castle. He wouldn't allow my bicycle
to come into "his" building. Now look, my bike wasn't a therapy
dog or anything: I just didn't want it getting stolen. He suggested
I lock my bike in a back alley behind the building, away from
any video surveillance. That was not going to be an option for
me. I'd heard too many "My bike was stolen" stories from other
travelers and wasn't going to jump through the hoops trying to
replace a fully loaded touring bike in Fargo, ND. Clearly, the
heat had gotten to me, and I was standing fast on my insistence
that my bike went wherever I did.

I asked the doorman to see the queen or the king of the
castle and the hotel manager arrived a minute or two later after the ball-busting Nutcracker whispered into the microphone
up his sleeve. My tired-biker hissy fit ended when I met Queen
Radisson, Hotel Manager of All Things. Once she saw the color
of my money, she let me bring the bike inside, no problem. "Just
don't clean your greasy chain with our white towels," she said.
I promised I wouldn't and informed her that I hadn't had any
intention to do so in the first place.

My room was on the fourth floor, and it was the highest off the
ground I'd been since landing in Seattle weeks before. A nice, long,
hot shower, a fresh set of clothes, a pair of street shoes, a bike safely

secured and stowed in a room, and a wallet with some money in it gave me a nice happy feeling in Fargo. I wasn't "that guy" anymore. Thankfully, the doorman had a short memory. He pretended not to know me the next time he saw me. I was a professional, I pretended not to be such a big baby the next time I saw him. But I think his mind was made up about me. You can never look at someone the same way after they throw a heat-induced hissy fit.

I stole over to the Sky on the Prairie, a rooftop bar that was serving up pint glasses of liquid golden deliciousness. But the Lord giveth, and the Lord taketh away: about three minutes after my waitress delivered my beer, she began putting the umbrellas down all around me and stacking all the chairs and bringing them to one side of the bar near the doorway like the building was about to capsize or something.

I was only few sips into that golden liquid of pure ecstasy when another waitress came over and delivered some horrible news: a lightning storm was approaching, and my rooftop seat was going to be confiscated due to the threat of "imminent" lightning strike. Ever notice that whenever someone uses the word *imminent*, it always means something bad is about to happen? Change is *imminent*. Job promotions are *pending*. Death is *imminent*, but birth is "any day now." Hotel management sent its sincere regrets, but "with Mother Nature out there doing her thing, there is really nothing we can do," said Sarah, my waitress. She added that she was very sorry to have to shut down all the rooftop fun. No matter. I was only good for one beer, if that. Up I stood and down I went on my reverse trip to the sidewalk. On my way out, I scored a hot lead on a Fargo restaurant that had just opened. I headed there for dinner, managing to reach the Boiler Room before the downpour started.

I rode all day on hot pavement and found myself in the Boiler Room for dinner just before the rain and lightning storm.

And rain it did. The people that followed me into the restaurant a minute or two later looked as though they swam to the front door of the place.

After a superbly cooked steak and a nice big fat glass of red wine, I walked the sidewalks of a city that looked like it had just been put through the rinse cycle. Fargo was a nice little city. I returned to my hotel room, and got hit over the head by the sandman. Sixty miles traveled in over four hours and twenty minutes through a ninety-five plus degree summer heat at an average speed of fourteen and a half miles per hour on a bike is one way to make sure your eyes remain closed all night.

The next day I awoke to bright sunshine and lingered at the hotel long enough to take advantage of the 'free" brunch that ran from nine to eleven o'clock. I sat next to a retired school principal from…Blah Blah, Montana! Yep, the woman was in town with her hubby for the Sons of Norway Convention, a bi-annual event, and she had lived in Chester, Montana, for more than thirty years. For those of you who can remember that far back, Chester, Montana, was the place where Daisy soused rooms at the MX Motel with the weapons-grade concentrations of liquid bleach. Yes, that's right: Spuds Café, Daisy was also the waitress with the mace, the cell phone, and the stalker. That's the town where there's nothing else for the kids to do but drink, smoke, snort, shoot, and trip. It was also the place I met Graham, the sixty-five-year-old Englishman who woke up early everyday to beat the wind and who had biked twenty-eight centuries in a row. I still can't believe Graham's pace or the fact that I ran into the retired Chester, MT, school principal in Fargo, ND. What a small-world experience in the big town of Fargo.

Before rolling that day I tucked section number four away and unfolded section number five and put it into my handlebar bag. "I think I can, I think I can" I said.

So Fargo, so Good-oh, right? Within an hour of leaving the Radisson, I got another pinch flat and was lost in a city with just over a hundred thousand people. I'd lived in a city of *eleven million* and never once lost my way, but there I was, lost in Fargo. I ended up asking directions from a couple of young men, one nineteen, and the other twenty-one. Both were bare-chested in cut off shorts and were propelling themselves around Fargo on long boards. They pointed me in the right direction and told me to check out some YouTube videos featuring long board riders.

"They are so sick! They go down crazy hills!"

I looked around me. I was in Fargo. The place was as flat as God's ironing board. I told them I'd been down some crazy hills myself on the Fun Mover. They were not impressed. They came to life and their eyes opened wide, however, when I told them about a particular hill outside Bismarck that had been recently paved and had about 2,100 vertical feet. They looked at each other and smiled.

"Wait. 2,100 vertical feet? Is that up or down?" the twenty-one year old asked me.

"Depends which way you are going, dipshit," his buddy laughed in answer.

"Oh, well I'm not good at math," was all he said in his own defense. His buddy jumped in again.

"It ain't math, Steve. It's physics, dumbass."

They had no way to get to Bismarck to ride the hill I'd described, so I suggested they might try bike touring as a cheap way to get there. Yeah, and while I was at it, maybe I should have suggested doing some community service or some door-to-door vacuum cleaner sales to make a little money on the side.

"Sir," the younger one said, "I know you say it's not much money to ride a bike or whatever, but when you have this much"—he held up his right hand with his thumb touching his index finger, the sign for "OK" or, in this case, for zero—"Anything more than this, which is exactly the sum total of all that I have, is too expensive."

The young man had a good point and clearly a firm grasp on the new math for his generation. Zero is zero, and there are no two ways around it.

After stutter stepping out of Fargo with the new information the shirtless dudes had provided, I hit my stride once certain I was back on route. I left North Dakota and entered Minnesota.

I ran headlong into a biking trio heading west, two guys and a gal. We all stopped and chatted for a bit on a quiet road surrounded by open fields. We exchanged a few introductions and gave each other the heads up on what to expect in terms of road conditions and bug conditions. I gave the first guy a bottle of bug spray that someone had given me just a few days before. I hadn't used it much and I figured he would need it more than I did. I told him if he was headed anywhere near Malta, he would really need it. I omitted any mention of Operation Lube Job where I had to apply Butt Butt'r in enemy territory, but I did warn him not to stop at the rocks that looked like sleeping buffalo without having first applied repellent no matter how hard he thought the wind was blowing.

"I ran into a shit storm of blood suckers on jet packs that laughed at a fifteen knot wind. Be careful man. The 'skeeters out there are the real deal. Watch out and don't stop rolling 'til you get inside somewhere. Damn bugs could airlift a loaf of bread if they had to. Don't mess around with those bad boys."

The trio had left Pittsburgh three weeks prior and spoke of seeing six eastbound riders the day before.

"A couple of girls, three guys, and another woman. The girls were from Martha's Vineyard," one of them said.

I laughed to myself in the knowledge that there was still no way I'd catch Manuel's pretty butterflies, not even with a mighty big breakfast bowl full of giddy the hell up and a hot steaming cup of get-the-show-on-the-road black coffee. Even if I'd rode all night and into the next day, I figured I'd still not even come close to catching them. "Ride on, beautiful bicycle butterflies," I said to myself, "I'll see the Atlantic long after you do.

As my man Clint Eastwood once said, "A man gots to know his limitations."

I rode all the rest of the way and stopped for dinner before securing a room at a local motel. Normally I secure a room first and then go out for a bite, but that night I was too hungry to spend time searching for a roof. I walked in to the first restaurant I came across and seated myself at a booth. I thought my waitress had lost a fight because she had what first appeared to be two black eyes. I looked around and saw the raccoon look on other women in the restaurant. Was I witnessing domestic abuse on a grand scale?

"It's just a thing here. Everyone's doing it. Last year it was blue hair, remember?" she asked me.

"No, I, I don't remember that," I stammered. Granted, the black eye liner made the blue in my waitress's eyes pop, but a little more liner I would have felt underdressed at a masquerade ball.

She directed me to a cheap motel and I slept like King Tut.

During the following riding day I came across a sign that read "Downer" and assumed it was the name of a town. Even though I'd never been to Downer, Minnesota before, I'd been to Downer a bunch of times in my life—when I was in New York City, once or twice in Massachusetts, and definitely towards the end of winter in New England. What a great idea it was to name a town after an emotion or, I'll take it further, a pleasant physical experience. What do you say we put "Bliss" or "Ecstasy" or "Positive Outlook" and maybe even "Orgasm" on the map and see what it does to people's worldview. I can just imagine the conversations...

"Hey man, where are you from?"

"Orgasm, New York."

"Cool. I'm from Foreplay, Tennessee. Never met anyone from Orgasm before. What's it like?"

"Well, you know, same old same old. It can get pretty intense, though. We have a big tourism industry. No one stays long, but everyone leaves happy..."

Fittingly, just after I saw that sign for Downer I came across a dead turtle in the road and figured I must have crossed into the town of Bummer. I double-checked the map and could not find the town of Bummer anywhere. I didn't care what the map said: to me that dead turtle sure looked like it was in Bummer town, or maybe it was actually visiting Eternity Ville.

It was difficult to say for sure; that dead turtle wasn't talking.

Chapter Sixteen

THE VIKING HAS LANDED, FEELING TIP TOP THEN FLAT

I landed in Alexandria, Minnesota on the 24th after a great ninety-six mile ride along the Central Lakes Bike Trail.

And the big news? I came across another corny hair-salon name: Hair-N-Beyond. Why do hair-salon owners give in to the temptation of puny word play? The thinking behind the names must go something like this:

"Hey, honey, I have a new business idea. Why don't we open a hair salon? Everyone needs a haircut every few months, right? We'll open up right downtown and give it a catchy name so everyone stops by, you know, because the name of the business is so funny. We'll make a fortune. What should we call it? Hair and Again? The Chop Shop? The Hair Lair? Been Hair and Back? *Wait.* How about Hair-N-Beyond?"

Motorboat owners are the same way with their *Boat-a-licious, Ahoy-Vey, SeaRenity, Tax Sea-Vation, Nauti Girl,* and *Sea-duction.* Horrible, horrible puns, but I still like to collect them.

Little known fact to most people. The Viking Café in Alexandria, MN, claimed to be the home to the "Best Omelet in Minnesota", so the next day I went to go to see what the fuss was all about and have my Jonathan Gold, food critic, moment. I mean come on, man. You bust out a boast like, "The Best Omelet in Minnesota," and you're certainly going to ping on my food radar and you darn well better be able to back it up. "Best omelet in the state" is some serious trash talk and I had made my way to the Viking Café specifically to see what gives. Not included in the hype, however, was the fact that they stopped making the best omelets in MN at eleven o'clock in the morning, hard stop. I rolled in at 11:07 a.m.

"No omelets for you," was all Brenda said.

Maybe I'd experience the gastronomic delight on my next trip through, maybe I wouldn't. I opted for the chocolate milkshake, the BLT, and some chicken soup, which all tasted just fine to me. I got to admit that all that delicious food at the Viking Café kind of put me in a Viking mood. I wanted to get on a ship, sail the seas, and pillage other places and burn villages down just for the fun of it. But, realizing that all that kind of behavior was, like, so 750 AD, I decided against it.

Before Viking out—I mean biking out—of Alexandria and conquering new worlds, I walked the streets and found Alexandria to be a very nice town. I came across a thirty-foot high statue of a Viking that the locals call "Big Ollie", but I named him "BFV", short for "Big F^%$ing Viking."

Another curiosity I came across was a retail store unlike any I'd ever seen. It was there on Main Street, right across the street from the Viking Café and it offered, of all things, vacuum cleaners and sewing machines for sale. That was a rather odd pair of offerings in one store. How many times in your life have you left your house to buy a sewing machine *and* a vacuum? Fewer than one I'd imagine. What was their pitch? "Come on in. Our vacuum cleaners suck, but our sewing machines sure don't—they're a stitch!" The place had no fewer than thirty sewing machines on display. Every single home in Alexandria must have had some pretty serious window treatments, quilts, and closets full of handmade dresses in order to support that kind of retail display area dedicated to that many sewing machines.

I took off and headed east. All systems go: it was a good day for a ride, my stomach was full, and I was well rested. Body felt strong, head was clear. Things were going my way. Bonus? A few miles outside Alexandria, I saw an ad for an electrician: "Electrician. (Area code) Phone #, then *Jesus Is Lord.*" I'd been looking for an answer to that question for a while, so I was naturally delighted to get an answer to it. Jesus *is* Lord. Well, that settles that.

Or does it? On my way out of Fargo a few days back, I had seen a bunch of folks standing around downtown on a Sunday morning, holding signs up that read, "Come meet an Atheist." At the time I was too preoccupied with finding my way out of Fargo to actually stop and meet an atheist, but I wished I had. I know this is a bike book, but I'll weigh in on the God question by mentioning that I am not certain those atheists had it right. They *might* not have thought everything through. First off, how can you look at all the beauty in nature and in the world and not declare, "There is a god"? Do atheists believe that a sunset over an ocean is just a big fat coincidence of color, moisture, and light? Ok, but how can anyone believe the kindness of a stranger's smile is just some random thing that came along from the great expanse of the universe? Were a swimsuit model or a perfect bowling game just bound to happen eventually, or were Drug Geronimo and his German buddy praying to Mother Sun and Sister Sky for no good reason?

Personally I've often wondered how sunsets, landscapes, great horned howls, miniature labradoodles, and all different races of people ended up on the same teeny weeny little blue planet dangling in the dark void of an endless space and rotating around a sun 93 million miles away from it -- precisely the right distance from said sun to support life. How can that be considered coincidental? How is it possible that all those things came about if not by some managed force or all knowing Creator? It was an interesting subject that I'd have loved to have the chance to discuss with that "Jesus Is Lord" electrician and those Atheists, but I had to roll. I was out of time and on a tear through Minnesota, a beautiful state that the Bible thumpers believed God created and Atheists believed happened by accident.

The following day's ride, a fifty-mile jaunt, was easy, mileage-wise but all fifty of those miles left me, once again, too pooped to pop. (Hey, this is a bike book, what did you expect? This sort of thing happens every single day.) But that day, I think my legs started out a little fagged from the ninety plus miles I'd pedaled the day before. I continued along the Northern Tier route, which offered great views and few cars—truly the best stretch yet.

I came across another bike tourist headed in the same direction. It was Larry, a retired teacher from Kansas City, who, as a life long touring cyclist, was very familiar with the trials and tribulations of bike travel. We'd seen each other along the way for the last couple of hundred miles. He had introduced bicycle touring to his daughter when she was only twelve years old: they took a three week tour together on a tandem bike before she graduated to her own two-wheeler. Over the years they had crisscrossed Michigan six times and completed a few other tours as well. Now twenty-nine, his daughter no longer rode much, but Larry had set his sights on his granddaughter and hoped to one day do some riding with her in tow. I had the good fortune to share some of Larry's first ever cross-country ride and to enjoy some of his humor as well. He also rode a lot at home. Larry rode a bike all year round and had commuted by bicycle for most of his adult life. He determined that, for him, the best commuting distance was twenty-five miles each way.

"Either way," he told me, "longer or shorter commute, if you ride a bike everyday, you keep a base that you can build on."

Though Larry and I were both heading towards Maine at roughly the same speed, we'd been leapfrogging each other over the course of the last couple of weeks. He was ahead of me and flagged me down as I passed by his picnic table on the Woebegone Trail bike path. I swung back and joined him for a quick break. Larry was sharing a picnic table with an ex-army guy named Mark he'd just met. Mark swore he "never took a vehicle unless absolutely necessary."

Mark was shirtless and had a tattoo that covered his entire beer belly. He was quietly working his way through a ham sandwich and a can of ginger ale. A quiet man, Mark was built like a brick shithouse and wore a ponytail on the top of his head "to cover up a bald spot," he said. He was built Army Strong and seemed to have his anger on a low simmer. I got a bad feeling from the guy: something about his eyes indicated preponderance for violence. He won my vote on Most Likely To Snap For No Apparent Reason and Kill, Kill, Kill.

While we were all at table chatting about weather, biking and camping, Mark looked at the time on his phone and realized he had to go to pick up his girlfriend then go to a picnic in his van, so he was off. I guessed it was "absolutely necessary" for him to do so. Good riddance. He seemed like a person that would be very familiar to local law enforcement.

I finished what I was eating and left a few minutes later, leaving Larry at the picnic table sitting alone, happy as could be, continuing to enjoy his break. He was going to linger and maybe lob a call in to his wife Denise. Though we didn't know each other very well at that point, Larry and I found common ground early in our friendship: we both agreed it was a good idea to call home when time allowed and it was good practice to stop for an ice cream whenever the opportunity presented itself.

I put my money where my mouth was in Osakis, Minnesota; I stopped into the Tip Top Dairy Bar for an ice cream. It was a block or two off the bike path and I found it like a homing pigeon might find a roost in a foreign land. I got there by instinct and ordered up a soft-serve cone. The lady who handed me the cone turned out to be the mom of the two kids working in the kitchen. The guy behind the store in the midst of dismantling a kitchen fan to get at the blades cleaned was the owner, husband, and father of the two kids. He and I met when I took a seat the picnic table and started in on my soft serve. He was doing a damn good job at cleaning that fan. I asked him why one of his kids was dressed in a sundae outfit and the other wasn't. .

"That's my daughter Maddie. She just graduated from high school a couple of weeks ago, and all she wanted for a graduation present was a twenty-seven-dollar foam costume that makes her look like a giant ice cream sundae. I told her she could have anything, but all she wanted was that. She's been wearing it every day since."

He asked me where I was going and whether I wanted a picture with the human sundae as a keepsake of my visit to Osakis.

I said, "Sure, why not."

So, after her mom made me a thick shake, I threw an arm around Madison, the Human Sundae. Her mom shot the photo on my phone.

That was it. I got my phone back, stashed it in my handlebar bag, and started getting my gear on which included my bike helmet, CamelBak, and cycling gloves. Madison returned to her post at the "Order Here" window and began furiously writing something down on a piece of paper.

"Nice to meet you. Take care!" I called out with a wave to the family crew and a Tip Top Dairy Bar review. "Thank you for the delicious ice cream and the best thick shake I've had on the trip."

"You're welcome," said the mom.

"Ride safe," said the dad.

"Wait!" cried Madison.

I walked over and saw she was still writing something down.

"You might be the first person under twenty I've ever seen use a pen," I said. "Don't all teenagers text?"

"Texting is overrated," she answered, and then she slid open the order-window screen and handed me a folded note. Her mom and dad, who moments before could not have been nicer, stood behind her giving me a little bit of the hairy eye as if I were asking their cute young daughter to climb into my rusty van to help me find my lost puppy.

"Here," she said, "Have a safe trip."

It was an awkward moment. I fully endorsed the fact that the parents were protective of their kid. They didn't know me from Adam. And what was their kid doing passing me a note? What had I done to deserve any of her attention? I was uncomfortable receiving folded a note from a teenager. The last time a teenage girl gave me a handwritten note was when I was a young teenager myself. Joanne S. had written me a nasty missive for some social slight I'd unknowingly delivered to her the day before and she'd spent the whole night writing out her I Hate Tim Fahey manifesto in pink ink.

Madison's note that I opened a thousand yards away? "Have a safe and beautiful journey! Julie and I will keep you in our thoughts and prayers! Lots of love from the Tip Top Dairy Bar. God bless!"

Wow. That note and those well wishes I'd take any day of the week, any week of the year. What a great young woman. Thanks to her, I was walking on air. I was surprised and complemented she'd taken the time to scribble down her well wishes and pass them along. Ah, the power of the printed word. She lifted my spirits higher than any ice cream cone with a thick shake chaser ever could. I'll won't forget her or her family or how great things tasted at the Tip Top Dairy Bar.

Yes, I was feeling great...until my back tire got a flat not five minutes later. Ah, the ups and downs of bike travel—feeling tip top one minute, flat the next. That flat didn't get me down, though. Those well wishes from a human ice-cream sundae were so unexpected, welcomed, and appreciated. Nice young woman, Maddie, and a solid family. You don't see that every day.

Larry caught up to me and pulled over to chat while I repaired my tire. He, too, had stopped in for an ice cream in the same town, but at the hard serve place a few blocks over from the Tip Top. I told him about the note. We shared a laugh at Fate.

Right there, while I was changing my flat tire, Larry said, "'Feeling tip top one minute, flat the next?' That's good stuff, Fahey. You know, you should write a book about this little adventure of yours."

Larry and I pedaled together for a while then parted company when I decided to push forward to Albany, MN, population 2,561. By the time I arrived, I was just *done*. I woke up the next day and could not count to one. Yes, biking fans, I was stuck at zero and wasn't going anywhere. I tried to shake it off. I drank a cup of the liquid black stuff that normally reached into the deep, dark recessed parts of my brain and ironed out all the wrinkles, but even a couple of cups of morning coffee couldn't get the lights to turn on in my attic. Ye olde bike body told me, "Today is a zero day. You shall rest."

And so it was done. I did rest. I took a zero in Albany.

I'll admit it: Albany, Minnesota, would not have been my top choice for a place to spend a zero, but there I was with one. After getting a nap in after breakfast, I decided to do something else besides lie around all day, so I played golf. Thirty-six dollars rented me a golf cart, a set of clubs, and permission to drive the back nine at the Albany Golf Course, a real dog track of a half loop. I kept on looking back down the un-fairways I'd strolled half expecting to see a mechanical rabbit screaming up towards me with a pack of greyhounds in numbered pennies giving chase, but I saw none and was left alone on the back nine to whack away at a little white ball and follow it wherever it went.

I bought six prewashed golf balls that someone had found, washed, and put in a bucket at the pro shop, waiting for some cheapskate like me to come along and buy them for a buck fifty each. They looked like they were round, but they sure played like they were square shaped when I hit them. Not that the shape of the ball mattered much; I've always swung like a rusty gate and putted like a blind fool. Round or square, the golf balls I hit don't go where I want 'em.

All the exercise I'd done had no positive effect on my golf game—I was still terrible. For those looking to be disappointed, my game did not disappoint. I started playing at the age of thirty-five, thirty years too late to become any good.

It took a couple of hours, but nine holes came and went and at no time was the course record in jeopardy.

On my way to returning the rented clubs and the golf cart, I strolled though the golf shop past the racks of hats, clubs and golf clothing for sale. My Bullshit Meter went off and got pinned in the red zone, triggered by all the marketing bullshit.

Labels on everything from clubs to shoes touted some new-fangled way of lowering a golf score. What a bunch of crap. All the hype around the golf equipment is just that—hype. In the game of golf like the world of jazz, "you don't have a thing if you don't got that swing." Clothing and clubs don't contribute much to improved performance. Have you ever seen the hickory shafts the legends of the game used to set some of the records that still stand? Yeah? Well, I rest my case.

I got to thinking: Why doesn't anyone introduce a line of golf clothing for duffers like me? Someone should and they should call it 'NeverPar.' I liked the sound of it immediately. The target market for NeverPar clothing would be the hacker, the guy who knows he doesn't have a chance in hell to score well, but still likes the game enough to give it a try and play anyway, for different reasons. The duffer plays for the pure fun of it and maybe just to get away from things for a while. NeverPar wear would be the logical choice for the municipal-course regulars who swing too much, drink too much, and smoke too much *during play*. The tagline? *NeverPar. You know who you are.*

NeverPar shirts would be blousy enough to hide man boobs and belly paunch and be long enough in the shirttail to hide ass crack when the wearer retrieved his ball after a five putt or when the wearer sits on his barstool at the 19th hole wallowing in post round sorrow. Sure, the Nike GOLF clothing is "engineered" and has materials that "wick away sweat and provide the wearer a more uninterrupted, untethered, unconstructed golf swing," but we NeverPar guys wouldn't need all that. Hide my paunch, cover my ass crack, give me some more room in the shoulders and we're good. Attention Mr. Four Putt, Mr. Duck Hook, Mr. Slice, and Mr. Chip Shot into the Bunker—your golf clothes are ready!

After nine holes of disappointment, frustration, and dashed hopes—that is, after nine holes of golf—I went for a late lunch in Albany and sat next to state representative Paul Anderson at the counter. He was a good guy and someone I would've voted for. It's funny, tons of people see the same thing happening all over the United States, but no one seems to be able to do much about it. When you are in a republic, it sure hurts a lot when the folks you vote in have their own best interests in mind, not their continuants'. Mr. Paul Anderson had his hands full dealing with the rain and flooding in Minnesota, something that I had not seen much at all of. He was taking a lunch break from trying to acquire emergency funds from Washington, DC. He wanted to help some of the areas of the state that had experienced the worst of the storms and the worst of the destructive flash flooding.

The weather was not the only bad thing going on, climate-wise. Paul informed me that the Democrats had taken over Minnesota a couple of years back, and in Paul's view, things were getting increasingly worse in terms of people becoming more addicted to handouts. More and more citizens were sucking off the government teat. Paul got frosted at the ninety-six weeks of unemployment coverage.

"It seems people are being paid to *not* return to work." (Actually, Paul didn't say that. I put it in quotes because I paraphrased what he said.)

Because I had a lot of zero left on my hands (it was only 1:00 p.m. when I finished lunch), I walked around a bit and had more of a chance to speak to a variety of people while in Albany. I met a woman who worked at Edward Jones Investments and was a part owner of the hotel I was staying in, and I also met a diner waitress who had gone to the state championships for discus and shot put—but you'd never guess it to look at her. She wasn't the classically stout and powerful shot put type; instead, was more lanky and lean. I wandered over to a bakery after lunch and chatted with the owner and her dad. I scored a fresh baked doughnut or two as well. Clearly I suffered from TD: talking disease. I figured I'd better shut up and stop talking so much if I ever wanted to finish my ride. I noticed when my legs stopped moving, my tongue tended to start wagging.

Maybe the following day would be a zero day for my mouth.

Chapter Seventeen

B'fast At The Contagion Café, An Ex-Con, A Search For A Twist

The following day was really strange, just the way I liked them. I pedaled seventy-five miles, most of them weird. I crossed paths with all sorts of people, too, on that 27th day of June. It was a random set of folks that only a bike can stitch together like a shuttle in a loom that weaves a fabric from many threads. I met a religious financial advisor, a fifty-three-year-old ex-con cement worker, and a woman whose nephew had lost all his teeth to his crystal meth addiction. Said nephew was working two minimum-wage jobs to save enough money to buy a set of dentures to replace his long gone choppers. As she figured it, it would take him *ten years* to save enough money to get some teeth. (I resolved to think about that guy whenever I started to think I had problems.) Also, I came across a slow-moving waitress, a hooker's brother, and a farmer who hunted wildflowers for the Audubon Society.

Let's begin with breakfast.

I walked into a coffee shop and took a seat at a table by the window. Everything seemed normal at first; tables were set, Muzak was wafting gently through the air; the place was mostly empty after the breakfast rush. Four customers, two together, two apart, sat stone still and, if they spoke at all, they spoke quietly.

The waitress brought coffee over and asked if I needed a menu. I didn't need one to order the same breakfast I'd had for decades: three eggs over easy, whole-wheat toast, no home fries, bacon, and a glass of OJ. With no wheat in the place, I was told they served "white only."

So I ordered the Jim Crow toast in lieu of the whole wheat. I hoped it was better than the coffee they served. Even a coffeeholic like me had a tough time drinking it.

No one uttered a word after I placed my order—not even the couple sitting together by the window. Guess when you live in a town as small as Albany and when you are as old as the hills, you eventually run out of things to say. People chewed their food slowly, their pupils were as wide as dimes, and all there except for me seemed transfixed by something out the window. I turned around to get a look at what was catching their attention: all I saw was a grain elevator across the street. I turned back to look at the other customers and there they were, all still staring out the window at that grain elevator, still expressionless. I wondered if they bothered to plug in their TV sets at home before sitting down to watch their favorite shows.

Muzak continued to play softly as the waitress rubbed a plate over and over again with a dishtowel. Minutes passed before I heard a bell ring and someone back in the kitchen say "Order up!" in a German accent. My waitress put her plate down and threw the dishtowel over one shoulder, grabbed my breakfast off the stainless steel countertop, and sauntered over to me. I noticed that her thumb touched my eggs, toast, and bacon all at the same time, and that thumb was the last digit to leave the plate after she'd put it down with a loud thud on the table in front of me.

Yuck.

She turned and started back towards the kitchen, but then stopped dead in her tracks. She arched her back, inhaled deeply, and put both hands over her face.

She stood like that for just a moment, then leaned forward suddenly and *sneezed* and *farted* at the same time.

A sneeze/fart.

In a coffee shop.

By my waitress.

I went, "Yuck," then "Ha, ha, ha" in my head. Sneeze/farts are Mother Nature's slapstick comedy and they are always funny in my book.

My waitress regained her stoic composure by standing back up and mumbling an "Excuse me" before returning to the stack of plates.

People acted as if nothing had happened. They continued to stare out the window in stone cold silence. Come on! She'd just given the world both barrels as it were and no one batted an eye? No one?

A word to the wise: Never trust anyone who doesn't laugh at a sneeze/fart.

She dried the dish. I ate the food. The only sound in the place was the Muzak and the ticking clock.

After downing two and a half eggs, most of my OJ, and all the white toast, I couldn't take it anymore. My Talking Disease was killing me, so I asked my waitress a neutral, open-ended question:

"How's life?"

She looked away from the grain elevator over to me and froze like she was a deer in headlights. "Life?" she responded as she awoke from her daze. "How's life?" After a few seconds, my question seeped into her cranium.

"Oh! You mean *my* life? How's my life?"

I nodded yes to her.

"Oh, it's OK, thanks. I gotta be honest with you, though," she said and made a face like she'd just tasted something she didn't like. "My life would be tons better if I hadn't woken up with tummy problems this morning. I was throwing up all last night, but still had to come to work 'cause Sally had the day off and she's visiting family up north."

I stopped chewing immediately and looked down at my plate. There was a half an egg and one piece of bacon left on it. Little Miss Tummy Upset was the very person who'd thumb-served me my breakfast, the very same breakfast that I was now mostly finished with. I put my Health Inspector's hat on and looked around the coffee shop with a new set of eyes and was disappointed by what I saw. There wasn't a hairnet in the place and the handling of food had already proved to be nowhere near up to code. They could have called the place the *Petri Dish Diner* or the *Contagion Café*.

While looking down at what was left of my breakfast, I pondered my next move. Should I finish what the sneeze-farter with the tummy problems had thumbed, or should I shout an outraged, "Are you kidding me?" and stomp out of the place?

What the hell—in for a penny, in for a pound, I always say. I rolled the dice and cleaned my plate, come what may, figuring I'd already ingested whatever she was suffering from. Maybe all the biking I'd done boosted my immune system. Fortunately I had a ten-spot ready when the $8.55 bill showed up, so no contagious cash would be handed back to me. My deposit of the ten large on the table was the only clean exchange I experienced at that coffee shop. I left my payment along with a hurried "thank you" and got the hell out of the place before I, too, began to find the grain elevator fascinating and before I went mute and began chewing my food sideways. I caught a stare when I tried to open the exit door with my elbows. I didn't want any more "tummy bugs" on my hands.

I'd left my bike locked and leaning against a tree, clearly visible by the front window of the place. I unlocked it and got ready for the road by putting my gloves and helmet on. The couple sitting by the window inside the coffee shop of health horrors was only about five feet from me on the other side of that big pane of glass, but it didn't appear they saw me as their eyes were still glued to that grain elevator. Set the ring tone on your cell phone to the "Sci-Fi" tone and then have someone call you. Yeah, it was like that. If the Weird Vibe Coffee Shop had a theme song, that was it.

I shot off out of there —off route.

I rode ten miles before I realized my mistake. Instead of turning back and turning a ten-mile mistake into a twenty-mile fix, I decided to try to work my way back on track from where I was. Lost, I stepped into a restaurant/bar and asked the first person I saw for directions. He was a farmer covered in dirty overalls and apparently just in from a morning's work in the fields. He also happened to be an amateur photographer and a self-described "wildflower hunter," the most successful flower hunter in the state. He spent his off hours searching for and photographing never before seen wildflowers and posting his photos onto the Audubon website. He was extremely articulate and delivered me a set of directions that were clear as a bell. He did not waste one single word when giving me his fairly detailed and highly accurate instructions. It was an impressive feat. I was back on the right track in no time.

The next part of my day was spent on the Wobegon Bike trail in central Minnesota, a recreational pathway host to walkers, runners and bicyclists. A guy on his bike caught up to me and we struck up a conversation about my loaded touring bike ("Why are you carrying all that stuff?") as we rode shoulder to shoulder for a while. A good guy, Steve R. was training for his fourth upcoming Habitat for Humanity fundraising event. He was a financial advisor by profession and do gooder by vocation. He assured me his suggested way back to the Northern Tier route was not only the fastest but also the best as it included a stop in his kitchen for a cold drink. He was right: he saved me some serious time and effort. I continued up past the hydroelectric dam that was overflowing due to the massive amount of rain that Minnesota was having at that time, although I hadn't seen much more than a drop of it fall from the sky in a while. It was strange: farmers were worried about the lack of rain behind me and worried about historic flooding ahead of me.

Once back on route, I settled into a relatively good pace considering the fact that I had a headwind to deal with. It was another afternoon of hard mushing, compounded by a series of wrong turns. Pilot error can be frustrating—especially when you are the pilot and only have yourself to blame for your own glaring stupidity.

It got a little hot that afternoon, so I thought it might be a good idea to stop and rest under the shade of a magnificent tree with a broad canopy of hundreds of leaves the size of car headrests. The idyllic tree stood near an innocuous-looking house with a barn out back. There happened to be a tantalizing green grassy spot underneath it, buried deep in the shade near the trunk of the tree, the perfect place for a bit of picnic lunch. I noticed a truck parked outside the small and tidy house with a split-rail fence along the road. The barn doors were closed.

Then I saw the two-foot-square sign posted next to the mailbox out front that read: Bio Secure Area. A closer look revealed that the place was *too* perfectly tidy—not a weed in the lawn, not a scratch on the squeaky clean twenty year old truck. There was a second fence I hadn't seen at first: it was a fence behind a fence and it was made of a thick gauge razor ribbon and, here's the kicker—it was an electric fence. Man, if the razors didn't stop you, the juice sure would. I stopped rolling and put a foot down to take a longer look at the most likely secret government sponsored bad idea. Surveillance cameras were mounted on every corner of the barn, and every window in the house had its lace curtains drawn. One of the cameras rotated toward me and stopped.

"What the hell goes on in there?" I wondered. Was Dr. Evil crossbreeding cows and pigs to make milk taste like bacon? Or was this place a lair for some hyped up hacker hoarding bioweapons? Who knew? I got the hell out of there. I don't like it when surveillance cameras swing my way and stop.

A bit later I passed St. Elizabeth's Catholic church with a sign outside that read, "Gun raffle drawing tonight! 7:00 in the church basement!" No further proof needed: I was in guns-and-God country for sure. I also just happened to be in the writer Garrison Keillor's hometown. He had found inspiration for his books and his radio shows in the local culture and in the people of the area. At first, the place seemed bland, but scratch the sur-face, and the characters will come a-running.

Towards the very end of my ride that day I was looking for a Super 8 motel. I knew I was close, but I just could not find it. During my search I came across a cop directing traffic around a construction site. He was a man of few words: when I asked him for directions to the Super 8 Motel, he pointed the way with an arm and an index finger. I guess in his case it was easier for him to use his arm than his tongue. I thanked him and started off in the direction he indicated.

Then, completely unsolicited, he told me where the town strip club was.

"Strip club is a block or two down on the right. Just saying," he added.

Less than a mile later I was standing in the parking lot of the Super 8 Motel talking to guy named Donny who was an ex-con, the same guy I mentioned in the very second paragraph of this book. Donny and I shared a birth year and month: we were born ten days apart from each other. He was four inches shorter than me, half again as wide, and solid as a fence post. He said he used to fight a lot in high school.

"Where did you learn to throw a punch?" I asked him.

"Hockey!" he replied.

Donny was grilling up a mean shish-kebab dinner in the back of his pickup truck outside the motel. He had the onions, peppers, steak, and olives going. It smelled delicious. He drank as he cooked, stealing swigs of brown liquor from a paper-bagged bottle he had stashed next to the grill. A couple of lean beer-swigging guys in their mid-twenties were nearby, smoking cigarettes and sharing a phone.

"If you assholes want to smoke, stay the hell outta my kitchen, and my kitchen, by the way, is three car spaces in every direction from the back of my truck. I don't want these kah-bobs stinking of smoke."

"Ok, Donny," one of them said with a smile, "Whatever you say boss."

They worked together as a cement crew with Donny playing crew boss in charge of the finish work. They did commercial hog barns, cattle barns, and sometimes they constructed support pads (at $1 million each) from the ground up for the huge wind turbines I'd seen spotting the landscape. Donny and his boys worked mostly in South Dakota and Texas, but were up in that area "on special assignment" doing renovation work on hog barns to bring them up to code. New sanitation rules mandated old hog barns be updated with fully slotted or partially slotted floors that would allow the flush or scraper manure handling options to more easily move and store manure outside the buildings and away from where the pigs lived.

"Pig welfare issues, Timmy. That's where the money is."

I asked Donny how he got into the cement finishing business and he told me in two words: "Had to."

Donny went to jail for selling drugs. In at the age of thirty-seven, out at the age of forty-five. "I spent nine years in jail, Timmy, nine long years and after I got out, finish work was all I could get."

I was going to correct him on his math, but I figured he was the one with all that time to count, so I didn't dare. After being released from prison, Donny had drifted around for a bit, and then landed the cement job. His prison time had learned him, he said.

"I'll never do time again. Inside ain't no life. Want some blueberries?" he asked.

I took the small green cardboard basket of blueberries and took a palm full.

He continued. "I never saw the prison from the outside. I was dropped off at night and picked up at night. I heard cars drive by the whole time I was in and all I wanted to do was go somewhere, anywhere, from where I was. I told myself that I'd be in one of them cars one day. Last year I almost was."

He was with his boss on a scouting trip to the area, but his boss didn't know he was an ex-con, so Donny didn't want to insist they drive by the prison for a look. He never got to see the place from the outside. For what I am sure was the only time in his life, Donny missed going to prison.

Cocaine trafficking had put him there. "Timmy, I was living the life! I was having two girls at once, drinking champagne, boozing, eating lobster sandwiches, Timmy! And I got all the free rails all the Donny Train wanted." Donny was using both his thumbs to point to himself. "It was the life, Timmy!"

Yes. What I liked instantly about Donny was that he referred to his former party cocaine drug dealing self as "the Donny Train."

"Timmy, I had sixteen cars! Jeeps, Land Rovers, a Cadillac. I had a 1968 Mustang, mint! I owned three houses, but then I got caught. If it wasn't for that snitch, I'd have those years."

I told Donny he'd still had those years, but he'd just spent them in a different place.

"You know what I mean, Timmy." Donny took a pull from his brown paper bag and put it back next to the grill on the back of his pickup truck. He turned to the two guys drinking beer and smoking cigarettes a few yards away. "Which one of you two assholes likes it well done?"

The lady who checked me into the hotel was the aunt of the crystal meth addict I'd mentioned earlier. Off the drug for a decade, her nephew had no teeth and was working two jobs to save enough money for a set of dentures. He was thirty-seven and "biked all the time to clear his head." Man, what a tough go. As if that weren't enough, Tony, one of the young guys on the crew hanging with Donny in the parking lot, told me he had an older sister living in Las Vegas who was also a meth addict. I'd heard crystal methamphetamine addicts lose weight and teeth. I wasn't sure why the teeth fell out, so I asked.

Tony explained that battery acid is often used in the distillation process and it "wreaks havoc on the soft tissues. Gums recede and your teeth fall out even if you don't smoke it." Tony knew more about the crystal meth manufacturing process than the whereabouts of his own sister. He hadn't heard from her in two years, but last he heard, she was living on the streets and "was probably hookin' to live. She and I weren't never close, but no one deserves that," he said.

I dined at Dairy Queen, devouring a Flame Thrower double cheeseburger with bacon, a thick chocolate shake, and a small order of fries. I also had enjoyed some of the fresh watermelon and blueberries that Donny was serving up from the back of his pickup. Earlier, I'd had teriyaki beef cubes (like beef jerky), and I must have had half a pound of trail mix. Whatever the food and whenever available, if you are biking, you better be eating a lot of it. Miles don't come free.

That's it from Lake Wobegon. An interesting day indeed full of cross connects from different walks of life. I was out like a light that night.

As different as all those lives were the day before, the next day was Saturday for all of us. Some people slept in, some people got up early to go for a run, and some, like me, decided to bike two hours and forty-one minutes against the wind to cover thirty miles before lunch. Yes folks, that not-going-my-way wind was back in force again.

I arrived in Osceola in search of a lunch place and went inside a store that sold ice cream and antiques. (I'd love to read that business plan.) Turned out they did not serve lunch, so I pulled a 180 and left the store. Two ladies and a man looking were on the same mission I was. They had followed me into the store and fell in behind me as I paraded out, still in search of lunch.

I took my chances and turned left out the door, they took their chances and went right. Not ten steps later I spotted a lunch place on the corner on North Cascade Street and thought to let them know. I turned back and hailed them with a whistle that caught their attention. My whistle also caught the attention of a mom climbing out of a gray minivan with remotely operated sliding side doors.

"Oh, sorry," I said to the mom. "I wasn't whistling at you," I explained. "I was trying to get the attention of those two ladies and that gentleman up there."

The good-natured mom beamed a smile.

"No, it's OK. I do that to this little one all the time," she said, turning and pointing to a kid who wasn't there.

"Billy! Billy stop!" She bolted by me down the sidewalk in time to catch her fast-footed kid just before he stepped off the curb and into traffic trouble. Her Billy had made a mad dash to freedom when he saw the opening my whistle had given him. His mom had turned away for a second and the tike made his move.

They should have named him "Ghost." He had some serious exiting skills.

Karen and Phyllis were the name of the ladies I'd whistled to. They were lifelong best friends who had known each other since their grade school days. They weren't sisters, but were from the same same neighborhood and had recently attended the same jewelry party where they'd bought the same necklace. I told the two of them about the corner restaurant that looked promising. We all ended sharing a booth at the Mexican food place. Karen's husband, Bill, made it four in the booth after he parked the car closer to the restaurant.

They were good folks. They all shared a special bond—shared loss. Both women had lost a daughter in their forties, one to cancer, and one to a car accident eight and ten years or so before, respectively. They both said their lifelong friendship helped them carry on. Bill nodded in agreement.

Once their Diet Cokes arrived, they told me a funny story about the time they'd traveled to Newark, New Jersey in the late 1960's to visit their other high school friend, Susan, who was very funny in her day. While en route to New Jersey to visit their friend, Karen and Phyllis had to switch trains in New York's Penn Central station. It was their first time to New York and they wanted to see some of it between the train stops. They thought it would be OK to leave their baggage unattended on the train platform and went upstairs and outside for a few minutes of sightseeing. Their Trail Angel came in the form of a Red Cap (an Amtrak porter) who saw them leave their bags and stopped them from doing so. He learned where they were going and immediately took them under his protective wing, keeping a sharp eye on their bags for them while they stepped outside for a look 'round.

They still appreciated his actions.

They returned to the train platform about an hour later and caught their next connection. Before arriving in Newark, NJ to meet their friend Susan, the ladies switched into nun habit costumes as a joke.

"Well, you can just imagine!" said Karen. "When we got to Newark and met Susan at the train platform, she looked right by us at first and then just about fell down laughing when she saw it was us in those habits!"

That had happened years before, and their friend Susan now had Alzheimer's.

"So much of her sense of humor is lost now," said Phyllis looking down into her glass of Diet Coke.

But, no matter: their story brought a little of Susan back and it still made Phyllis's and Karen's matching necklaces shake at the same time when they chuckled about "those habits."

Karen's mom had been a "beauty operator" (I love that old term for a beautician), and they all used to get their hair done together. "Lots of sordid tales were told under those old beehive hair driers." They both chuckled again.

Bill just nodded.

All three were in town for the funeral of a hard-drinking, hard-living high school buddy of theirs. Their friend had been buried the day before.

"There was no mincing words at the funeral. People stood up and told the truth like it was."

They were trying to be nice about it, but to me, it sounded like the guy was a hard drinker who registered pretty high on the asshole meter. It didn't sound like the world would miss him much. Karen presented a laminated prayer card that she'd picked up at the church. It came complete with a picture of the smiling deceased and came with some prayer about the winds always being at your back and such. There were hymnal song lyrics below the photo and on the back as well. After a certain age, those damn prayer cards start to pile up like leaves in the fall. I had a growing collection of my own; the most recent one had my mom's name on it.

We all agreed that life goes by too quickly and everyone owes it to himself or herself to get up and do things before it is all over.

Quiet Bill came up with a story of his own. It dated back to New York in the mid 1950s. He'd been stationed in Washington, DC for a couple of years while in the service and was known to journey up to New York City with one of his Army buddies who had family Little Italy. He spoke of a weekend in NYC in which he stayed with the family of his Italian friend. He ate great Italian food the whole time. His friend's dad found out about Bill's love of Italian bread and gave him a large loaf as a parting gift to bring back with him to DC. Bill did just that and when he got back to DC, he put it into his locker to eat the next day.

Unfortunately, that night the cockroaches beat him to it and ruined the loaf. He did not get to eat even a single bite of it. I figured Bill must have really liked Italian bread to tell his story of a "Loaf Lost" (sorry for the *bun*...I mean, the *pun*) so many years later.

After lunch, I was back on the road, getting bitch-slapped by Mother Nature's hot, humid, steady exhale. I stopped into a restaurant for a short rest, which turned into an hour. I bought a Sunkist soda and drank it sitting in air-conditioned comfort. A soccer game was on the flat screen, and the place was full of people playing pool and drinking beer. Ah, air conditioning...

After a while, I got cold sitting there with the A/C unit blowing the chill my way and dropping the temperature of my sweat to what felt like near freezing levels. I stepped back outside and got to enjoy the rest of my soda in the company of a woman my age that had left city life along with her third husband. She was living...how did she say it? "A self-sustained lifestyle."

Her dirt-caked knees evidenced the work she'd done in her organic garden that morning. With all her "chemical free weedin' work done for the day" she was there enjoying a chilled glass of rosé wine and a Virginia Slim cigarette or two. It turned out that she'd lost her mom recently, too. We clinked a rosé glass and a Sunkist bottle in toast to two lost moms. The woman said her family "was coming apart at the seams about the money 'n everything." She said an alcoholic lawyer, now incarcerated for a hit and run, had drafted her mom's last will and testament and somehow his name had been included as one of the beneficiaries.

"My mom's will is full of more holes than a piece of Swiss cheese."

Her family's financial friction was fueled and fostered by infighting for the family fortune. It was a festering failure. A lot of F words were intentionally used in those last two sentences to describe the situation, but I'm sure that is nothing compared to the number of F words flying around at their family functions. Must be fantastic fun. I will tell you the key F word there is 'fighting,' as I was sure there was a lot of it going on.

I finished my soda and left the woman sitting there, sipping her rosé, and huffing on her cigarette, staring blankly at her shoes, her third husband inside, watching soccer.

While back in the saddle and making my way to Amery, I saw a billboard sponsored by the local bible thumpers: it was for a bible camp a few miles down the road. The folks who run those Bible camps wanted to "keep the SIN out of WisconSIN!"

As soon as I reached Amory, Wisconsin, I stopped at the Dairy Queen as a reward for making it across another state line. I had successfully battled the winds for a total of seventy-six miles that day and was pretty damn pleased with myself. Time for a treat.

I stepped into the Dairy Queen and a five-foot-seven inch tall, blue-eyed absolutely beautiful young woman of Swedish descent said the words that I did not want to hear.

"Can't give you the vanilla chocolate twist you want mister, sorry. We only got vanilla because the machine's broke."

I replied, "So, there is only vanilla?"

"Yes," she replied.

"Well, I guess I am having vanilla."

She paused and looked at me. "I don't know, *are* you having vanilla?" she challenged, her pretty little trigger finger on the dispenser button, her killer blues looking straight at me.

"Yes, I will have a vanilla, thank you." I was catching a pretty weird vibe from the young woman. She certainly had some sort of feelings for me, for reasons that were beyond me. Maybe there were some Daddy issues going on there, or had I ruined her day by asking her to do her job? I wasn't sure, but I think she was mad at me.

She faced the machine and pressed the red button under the VANILLA ONLY sign and the machine groaned and shat once into a sugar cone. A soft *plop*. She turned to me again. "You want a small or a medium? I can't make the large right now. It goes all over."

"Medium, please," I told her.

She turned back 'round and pushed the button again. The machine let out another large groan and, with its second push towards the cone, it was *déjà* pooh all over again, turning my soft-serve small into a soft-serve medium. Miss "Machine's Broke" took her pretty little finger off the poop button and pulled the soft serve cone away and thus formed that final, dainty little wisp of a curl that always falls to one side of the top of the cone, the final stroke of the soft-serve VANILLA ONLY sculpture. The cone was handed to me for $2.10 in return.

I really wanted the chocolate vanilla twist. Maybe I'd get one next time.

Day turned into night. Night turned into day.

I pedaled another thirty miles or so and made it to God Knows Where, Wisconsin, another town that had another Dairy Queen restaurant, and thus, another opportunity to score a chocolate vanilla twist cone. I was pumped about my chances.

Damn Dairy Queen. I asked for a twist and got denied for the second day in a row. I was given a two-letter answer instead of a three letter one.

"No."

A chocolate and vanilla twist "was not possible" at the Amery DQ. The counter kid told me "It either comes out vanilla or chocolate. We tried to fix it, but that didn't work, so now we'll have to call a professional."

I said, "OK, I have a solution for that. Chocolate on the top."

Wouldn't you know it? The kid hit both buttons and the damn thing came out all chocolate with a smear of vanilla at the very bottom. It was hopeless. I remained optimistic that I would soon be handed a decent twist, but now I wasn't holding my breath: obviously professional soft-ice-cream-machine mechanics were in short supply in those parts.

As tragic as the Dairy Queen incident was, even more harrowing was the fact that the motel I had my eyes on had no vacancies. I walked into the hotel lobby just before a storm hit hard and the rain didn't let up for hours. There was not room at the hotel I was standing in, and there was no room at any hotel I could get to. For the first and only time of the whole ride, I was up the lodging creek without a paddle.

"We have a reunion, a funeral, and a wedding, so, as you can see, we got a whole lot goin' on here," said Mary, waving her hands around manically, pointing to the lobby of the Forrest Inn and Suites. I looked at the lobby where she pointed. There were two old guys watching golf on TV.

It didn't look too crazy busy to me.

Mary, the hotel manager on duty, was the only person working at the Forrest Inn. She said they were fully booked, but they were also "all about hospitality," so Mary scored me two pillows, a blanket, and the floor space in the storage room for the night after OK'ing it with the owners who "were off site, kickin' back poolside somewhere," according to my hostess with the mostess.

Mary talked openly about the possibility of me grabbing a shower the following morning when a room would became available. I hoped she wasn't teasing, because my armpits overheard mention of the word "shower" and became very interested in the chance to swim in hot suds for a while. It was going to be a full on stinky and sticky bike man situation until morning. In Drug Geronimo's terms, "Biking Bear needed indoor waterfall to smell less like bear, more like Barbie."

Mary had been very kind to put me up. I ran into some of the nicest folks on this trip—some of them even liked to help strangers keep out of the rain.

With God's washtub still being poured out outside, I settled onto a couple of polyester blankets laid over a paper-thin rug over a hard-as-a-goddamn-rock cement floor in a storage room slash administrative office at the Forrest Inn in Amery, Wisconsin. It was not the most comfy accommodation, but beggars couldn't be choosers. I went to bed thankful to be inside, warm, and dry.

But I got too warm and too dry about ten minutes in. There was a fridge in the small cinder block room that acted like an oven and dehydrated me to the point of risking mummification. That fridge gave the ancient Egyptian priests a run for their money: it ran all night long in twenty minute on/off cycles and would exhale warm dry air into the small confined room. The refrigerator coils acted like a heater that heated the room up to about ninety-five "dry-grees" and it sucked up all the moisture within ten feet of it. It recycled the same air all night long because the door was closed and the only window was locked shut.

I awoke with a lower back that was stiffer than the rebar Donny and his crew used to reinforce the hog barn floors they built. I looked around for the film crew, and as soon as the director showed up and shouted, "Action!" I was ready to say my line: "I've fallen down and I can't get up."

Good news did not await. The weather was clear, sure, and the storms had moved on, so that wasn't the issue. The thing that killed me was that no one had checked into the suite right next to the storage room where I'd suffered all night. There was a big king bed and a walk in shower not ten feet from me the whole time. After spending the night in Storage Closet Hell, I'd been informed that Heaven was right next door. Mary keyed me in to the unused room and I grabbed a shower. My armpits were happy.

"Tim, I am so sorry. The room was reserved, but the people hadn't checked in yet when I went to bed around midnight, but you never know. If I'd given you their rented room and they arrived late in the middle of the night to find you in the bed they'd reserved, well, there'd be hell to pay."

She had a point.

After cleaning up, I mingled with the other hotel guests over the continental breakfast in the "breakfast area" which was the part of the front lobby that had the kitchen tile flooring, the under-the-counter refrigerator, and the on-the-counter toaster.

I mixed in with the other guests of the fine establishment. It was tough to guess who was heading out for the wedding, the funeral, and the reunion. All looked pretty snappy and ready to celebrate some stage or another of Life.

On the other hand, it wasn't hard to tell which guest had had the worst night's sleep. All I had to do was look into a mirror to spot him.

While waiting for my cinnamon raison mini bagel to toast, I met a ham radio operator. Yeah, the guy was just hanging out, waiting on a bagel of his own. I would have had no idea he was a "hammer" had he not mentioned it three times before my bagel could make it off the conveyor belt and slide out onto the tray. These days with email and internet connectivity so commonplace, I considered the ham radio to be a relic of a distant past, sort of the 1950's equivalent to social media 1.0. I asked him if he used his ham radio to make his hotel reservation and he said, "Oh hell no. I just called them up on the phone. I keep my ham radio around to be able to communicate with others when all other types of communication go up in smoke. Me and the Mrs. have a solar backup so we are good to go under any circumstances."

It turned out the Hammer was there to attend a neighbor's funeral. Said he travelled two hundred miles to bury the guy who'd lived next door to him. He'd made a weekend out of it. "The wife" and he were going to see what Amery had to offer and, while he was at it, "pick up some supplies."

He told me he was "preparing" and his self-described "skill-set" wasn't "just 'hamming' on the radio." No, there was more and he was there to reassure me of it.

He stated quite clearly that he knew how to "grow vegetables." (I do, too, by the way—you plant their seeds.)

He told me he could field dress a deer "in, like, nine minutes."

He could do other things like shoot guns. He'd practiced shooting guns out every window in his house during both the daylight and nighttime hours so he'd be ready "to surprise any unwanted guests coming down his driveway looking for food after the End of Days began."

I asked him how he'd know what day it was on his calendar after the End of Days started.

"Don't need a calendar after all Hell breaks loose, as Hell hath no schedule. Just because it is nighttime where you are don't mean it ain't go-time for Satan. When the grid goes down, the Devil comes to town. And don't think She won't. Hell, they had a brown out just the other day next county over. That there's a sign."

I. Love. Bike. Travel.

A prepper who had ham radio, vegetable farming, and field dressing skills? That was a first for me. I walked away from him to put another bagel in the toaster while the grid was still up and running. I thought it was a good time to fatten up while times are easy and there was still some juice in the wall sockets.

Mary ran out of paper plates halfway through breakfast, so I immediately offered to go fetch some more from across the street, right past the Just-A-Hair Away salon. I got three hundred paper plates for forty-six bucks. It was a very stupid way to spend forty-six dollars, but I wanted to show my appreciation to Mary and to the owners of the Forrest Inn and Suites for the free night's stay. Not only did Mary work there seven days a week, she lived there twenty-four hours a day, and had since the previous September. She had three days off coming up and was looking forward to visiting her family up at their cabin. What did she do in the off-season? She said she got "some reading done" over the past winter and did some "special projects" (painting, extra cleaning, etc.), but she'd been "Super busy as a beaver since the weather turned nice."

She either loved her job or was part of the slave trade, I couldn't tell. It was beyond me why anyone would want to live at work with no time off for over a year.

Little known fact about Mary: she did a little coffee retailing on the side.

"Tim, if you plan to run a successful mail order coffee business, you'll need more than a few freeze dried packets of the good stuff. My side gig relies on good systems for sales tracking, customer mining and goal setting. As an independent contractor, it's up to me to meet and beat company challenges and personal sales goals. That's where you come in. I am talking about a ground floor opportunity here, Tim."

Lucky me, she invited me in on some of the mail order action. If I could get just four of my friends to drink freeze dried instant Chinese coffee from halfway around the world, I could become one of her "official distributors." After hearing Mary go on about the special brand of coffee only available through her growing "distribution network of friends and family—a real virtuous circle of corporate and social responsibility," she let me sample the product.

Ah, but there was more: the coffee wasn't just coffee. It had "secret, ancient Chinese medicines made from rare herbs that were added to it for better taste, more wellness, and, thus, bigger benefits."

"Coffee with benefits?" I asked. It sounded like a dream come true. Where do I sign up for a cup of that liquid happy-happy? What a great way to start every day: coffee with benefits.

"Of course I will try a cup, Mary, thank you," I replied while rubbing my lower back to help get blood circulating into the problem area. The cement floor had kicked my ass the night before.

Whoa. After a cup of the black stuff, I became hyper-aware and my sense of hearing doubled and my sense of smell quadrupled. I could identify the bagel type in the toaster fifty feet away (cinnamon raisin) and I could hear what the young people next to the far window were whispering about. (They were whispering about the rehearsal dinner they'd both gotten drunk at the night before and were both a little embarrassed about sleeping with each other...again.)

Bonus? Those magical herbs and whatever the hell else was in the coffee put my intestinal track into super hyper overdrive. Not only did I feel better and more aware, but also I had to go number two about a minute and a half after finishing my sample cup. That coffee served to cut my morning splashdown time down significantly. Maybe I'd try another pouch of that magic thunder down under powder the following morning as well. A life-changing plan was emerging from my mental mist. Maybe I would start each and every day with a sleeve of Mary's Magic Chinese Instant Coffee.

She gave me two sleeves for the road and I promised not to open them unless I was near a working toilet. She laughed nervously and moved away. Honestly, they should call the stuff "Coffee to Go" and maybe do a cross-marketing effort with the toilet paper people. "Drink our coffee and get ready to roll."

A big idea here, folks, big idea...

Hyperaware from one sleeve of online-only coffee made in China—a trusted name in food manufacturing—I almost got lost leaving Amery, but once I found Country Road E/G and was on the route again, I got rolling at a pretty good clip. I'm not sure if my exceptional riding pace that day was due to the coffee itself or the "rare herbs" like lisdexamfetamine, methylphenidate, and amphetamine undoubtedly included in the coffee I'd sampled, but, regardless, I covered some ground that day.

Whatever it was in that coffee, I was good to go in every sense of the term.

Chapter Eighteen

SHAH-WHEAT CAR, A HEARTBROKEN GNOME ON THE RANGE

T'was a picture-perfect day to ride, with Mother Nature's wind briskly pushing me along like an empty plastic Wal-Mart bag skipping across a deserted parking lot. Yep, I had the wind at my back and the sun in my face. It was the kind of morning I didn't mind getting out of bed for. There was even a well-placed convenience store on the side of the road right when I needed a break, so I swung into the parking lot and dismounted.

Ah, a bonus awaited me. There was a bench in the shade!

I was sitting somewhere about twenty miles outside Amory, Wisconsin, drinking an over priced chocolate milk, and loving life when up drove a gangbanger in a 1984 Monte Carlo with eighty-six thousand original miles and twenty-inch dubs that must've cost the owner $2,400. It was a cool-looking car. The driver and I exchanged hellos, and surprise, surprise—he'd bought it from the guy who'd bought it from his cousin.

"Really?" I asked.

"Yeah, the guy I bought it from never got the title. It was, I guess…yeah, the title, from my cousin before he went to jail. So, I picked up my cousin at his place after he got out, and I went to the DMV with him to get the title from him, even though I gave the other guy the money for car."

At that point, it had been at least two thousand miles since I'd seen anyone wear his or her baseball cap sideways. He looked over and gave the car a loving glance. "I have had many cars: a 2008 Monte, an '04 Ford Mustang ("It sucked"), a '92 Prelude…"—he went on for a minute or so—"…but I really like this one. I think I'll keep this one for a while. A friend of mine told me he'll sell me some lights for the bottom illumination for twenty bucks, so"—and he turned back to me—"so how can I say no to that, man?"

How not indeed.

I asked if I could get a picture of me next to his car, because it was made the year I'd graduated from college.

"Sure, man," he said. "I'll take your picture. Wait. Do you want to sit in the driver's seat?"

"Hell yeah!" I said. So, for you Monte Carlo fans out there, here's a shot of the author kickin' back in a *shah-wheat* 1984 Monte with a 305 under the hood, keeping it real and giving a major boost to my street cred. I knew the guy who bought the car from a guy who bought the car from another guy who was the first guy's cousin who did a ten-year stretch for manslaughter. Boom! So, the next time you see me in a jacket and tie at some fancy party on the coast of Maine or at a book signing in NYC, just know that I am not in the game, but I know a guy who knows a guy who *is* in the game.

Even though I am not into cars (I see them largely as a way to get from Point A to Point B), I enjoyed talking to the owner of that '84 Monte Carlo and learning about all the other makes and models he had owned over the years. His passion for automobiles was infectious. When you come across someone who is passionate about something, it doesn't matter what that something is as passion is usually contagious. He was a good guy who happened to like cars a lot, not bikes.

"Where's your engine at?" he chided, looking over at my ride. "You know they make engines, right Homes? You put gas in 'em, start 'em up, and you go bro, anywhere you want, bro. Whatchu got against engines, Homes?"

I laughed with him.

Well, to each his own. He took off with a wave and a splatter of dirt to show me "what a 305 under the hood could do." I finished my chocolate milk and took off on the bike real fast, to show the world what a 53 year old could do.

I randomly met up with Larry again, the retired teacher from Kansas City. I was supposedly faster than the very well traveled Larry, but every time I passed him, he was up ahead of me somehow a day or two later. I'd passed him four times in the past two weeks.

So who's faster—the turtle or the hare?

After I climbed out of the Monte and got back on my bike, the morning passed by and the afternoon came along right on time. Larry and I decided to split a room in Birchwood because one room is cheaper than two and one room split between two is only a little more than the cost of a crappy little tent site in the middle of a bunch of dirt. Costs aside, for one guy in his fifties and another guy in his early sixties, the room beats tent every time.

We rolled right down Main Street in Birchwood in search of accommodation. I could hear music coming from somewhere, and then it came to me: *they pipe music in on Main Street.* Speakers on telephone poles played Herb Alpert, Broadway tunes, Sinatra. It was kind of eerie being surrounded by the only buildings that had not burned down with the rest of the town in 1905. Larry and I stood quietly next to the buildings, listening to the music and taking the definition of surreal in with both our eyes and ears. No one else was there. We stood alone in the middle of Main Street with Sinatra singing, "Fly Me to The Moon." It was another Twilight Zone or Sci-Fi ringer tone moment.

But the day got even stranger, so read slowly and get every detail, because what happened next was classic and one of the funniest episodes on the trip.

Larry and I secured room 204 on the second floor of the Who Cares Any-the-Fuck-Way Inn, a.k.a. the Birchwood Inn. After seventy-seven miles in the saddle, I didn't care what the place was called. I wanted good water pressure in the shower and a decent bed on which to enjoy uninterrupted sleep. There was no elevator, naturally, so after a long day, we had to carry our loaded bikes up a flight of stairs. That was our Last Jab of the Day.

We cleaned up and wondered over to a restaurant right next door called the Bear Den where an eighteen-year-old Julia Roberts look-a-like named Ellie Z served us delicious dinners. She was heading off to school in the fall to start the next chapter of her life.

"I'm psyched," is all she said.

Larry and I returned to room 204 for some TV and some phone calling home to the wives.

I was just dozing off on my side of the room when I heard something heavy hit the wall behind my headboard. There seemed to be a bit of a commotion going on in room 205. We heard muffled voices, a door opening, and then very clearly, "Fuck you! I don't fucking believe you! If this is the way you want to live your life, that's your fucking problem. Don't you *ever* come back home! Fuck you! I don't believe you!" Then there was the unmistakable sound of a conversation ending poorly—a slammed door.

The mirror on the wall in our room shook at the impact. That door slam was an audio exclamation point at the end of a loud argument between a pissed off woman and a guy who'd made some sort of bad decision in room 205. It seemed to me that his future ex-wife had caught him red handed doing something he shouldn't have been doing. What that was exactly was anyone's guess.

After slamming the door behind her, the soon-to-be-formerly betrothed woman had a choice to make: turn left and pass by our window and let us catch a good look at her, or turn right into the night, never to be seen by your author.

I shot off a quick prayer to St. Louie, the Most Holy Patron Saint of Left Turns. My prayer was answered: she hung a Louie and shot right by the window in our room overlooking the parking lot.

I could not recall being happier.

Now don't get too excited, dear reader: I only got a quick look at the woman because her rage-fueled pace propelled her by my viewing station at a pretty good clip. From my perspective, she shot by like a duck target at a county fair shooting gallery. Luckily, I still managed to catch a good enough gander to be able to ID her later in a lineup if I had to. A floating head of bottle blond hair suspended over a worn out pair of acid washed overalls sailed by at just over five feet off the ground. She had shoulders like a garden gnome and no neck whatsoever. The first two words that popped into my brain were "Hydrogen peroxide." They were quickly followed by "short" and "pissed off" and then, of course, the question came, "Where's her neck?"

That woman was one of the most neck-challenged people I'd ever seen. It was her best or worst feature, depending on what you are into. Her chin bumped into the top of her T-shirt. She never got a scarf or a necklace as a present. If she wore a collared shirt, she'd have to unbutton the first two buttons in front in order to eat a sandwich or suck on a straw. Give her a rope to hang herself and she'd be no closer to death. I mean *no neck*: she couldn't turn her head without her shoulders moving. OK, you get the point. I'll stop here. Well, maybe just a few more: If you wanted to blindfold her, you'd make her wear a turtleneck. She couldn't chew gum without bouncing her boobies. If she shrugged her shoulders, her friends would think she lost her head. And how in the world could she fold a beach towel?

Ok, that's it. I'm done, don't got gnome more no neck jokes...

I asked Larry to hit the mute button on the TV so we could confirm her departure from hotel property. We were relieved to hear the sound of her *clomp, clomp, clomp* fade down the same outside staircase we'd carried our bikes up earlier that day. Her clomps ended with another slamming door, this time it was the driver's side door of her vehicle. An engine roared to life and we heard her speed away.

We never got her name, but she was one short, bulky blonde and one very pissed-off neck less sack of prairie gnome. She was one long white beard and one floppy red hat short of being an actual Gnome on the Range with a broken home on the range... if you think about it and see things the way I did.

After Larry and I shared some nervous laughter, we considered our situation and slowly came to the realization that we might be in a bit of a tight spot, as we grew more concerned about our close proximity to ground zero. What would happen if Miss No Neck returned, loaded for bear and not smart enough to make it back to the right room to avail her revenge? Both of us were dead sure that pint-sized piece of prairie love had a sound working knowledge of orbital sanders, nail guns, and chainsaws and was better versed in the ways of potentially lethal hand tools and shooting and stabbing weapons than both of us put together (which wasn't saying much, but still.)

What would happen if Her Gnome-ness boomeranged back with a loaded shotgun? Would hot lead make it through our shared wall as easily as the sound and impact waves had earlier? Were we facing bystander risk by sheltering in place next door to a soon-to-be dead dude? We didn't have a clue what Bummed-Out Blondie was capable of. Was she the type to return armed, dumb, and dangerous? How accurate a shot was she? Might she douse her anger with a fifth of gin and pass out, or would drinking gin for her be like throwing gasoline on a fire? Would she return with intent to kill?

Questions and consequences hung in the air.

Worse yet, we also didn't know if she could count all the way up to 205 twice in the same night. Personally, I wouldn't want her to get impatient around rooms 203 or 204...as *we* were in room 204. I could just imagine her thought process after getting all liquored up and making the return trip to "room 204, or..." she'd say to herself, "Or was it 205? Well, shit. It might be 204, but it could be 205. Ah, it don't matter. All the doors look the same at the Who Cares Any-the-Fuck-Way Inn. I will kick them doors *ALL DOWN* and see who's inside doin' what and why. If there is a man behind the door, I'll kill him regardless. Motherfuckers are guilty of something! All men are dogs. Gnome POWER! *Anything with genitalia outside its body dies tonight!*"

I had traveled way too far to be accidentally taken out in a marriage-gone-wrong scenario. I say, "Respect the gnome, man." and I also say, "Never fuck around on a no-neck woman." Sure, that sounds like a country song that I'll have to write at some point in the future, but both of those just happen to be two of the many rules I choose to live by.

Anyway, Larry and I didn't want to become collateral damage, so once the dust settled in the parking lot, I got the hell out of my bed and went down to the clerk in the main office for a new room assignment. Our new room was 109. It was on the first floor, at the end.

"Yeah," said the clerk in response to my recounting of the last few minutes. "That lady called here earlier looking for him. She sounded kind of mad."

"Sounded *kind of* mad? Look pal, if she were any madder, we'd all be in body bags right now. If I were you, I'd watch your six," I told him. I took the new room key off the counter and returned upstairs to pack.

We decamped from 204 and settled into 109.

I don't know who the guy was in room 205, but a part of me wanted to knock quietly on his door and say, "Hey, buddy. What's up, pal? Hey, gonna swing your door open here just a bit to let you in on a little suggestion me and all the rest of the guys on the planet have for yah. I don't want gnome trouble; so don't go throwing any heavy objects my way when I come in. Hey, man, yeah, just saying that when you live in a town of 234 people, you might want to point that hood of your truck *out of town* before doing something you should have learned not to do at Bible camp."

But I didn't say any such thing. I was learning how to hold my tongue on this trip.

Monte Carlos, Julia Roberts look-a-likes, and neckless pissed off gnomes: bike trips take you further!

On the morning of July first, Larry went one way and I went the other. He took off for Glidden, Wisconsin, fifty-seven miles away, while I detoured slightly off route to a bike store with my DIY ("do it yourself") tail between my legs. I'd tried to fix a brake problem I'd had for the past couple of days or so with the tools I had with me, but my attempts came up short. So, instead of hanging with Larry who was great company, I was off on my own again as my brake problem couldn't wait. The weather was threatening that day, so I figured I'd better address the brakes before the slippery stuff poured down from the sky and lengthened my stopping distance from pathetic to infinity and beyond.

As luck would have it, there was a first-rate bike shop not that far out of my way, and the doctor was in. Nick, the mechanic, was six feet five inches tall, ten years older than me, and still racing mountain bikes and competing in Ironman competitions. His kids were all Olympic athletes or runner up Olympic athletes.

My gene pool was slightly different. I hadn't mountain biked in years and I doubted any of my bloodline was Olympic grade. But it wasn't my fault; Faheys were bred to remain *in*side the pub.

Nick put my rear wheel back to true, fixed the brakes, and, at my request, switched my cassette (the back part of the gears). *Wow*—new bike! I bought a new bike helmet, some trail bars, and new foot beds for the bike cleats. I was on my way to another two stores to get a bedroll and a skullcap. Larry had turned me on to the skullcap-under-the-helmet solution for preventing sweat from fogging up riding glasses. It did the trick.

After leaving the bike shop with new equipment, I felt like I had undergone some sort of very successful bicycle colonoscopy. For the umpteenth time, I felt like a new man on this trip. The new cassette was for a mountain bike, but it worked just fine on my touring machine. Now my bike could climb a tree if I wanted it to. Wish I'd had it for some of those Rocky Mountain summits.

The rain showed up, and instead of feeling like a new man, I felt like a wet man. By the time two thirty rolled around, the sky was covered in a blanket of dark-gray clouds and it was weeping. By three o'clock, the weepy tears became a crying deluge. There were very few cars on the road, which, thankfully, greatly reduced the chances of me being hit by one. Even with all the rain and clouds, the outdoors was incredibly beautiful and worth all the effort of enduring it. After all those miles I'd pedaled, the beauty and the richness of the color of the landscape still stunned. My iPhone was no painter; real life beats digital rendering every time, but I guess that's why you have to get a bike of your own and come see it for yourself. The colors, the smells, the landscape, the drama, the humor, the food and the fantastic people are not to be missed.

I swung into the Clam Lake convenience store and…there was Larry, dry as a bone, warm, happy, smiling, and bug-free. What a contrast to my situation. He'd been marooned for two hours, smartly waiting out the storm under the cover of the convenience store roof. That was the only way I'd caught up to him after my bakeshop detour. For the previous two hours I had ridden through monsoonal conditions: the roads were rivers and the clouds dumped rain as steadily as water comes over a waterfall during a spring thaw.

The air conditioning of the convenience store quickly made my soaking wet clothing feel like ice packs. I dug out some dry clothes and changed into them behind a locked men's room door. Dry clothes did not help boost my body temp much: I had to find a way to warm up. I had no idea how fast air-conditioning and rainwater could cause hypothermia, but it started to settle in as soon as I'd stopped pedaling and stepped inside. I could feel it. Fortunately, I nipped hypo in the bud by swapping out my wet clothes and getting my arms and legs moving. I walked the store isles waving my arms and kicking my legs sideways like I was auditioning for a starring role in "The Pirates of Panzance."

I didn't get a callback. I didn't want the part anyway.

Together again, Larry and I waited another hour or so for the rain to stop, then mounted up for the last seventeen miles to Glidden, where we split the fifty-dollar room and walked over to the Green Lantern restaurant, me for the rib eye steak, him for the chicken. Both of us were delighted with our delicious meals. Steve, a fifty-eight-year-old grandfather of two and a crane operator for thirty-seven years, joined us halfway through our meal. We'd met him earlier in the hallway at our near-empty motel, and, as the Green Lantern was the logical place to eat (walking distance from the hotel, good reviews), we ran into him again. Steve was the only other lodger we'd seen in the hotel and the only other customer at the restaurant.

Steve talked while I polished off the second half of my rib eye. Years and years before sitting down with us at dinner, he had gotten his now dead ex-wife pregnant at "barely eighteen. She was crazy," so he divorced her at age twenty-one. He saw her die of lung cancer at age forty-eight.

He said, "She was a beautiful, but an exceptionally vain woman. The very thought of her losing all her hair was enough to kill her. She got herself a nice wig before she died, though. It was a nice wig."

Now Steve had two granddaughters. His daughter "waited" until she was twenty-three to have her first kid.

"Waited?" I asked. "Back east, 'waiting' means thirty-five."

"Well, my daughter waited half a decade longer than her mom."

That's all, folks. The United States lost to Belgium 2 to 1, so we were out of World Cup competition. I was so bummed that I couldn't write. I was getting a bit long-winded anyway, but the little bike trip of mine had continued to deliver fascinating characters each and every day. The variety appeared endless.

Chapter Nineteen

FEELING LESS THAN THEN MORE THAN
WELCOME IN PRESQUE ISLE

The next morning Larry was off to meet friends who lived a few miles off route. He took off right after breakfast. I returned to the room for a little more shuteye.

A few hours later I was riding again. I continued pedaling the Northern Tier and arrived at a crappy campsite called Big Lake Campground in Presque Isle, Wisconsin at around six thirty, both tired and hungry. Make that the *Big Mistake* Campground. Bloodthirsty bugs numbered in the billions and the whole place needed a weed whacker army to parachute in from all directions to attack the overgrowth from all sides. There was a camp host, or more accurately, a camp Zoologist/ Botanist of Insect and Weed World who'd stepped out of his RV looking like he had broken out of rehab and spent the better part of the past month trying to make up for lost time during his brief experience with sobriety. He was just as disheveled as Walter Matthau in *The Bad News Bears* and just as welcoming as Jack Nicholson in *The Shining*. One look at him, and I didn't need to ask—clearly there were no showers, toothbrushes, Laundromats, fresh food sources, soaps, shampoos, or shaving kits anywhere near Big Lake Campground. He was a walking human billboard of what can happen to you if you spend too many days at the Big Mistake Campground.

He initiated conversation by asking where I was from.

"Maine," I replied.

"Does it say you are from Maine on your driver's license or some other government issued ID?" he asked.

"Yes."

"Well, then normally the charge is twelve dollars a night, but because you're from way outta state, it will be fourteen."

As he was filling me in on the two-dollar tourist tax, I kept slapping my legs to kill mosquitoes. Each slap yielded multiple hits. During his short pricing commentary, I must have sent twenty mosquitoes to their graves.

"Man, the mosquitoes are really bad around here," I said after he made sure I understood the two-dollar "way outta state" penalty.

"Yes, they sure are," he replied, following up his response with some local humor that really must have torn them up at the local store where the camp warden purchased his plastic five gallon jugs of well vodka: "Our mosquitoes are a mite...*friendly*, aren't they?"

I was pretty low on fuel and a tad shy of water, so at that point in my day his sense of humor didn't fly so well with me. Nothing says, "Welcome to our state" more than an upcharge and a bad joke. Bah, humbug. That place was certainly not my fav.

Before forking over my hard-earned fourteen bucks, I thought I'd take a slow roll through the place to get a good look around. I wanted to know what I was paying for.

His dismissive backhand wave was his way of saying, "Sure sir, go check the place out and when you come back you can let me know what you think."

If the place passed muster, I'd be back to pay. If it didn't, I'd just roll away.

I'd been assigned to site number twenty-five, but he'd "make the necessary adjustments to the paperwork" if I preferred to stay at another site.

"Can't miss it," he said, "it's right by the boat launch."

I went into the campground. What a damp, dumpy, shithole of overgrowth and mosquito swarms. I rode by the other campsites as I made my way up to twenty-five and saw entire families in tattered clothing with missing teeth sitting around smoky campfires staring back at me with faces that looked like they belonged on the F.B.I.'s Top 10 Most Wanted List. I'd have been willing to bet "Dueling Banjos" was both their favorite song and the soundtrack of their lives. There was definitely a super creepy vibe going on at the Big Mistake Campground. One particularly dirty pocket of assembled campers occupied tent site 23. They had a fire going and were using a tree branch as a rotisserie to cook a *squirrel.*

Yes, you read that right. A squirrel, as in, "Hey, Jeb, what's for dinner?"

"Squirrel. Found it on the ground, dead as a nail. I got it cookin' right now on the row-toss-her-ree. 'Row-toss-her-ree.' That's a fancy French word for 'branch' in case you were wondering'."

I am not kidding. It was definitely squirrel on that stick.

(SFX: Dueling banjos)

I found tent site number twenty-five, the one I'd been assigned to, the one that all of the other people in the camp had passed up before selecting other sites that they could call their own personal Hells. Lot 25 was conveniently located next to both the communal bathrooms and the boat launch and the whole compound was a true pimple on the ass of Mother Nature. Lot 25 was just a bunch of dirt and rocks with thick weeds growing up to my bike's axles. The tent site he'd assigned me had more slope to it than the boat launch. The guy living in the camper was crazy if he thought I'd stay there for the night. The kicker for me was the broken picnic table covered in moss and broken tree branches. The picnic table itself was a splintered piece of junk shoved deep into the bushes. Site number twenty-five wasn't a campsite—it was a wet, weedy graveyard where picnic tables went to die. The table was sap-stained from the trees above, trees that had dripped sappy tears at the knowledge that they had to spend their whole miserable tree lives rooted in the place known to me as the Big Mistake.

Those trees might have been stuck there, but I sure as hell wasn't.

With the bodies of fifteen dead mosquitoes on each leg and blood on both my hands from killing them, I pulled out my phone and made my second call ever to Warm Showers.

And thank God I did. Not ten miles and forty-five minutes later, I was standing in a bug-free bunkhouse above a garage that Joan and Bill H. had just recently completed the renovation on. They were on their way out to dinner when I called in my camping Hail Mary. They could not have been nicer. Joan told me to come on over and make myself at home: they would return after dinner and meet me then.

Man, oh man. What a stay! I got there, changed clothes, freshened up, and headed out for a civilized dinner at a nice lodge just a few hundred steps away from their place on a private lake. I met the daughter of the guy who wrote the Buckshot Anderson books, a man who spent time in the nearby woods as a kid then wrote stories about his experiences. I bought one for my son George after I got back and read it aloud to him. He loved it.

By the time I returned from my dinner, my hosts had returned from theirs. We shared some stories over tea and homemade cookies. Take *that*, 'skeeters. Next up were a warm shower, a bed, and a straight-through night's sleep.

My gracious host and hostess were not done with me yet. After sleeping like a scared opossum all night, I got up and made my way over to their kitchen table. Joan made a killer breakfast of buttermilk pancakes and lots of maple syrup. Good coffee was had as well.

We all sat and chatted up a storm that lasted clear through 'til lunch. I had them laughing at my bike adventures, they had me laughing at the stories they told. Joan kindly made Bill and me grilled-cheese sandwiches with her homemade bread and "just a little butter"—yeah, like a cow's morning output's worth. Delicious.

It was a joy to be wrapped in the warmth of their hospitality. I was their first ever Warm Showers guest, and I will admit that their invitation for me to stay on for a couple more days was *very* tempting. They had a wonderful home and the only sandy beach on a beautiful lake. I can report with confidence that the place is absolutely beautiful when the sun is shining and a breeze is gently ambling by.

Their two-hundred-foot driveway was one of the hardest two-hundred-foot stretches of the whole trip because all I wanted to do was turn around and hang out with them for a day or two more. Great people!

The following night was different. Home cooked meals, cookies, pancakes, and all the peace and quiet I enjoyed while staying with Joan and Bill were in the past: none of those things followed me to the Super 8 in Eagle River.

I showered up and stepped out for a dinner at a chain restaurant and ended up meeting a nice young couple, Travis and

Angelina and their two kids. They were in the area to visit relatives in the North Woods. Travis worked in the cheese manufacturing industry and was responsible for all the robots that helped move the cheese along the conveyor belts. On his time off, he ran. He could do eight-mile stints like it was nothing. Angelina was no slacker, either. When she wasn't walking down a runway somewhere or giving birth to beautiful children, she was running half marathons herself. Their kids were literally following in their parents' footsteps too, with some races already under their belts even before their oldest was ten. Mom and Dad didn't want them to run too much though, because they'd heard too much running was bad for young, growing bones.

I needed to stop sharing. Those poor folks were just out to dinner and I came along. They kept on asking me questions, so I kept answering. I talked too long to them. I was like the Thing That Would Not Shut Up. Good grief.

Fourth of July was the next day and it found me on my bike at 7:00 a.m. and in a my first doublewide trailer that night. I went off route and made it to Townsend, Wisconsin, the every-year-for-two-decades July Fourth vacation spot of my old Boston biking buddy David Levison. He was there with forty other family members. When he found out I was only thirty miles away from his family camp, he invited me over for a visit. I happily veered off course to meet him and join his family for some July Fourth celebrations. There was water skiing, tubing, food, ice cream, and a two-hundred-pound dog—the whole nine yards. It was fun and I couldn't believe Dave and Heather were out in Wisconsin *just* as I was passing through. You can't plan this stuff...

After all the fireworks left the sky, the thousand plus crowd of onlookers shifted out into the parking lot and climbed into their cars. Some of the young kids had already fallen asleep in their chairs. I joined the parade that exited the parking lot and made it safely back to the Levison's place.

If you ever wondered what happened to your TV from the early 1970s, I found it. It is in the doublewide trailer in Townsend, Wisconsin, that I woke up in on July 5th, 2014. The ancient TV at the foot of my bed was as dusty and unused as the trailer itself, and both were throwbacks to a different time, a time before the main house, two car garages, and the tree house were even there on the property. I looked past that TV set and out the window to a new day. My internal alarm clock had me up earlier than anyone else, so I made my way from the trailer to the big house and quietly slid the sliding glass door open, stepped into the kitchen, and poured coffee into a cup and milk over a bowl of cereal.

The living room looked like some sort of dog bomb had been detonated the night before. Five or six dogs were lounging on couches, on chairs, on the floor and even on the coffee table. Half a dozen pairs of big brown eyes followed me across the kitchen, their heads not moving. While I crunched and sipped, the house slowly awoke around me. House dwellers began to stir, going from horizontal to vertical and slow parading into the kitchen just as I'd done a half hour or so before.

One of the parade members had four paws and weighed more than two hundred pounds: the huge Saint Bernard came over to me and put his big head right on my lap. He just stood next to me like that for a while. He was a good old soul of a dog. I gently moved his massive head off my lap and stood up, forcing the big ol' fella out of my space. As it turned and strolled outside, a foot-long drip of drool spilled out from under his mouth and swung back and fourth in a walking motion with every step. That dog was a large and noble beast, no doubt, and a very good-natured one, too, but the drool dripping down from the mouth of that gentle giant would take me some getting used to. I was glad he hadn't drooled on me.

After breakfast I packed up and said my good-byes to people. Dave had kindly offered to give me a lift back onto the Northern Tier route which saved me thirty or forty miles of riding. I climbed into his brother-in-law's Harley Davidson Ford F-150 and headed back to the route I'd left the day before.

While backtracking the thirty miles, we stopped to take a picture of a road sign Dave had always wanted to photograph. Old Dump Road (left) and Happy Lane (right). Classic. Old Dump Road and Happy Lane represent a decision we all face every day. You can decide to be happy and take Happy Lane or you can decide to be sad and take Old Dump Road into the dumps.

It's your call. Every day.

A few miles later, we stopped again, this time for a second breakfast. All too soon after breakfast, though, I was waving good-bye to Dave and watching the taillights of that Harley Davidson Ford F-150 truck get smaller. I was back on track and once again totally alone in the saddle at the crack of noon. It had been great catching up with Dave and Heather and sharing the company of their extended family. What a fluke to see a bike buddy from "way outta state."

What a rest of the day. Good Lord Baby Jesus: did the wind have it out for me, or what?

The wind slowed my progress to four miles per hour at one point. I covered eighty miles in seven hours and forty-five minutes, with an average speed of twelve. The only reason my average speed was that high was because the last twenty miles, which I rode mostly in darkness, were perfectly positioned for the wind to push me along. Around mile sixty, I turned left onto a silky stretch of freshly paved road that led into Manitowoc. For the only time during the whole trip, I had a night ride. I was on a smooth carpet of asphalt with a warm summer wind that whispered me along. I knifed through the warm twilight toward the city, past all the closed car dealerships still draped in all their Fourth of July ribbon and red, white, and blue balloon finery. The night sky up ahead lit up with another fireworks display, my second in as many nights, that boomed and bloomed like a huge and colorful exploding flower bouquets that flashed over the city scape. It was a nice reward for hammering out the rotations all day against the wind and a nice welcome into the city limits.

I arrived at nine thirty, just beat, but I had earned another riding memory to stash away and think back to after the trip was over. God, it was wonderful. Riding those last fifteen miles toward a sparkling fireworks show was like a dream I didn't want to end.

I found a hotel and checked in. The next day I woke up in the hotel and checked out.

"Checking out of room 103," I said, putting my rectangular plastic room key down on the front desk. I had the bike gloves and helmet on and was dragging the Fun Mover along next to me. I was dressed in street clothes for the short shot to the ferry dock and the SS *Badger*, the ferryboat that would deliver me to my next state (Michigan) and a new time zone (EST).

"You ride a bike, huh?" asked the Quality Inn lady. "I do, too," she said, not waiting for my obvious answer of yes.

"Yeah, I lost my license three years ago on some stupid thing. Still paying it back, but I commute by bike every day—seven miles."

"DUI?" I guessed.

"Yeah. I'll never drive drunk again. I've learned my lesson."

I wasn't told the details, but she must have really impressed local law enforcement with her drunk driving antics to catch their attention. The cocktail lifestyle and open container travel seemed to be encouraged in the region. When I was in Montana (or was it Minnesota?) I'd seen people get out of their cars and leave them idling while they stepped into a bar, had a shot and ordered four Bloody Mary's in to-go cups. Maybe Wisconsin was different. I was glad to see that law enforcement was trying anyway. Drunk drivers kill.

The day was kind of a zero day for me, but not one without concern. I didn't have to bike very far to make the ferry, but I learned the Fun Mover had developed terminal cancer of the rear wheel: the back rim was coming apart, splitting on the rim where the spokes were attached. It wasn't broken yet, but it had to be replaced as quickly as possible. Hairline fractures were at the base of many spokes on my rear wheel. The front wheel was fine.

I packed up and headed down to the Manitowoc ferry that would take me across Lake Michigan.

"It is never too early or late for an ice cream" was becoming my motto (or one of them, anyway) on this trip, so when I saw the huge statue of a cow out front of a one-story building, I figured (correctly) there was ice cream inside. There were also some nuns there busy loading a cooler with individually labeled ice-cream cups for their bedridden and aging cohorts who could not make the journey to the ice cream store due to poor health. I stepped in and paid for all the nuns' ice cream. The N.I.C. (nun in charge) told me my good deed was very much appreciated and would bring some happiness to the three sick bedridden nuns, two terminally ill with cancer.

"We will all get together and pray for your safety during your bicycle journey. God bless you," she said.

Hey, it felt good to put twenty bucks put in the right place. Who knew? If I pulled more random acts of kindness like that I might still have had a shot at getting into Heaven.

On my way out the door of the ice cream store, I ran into a tandem bicycle riding couple named Bernie and Tammy. They were heading right past the ferry, so they offered to escort me "through the crazy, twisted maze of roads" to get there. I accepted their offer and fell in behind them. They moved right along on their bicycle built for two. I huffed and puffed in their wake for the mile and a half it took to get to the SS *Badger* and was glad to have them escort me and glad to see them go. I could barely keep up with them.

With two hours still in my pocket before the ferry took off, I crossed a drawbridge and ate at a local Mexican place, chatting up Spencer, a young woman who was painting the outside of the building when I pulled up. She said the place was open and added that she hoped to do some biking of her own before starting college the following year. She'd never left the state of Wisconsin except for once when she was younger, but she was too young to remember it. She was a good kid who was on her own and doing a great job at plugging along, making her way in the world. The Mexican place closed down a few months later. I wonder whatever happened to Spencer.

I returned across the bridge to make the ferry in plenty of time. The Fun Mover and I rolled right into the private room that I'd reserved (and splurged an extra forty bucks for). I fell asleep to the sounds of the *Lego Movie*, which was being shown across a narrow corridor from my room. The theme song "Everything Is Awesome!" lulled me to sleep.

As I went to sleep, the sun was shining, a little breeze was wafting, and the Fun Mover was soon to get a new body part. The prognosis was good. Everything *was* awesome.

The ferry across to Ludington was over before I knew it. I was pushed awake when the boat kissed the Ludington, Michigan dock.

The SS *Badger* made landfall at around seven o'clock that night. I had made no reservations anywhere, so I pedaled slowly down the main drag with my eyes peeled and my credit card ready. The Stearn's Motor Inn looked promising, so I turned in for a closer look. As I entered, a man and his wife were just leaving. I held the door open for them.

"Hey, how is this place? What do they get for a room?" I asked.

The guy shrugged his shoulders. "Sixty-five bucks. It's a flop."

I smiled to myself and walked in.

Home sweet home.

Chapter Twenty

A New Word, A New Wheel, Finally Getting In To Yale

I took my first round trip to nowhere and was none too happy about it.

After spending the better part of my morning in a bike shop trying to secure a proper replacement for my rear wheel, I departed Ludington with every intention not to return.

Yet I was forced to. My new ninety-nine dollar rear wheel, the only one of the correct size available in the only bike shop in town, wasn't up to the task. Sure, it looked round like a circle, but it was oblong and rolled like an oval. What a piece of shit. *Thumpity-thump, thumpity-thump* went the tire over any surface. It would quicken with acceleration or slow with deceleration. The sound and the vibration was super annoying and acted like a Chinese Water Torture instrument that took minutes, not days, to drive me batty.

So, I bit the bullet and headed back to the bike shop that sold it to me.

"We can fix that," the owner assured me, the bullshit running out of his mouth as freely as the crap coming out the backside of a bull at a rodeo event. "Your tire wasn't seated right on your new wheel. My bad. I'm sorry." After forty-five minutes of trying, he announced, "This is much better. This will work."

But it didn't. The guy had no fucking idea what he was doing. I needed to order another wheel.

It took two days for a proper replacement wheel to arrive, so I was stuck in Ludington with not much to do, but zero. (Yes, I just made the word zero, or the null set, a verb.) I napped, read, wrote, and spent some time at the way funky, supercool Redolencia coffee shop (in Latin, that means "nice aroma that evokes fond or nostalgic memories") and waited for a replacement wheel. Ah, the nonstop action of a bike trip.

I suffered a very slight glitch on my first night at the Inn. I heard some loud and strange folks check in and, from what I could decipher from the words strong enough to bounce up the back stairway, past my door, and into my eardrums, I had no interest in meeting them. There was a fetish convention being held in town and the Stearns Inn was giving group discounts. As a precaution, I thought I'd go old school and reinforce the door lock with the old tilted-chair trick. My precautions were completely unnecessary, it turned out; their fetish appetites did not include chillaxing with middle-aged bicycle tourists suffering through a midlife crisis. (Does anyone still use the term 'chillaxing' anymore? I haven't heard it in a while.)

Because I was not attractive to them (or to anyone else for that mater), I remained safe in my little sunlit flop, my tidy warm cocoon. I was in the perfect place to lie low and spend some downtime when my wheels weren't turning and my legs weren't pumping. I never found out which fetish had brought so many nice folks together, the guy at the front desk wasn't telling. Foot? Elbow? Bondage? I was left hanging. There were no signs of any fetishes in the lobby of the hotel. Maybe they all had a fetish for normalcy.

Sign me up for that.

While I was at the Redolencia coffee shop in downtown Ludington, I picked up a new word, and so wish I had been the one to coin it.

Stephanie, a red-haired forty-eight-year-old who had just broken things off with her boyfriend of eight years, was halfway through her latte when she struck up a conversation. She confessed that before her most recent breakup with her boyfriend, she'd been a decade married, and before that, there had been another eight-year relationship. Though she was divorced from her husband for many years, she remained reluctant to use the term "ex-husband" when referring to her, um, ex-husband. She didn't like the stigma, the "negative buzz" of the term ex-husband. "The ex part sounds like failure. Ex-con, ex-friend, you know?"

She continued with her point. "That prefix 'ex-' has a certain finality and sense of failure to it that I am uncomfortable with. I mean we had eight good years out of ten. That's a B minus grade. Not bad."

So she came up with her own word to describe her ex-husband. She referred to her ex-husband as her *wasband*. He *was* her husband, so now he *is* her *wasband*. Brilliant. I immediately agreed with her that it sounded better to have a *wasband* than an ex-husband. Wasband seemed less negative than ex-husband and a more humane way to describe a decade long marital swing and a miss.

Hearing a new word like *wasband* reminded me of a word my own nephew came up with a while back: *Exhaustipated.* I wish I'd coined that one, too. One day my nephew, then age 12, returned home from school and flopped down on the living room couch. His mom asked him how school had gone that day.

"Oh, Mom, I'm exhaustipated."

"Exhaustipated?" she questioned. "I've never heard of that word. Did you learn that at school? What does it mean?"

"Exhaustipated, Mom. I made it up. It's a combination of the words *exhausted* and *constipated*. Exhaustipated. It means I'm too tired to give a shit."

Genius. I am related to a genius—he's a nephew through marriage, yes, but it still counts. The kid was not even a rebellious teenager yet and he was coming up with words like exhaustipated. With a creative mind like that tucked under his skullcap, his future looks bright as a star to me.

So, you may ask, how did I spend my *second consecutive* zero day? Napping, that's how. After a big breakfast, I clocked nearly three hours the morning of my second zero with my eyes closed and breathing softly and woke up feeling refreshed. My fourth grade teacher at the Belmont Day School, Mrs. Smith, defined the word "regenerative" to me and used it in a sentence as an example. I remember the sentence: "The man awoke from a deep slumber and felt better. He had experienced a *regenerative* sleep." Well, on that day I was that guy. I was surprised at how tired I was and how much rest I still required on my second consecutive day off. The bonus? The Stearns Motor Inn had a three-day discount, so because I didn't elect to have any maid service upon check-in, the third night cost me only an additional five bucks that brought my grand total for three nights to $148.90.

The next day the replacement wheel arrived and it was free, thanks to the wonderful folks at Independent Fabrication. Hats off to them, they really came through for me. I wished I'd tried them earlier and not bothered with the half ass at the bike shop.

So, with my brand new replacement wheel, I was off on the Fun Mover, running as smoothly as ever. It was worth the extra day to secure the right part.

Life lesson: Never buy a ninety-dollar wheel for a touring bike. It is simply the wrong tool for the job. Any self-respecting retailer would not even consider trying to sell you one. The local bike shop also tried to charge me for the shipping of the wheel that had been overnighted free of charge. Some people. If I hadn't remembered to get my shipping deposit back, the guy would still have my money in his pocket.

With my new back wheel on, I was good to go. I enjoyed another great riding day, weather-wise. The Ludington bike shop that installed the rear wheel screwed up again and managed to put my rear gear shifter, called the derailleur, out of alignment. The place was a bike den of ineptitude. About ten miles in I discovered the problem. My bike needed some more attention and adjustment, and I wasn't the guy to give it as I lacked relevant knowledge and experience dealing with such devilish things as rear derailleurs. So I figured I'd ignore my DIY urges and stay clear of the problem until I crossed the threshold of a bike shop with a competent bike mechanic who'd graduated from derailleur school.

With two days rest, I was not exhaustipated. Goodbye Ludington, hello Baldwin, Michigan.

Tens of miles of riding later, I met Lisa who, with her husband, had purchased the Wolf Lake Motel in 2004. When Lisa saw me hesitate at hearing what I considered to be the high forty-five-dollars-a-night room rate, she turned on her sales pitch.

"Your forty-five dollars buys you a clean room. I am insistent about a clean room, and you can be certain that all the sheets have been changed and are freshly washed. Ain't nobody been sleepin' on them sheets on your bed 'cept you, I can guarantee that. There are some places I won't go, and having dirty sheets is not one of them—I mean one of them. I won't go there with dirty sheets. I mean I won't go to places with dirty sheets. Well, you know what I mean."

Probably noticing that the look on my face hadn't changed much since her sales pitch began, she pressed on in earnest. "Now, we are in the middle of the woods here. I cannot guarantee you won't see a spider or two." She had to say that "middle of the woods" part twice because an eighteen-wheeler driving past the place had drowned out what she was saying. 'Middle of the woods?' My ass. That semi truck sure wasn't.

Honestly though, the traffic noise didn't matter much to me. I grew up next to a highway outside of Boston and had spent a decade living on First Avenue and 79th Street in New York City. The sound of semis and sedans rolling down the road is like white noise and bedtime lullabies for me.

I decided to take the room behind door number three at the Wolf Lake Motel.

"No problem," I said to Lisa, "Clean sheets are what I'm after. I'll take the room for the night," I said, adding my Tim Fahey Completely Useless Fact of the Day: "You know, you can spend your whole life trying to avoid spiders, but you are never more than seven feet from one, even when you are flying in a plane. I think they are the most successful species. I just wouldn't want to run into a brown recluse. I was bit by one once."

Unprompted, Lisa then backed away from me and hiked up her baggy gray gym shorts to reveal a pretty large left thigh and a sizable scar from a two fanged bite. Lisa told me she'd been bitten once by a brown recluse spider, too, "right up here on my leg while I was driving home. Damn thing crawled out of a feedbag I'd put on the front seat and it got me. Hate them browns. I killed that spider with my right hand while driving my truck seventy-five miles an hour."

It was show-and-tell time: the fang marks were mid-thigh, but the shorts were pulled ever higher to reveal a much more sizeable scar that ringed her leg. She hiked her shorts all the way up and spun around like a hot dog on a heated stainless steel roller in order to show me the whole thing. After completing her three sixty spin, she dropped her shorts back down and continued.

"See that pink scar around my whole leg? The only reason I'm sixty pounds overweight and one leg is shorter than the other was because of the complications resulting from that brown recluse bite."

"Infection got to it, and the doctors had to take an inch off 'round up here." She pointed. "See that scar? Yeah, you've seen it. I can tell by your face. Well, it goes all the way around like a tree trunk. Not sure you could tell that. Sometimes the droop in my ass cheek gets in the way of the scar, but it does go all the way around."

Once you've seen the tree-trunk scar on a woman's upper thigh, social barriers have been irreversibly broken down. She showed me hers, so I showed her mine: my scar was much less dramatic, as my brown bite never got infected and never reached the point where I had to get operated on. Guess I was a little bit of a Scar Pussy as well as a Motel Pussy; she had to look hard to find it even after I pointed right to it on my right calf. I think she just pretended to have seen it when she said, "Oh yeah, I see it now. Wow."

For better or worse, Lisa and I were BFFs at that point. Lisa was extremely helpful, thoughtful, and earnest in her passion for clean sheets. After I checked in she offered to do my laundry and to drive me three miles to the closest restaurant for a hot meal. She even offered to loan me her cell phone as a hot spot. She was by far the nicest hotelier of the whole trip. She was what all hotel management ought to be: caring and nurturing. We were brown recluse buds that shared the same firm stance on clean sheets. Now that's something you can build a lasting relationship on. My girl Lisa and I were proof positive that people with seemingly very little in common, like a biker and a hotelier, can find common ground.

After dropping my panniers on the floor and flopping down onto the sheets Lisa had guaranteed clean, I thought about my next step: dinner. I didn't want to bother Lisa with a ride down the road; it was very kind of her to offer me one, but I could see that she had a couple of kids running around that would need to eat some dinner soon, too, so I dug deep into my saddlebag and found, at the very bottom next to an inner tube, a beat up bag of ready mix something-or-other. I think it was Mexican rice and beans. It wasn't the best food I'd ever tasted, but without a restaurant within walking or reasonable biking distance and with me being reluctant to trouble Lisa for a ride, that packet of food was to be dinner. I fired up the jet boiler, boiled some water, and voilà! A welcome starchy mix of carbohydrates was laid at the feet of the Bike God, and the Bike God ate every single bit of it.

As I slipped into a food coma about ten minutes later, I considered what I'd just consumed. It occurred to me that I had no recollection of where the just-add-water meal had been purchased. Did Dave give it to me on the day he left? No. Had I bought it on May 15th in Anacortes, WA? Not sure. Too tired to dig through the trash for the nutritional information on the packaging, I had no idea where the food came from, what the ingredients were, or even when it was made. I wasn't even sure what country it was from or what the suggested serving size even was. Was there an expiration date? Bike *God*? Try Bike *Idiot*. When you are your own engine (which everyone is), you should be careful about the quality of the fuel you put in your tank. And that goes whether or not you are riding a bike across the country or across town.

The night flew by in the blink of an eye. One blink, actually. I closed my eyes then I opened them the next day. That's one blink.

I said my goodbyes to Lisa the next morning and mounted up, bound for the restaurant three miles away she had offered to drive me to the night before. I found it in short order and ordered up breakfast from a short order cook.

With a satisfying breakfast in my belly, I headed out on the road once again. I wished Lisa owned a whole chain of $45/night motels that provided clean sheets and that put her at every front desk to welcome me. She was a wonderful woman and I'd be her most loyal customer.

As I rolled through rural Michigan that day, I came across a grain bin standing three stories tall with the word SUKUP on it. I thought of something when I saw that word. With the economic hardship so prevalent in that part of Michigan, I was familiar with the fact that the state government had made it a common practice to provide generous amounts of social assistance to the many folks in the area who were in need of it. Welfare recipients received bi-weekly direct deposit payments into their state sponsored personal bank accounts and could access said funds through state issued debit cards called "bridge cards." When I saw that grain elevator with the word SUKUP blazoned across it, I suspected it might be the welfare state's way of offering subliminal career advice to its residents, on not necessarily how to *get* a job, but certainly how to *keep* one.

During the day I came across Pete Skinner, a fifty-nine year old celebrating his sixtieth birthday early with a Northern Tier crossing. We were both on the same road, going the same direction, at roughly the same speed—but he was better at it. He had a leg up on me: an ex-military man, he had kept himself in shape his whole life, so he didn't have to suffer through the pains I had at the start of my trip. He'd left Anacortes ten days *after* I did and he had still managed to catch up to me, no problem.

Pete and I rode together that morning and I got to learn more about him. His lifetime parachute jump count was north of *twelve hundred.* He used to train Special Forces units and S.W.A.T. teams in all sorts of weather, day and night, including HiLo, and LoLo deployment practice. The discipline and fastidiousness he must have had when packing a chute was evident in his approach to bicycle touring; every mile and a half he took a measured sip of water. He had a GPS unit mounted on his handlebar and a bike computer to help measure speed, distance travelled, distance remaining, that type of thing. He knew the exact location of every single item on his bike. Me? In contrast, I tended to ride until I was thirsty and then guzzle down water like an overheated camel at an oasis. I used maps and still couldn't find my ass with my own two hands. Every time I needed to get something from my bike, the search would begin with the words, "Now, where in the hell is my…"

Even after a couple thousand miles of riding, I still had no clear understanding of where anything was on my bike. Sometimes it took me ten minutes to find a toothbrush. In contrast, all Pete's gear had a place and everything was in its place. He rode a custom-made Co-Motion bicycle that fit him like a glove. I'd bought my bike because it was red and it looked cool. Hell, I bought my sleeping bag because it was green and puffy. As Mike the Bike would say, my bike had not been set up in "fine-tune fashion." Pete had a printout of every place he would be visiting for the rest of the trip. Me? I didn't know where I'd be sleeping when the sun kissed the horizon good night, so me hanging out with Pete was like a professional gambler hanging out with a certified public accountant. Although our background and organizational skills were starkly different, our shared goal was identical: reach the Atlantic Ocean in one piece.

After a shared lunch at a roadside restaurant, Pete and I parted company. He wanted to hang out a little more, maybe grab another cup of coffee. I took off.

I wish I'd stuck around long enough to at least begin my afternoon ride with him, because I went off in the wrong direction the minute I got back on my bike and spent the lion's share of the afternoon trying to get myself back on track.

That night I made it as far as Lake George, Michigan. With no motel around, I was forced to camp and to hope my back would survive another night on the ground. Though the trip had whipped me into shape, my lower back continued to be fickle and overly sensitive to hard earth.

If you've never camped before, let me introduce you to the idea of neighbor risk. When you choose a tent site, you should be aware that anyone, and I mean *anyone*, can drop in and set up right next to you. That includes carnies, ex-cons, drunks, people who think they are better than everyone else, young couples, perverts, old couples, nonunion guys, rednecks, hillbillies, hikers, and—worst of all by far—middle-aged cyclists like me.

I looked at the campground and figured what the hell; it had been a while since I'd popped the tent, and given the fact that I'd lugged it for nearly three thousand miles, why not use it on the eve of my eighth week on the road? "Time to keep it real and get back to basics," I thought to myself as I reluctantly made a left turn into the Lake George Campground, which had a sign out front promising access to a pool, Wi-Fi, hot dogs and hamburgers.

Lake George Campsites were…awesome! Clean, quiet, and well maintained—a welcome sight after sixty-five miles of riding. While there I saw only two other campers and the place was nearly 'skeeter-free. The showers were great and the food was filling. Even with more than thirty campers, trailers, and RVs there, the loudest sounds came from the songbirds. It was the best camping spot on the trip except for Steelhead State Park way back in Washington State. My neighbor risk was a non-factor: no neighbors showed up.

The following day, a Friday, saw me outside and upright on a bike for only forty-eight miles or so. I got the Fun Mover as far as Midland, Michigan. Just after getting there, I got lost again. It was embarrassing if nothing else, but I eventually met a local guy passing by in a Jeep. He'd slowed down to give me the thumbs up sign. He had two bikes on the back of his Jeep and a "Share the Road" bumper sticker. He was obviously a regular biker and he assured me that the route he'd suggested to get me back on course was bike friendly and direct.

I followed his directions to the letter with every intention of returning to my mapped route and adding maybe another twenty-five or thirty miles to the odometer before the sun set, but as soon as the Sleep Inn came into view, I knew my riding day was over. The Sleep Inn called my name, and I answered by sliding my charge card and driver's license across the counter to the woman behind it. She recognized my old Guilford, Connecticut address on my license and said she'd once hailed from Newtown, Connecticut, a town thirty miles or so away. Before leaving Newtown and moving to Midland, Michigan in 1972, she had been one of the very first graduates from the then-brand-new Sandy Hook Elementary School, which on December 12, 2012, became the scene of one of the worst school shooting massacres in our nation's history. I have never been able to get over the horror of that day—and never will. Those poor little kids and those teachers who tried to save them break my heart every time I think of the horror of that day.

The desk clerk suggested a restaurant a few doors down, and her recommendation was spot on. After polishing off the soup, the salad, the cod special, and many refills of pure cold water at Shirlene's Cuisine, I did the zombie walk back to my room on the first floor of the Sleep Inn, slipped into bed, and slept like a baby. The Motel Pussy hadn't slept very well in his tent the previous night, so there was some catching up to do. Man, that bed felt great in comparison to the ground I'd slept on at the Lake George Camp*ground*.

After my night's rest at the Sleep Inn, a hotel that in my opinion had lived up to its name, I got going at around ten o'clock.

Small farms dotted the route, but of all the bucolic sights seen that day, there was a clear standout. It was an anomaly, actually. Some guy had stolen a traffic variable message sign, reprogrammed it, and stuck it out in his front yard announcing, "ALIANS ARE HERE."

I guess all the spell checkers had left town.

The sign flashed the news in orange dots that we, the human race, are not alone. Astonished, I took a look around at the barn across the street and another one on the other side of the road. I was in the middle of nowhere, yet there was a guy with news that all humanity should certainly know about, and all he could do was put up a stolen sign in his front yard, misspell the news flash, and turn it toward a fallow field and an empty barn across the street? That's like putting a sign out that says, "Cancer Cure Here" in ten feet of water.

After taking a picture of the sign, I lingered a moment until I realized that with my bike helmet on, I might have passed for an endoparasitoid extraterrestrial looking for a host. My yellow-lensed wraparound sunglasses gave my eyes an almond-like shape. And my legs? Well, everyone who is anyone knows for a fact that all the aliens in sci-fi movies have long skinny legs. Why? Because all they do is sit around on their interstellar butts in space ships and fly at light speed to and from different galaxies. There isn't any gravity in space, so space dwellers tend to lose muscle tone quickly. What's the bottom line here? Well any moviegoer such as myself knows that alien technology is so advanced that aliens become horribly out of shape because they don't get enough exercise. Aliens don't work-out, and they don't have gym memberships. They don't even walk much unless it is towards the end of the movie when they get up out of their spaceship driver's seats and walk down a UFO ramp that always seems to have a fog machine and a bluish light source behind them. They walk the few steps it takes to collect any and all Earthlings who want to go on a one-way trip with them. Then they turn around and walk back up the ramp and into the fog to the sound of rousing music as the director rolls credits.

I got the hell out of there as fast as I could, fearing the home-owner might mistake me for another alien and lock me in his basement, determined to give me the same sort of probing the "alians" surely had once given him.

Fifty-two miles later with the wind against me the whole time, I arrived at a town called Frankenmuth, Michigan. I'll tell you: I was beginning to seriously doubt the thinking behind the theory that if you head east you are going in the same direction as the prevailing winds. I was calling bullshit on that one: it seemed to me that the wind had been against me 90% of the time.

A tourist trap, Frankenmuth was overflowing with visitors navigating sidewalks and checking out all the shops and themed restaurants.

I found vacancy at a huge inn called the Bavarian Lodge Inn after crossing a covered bridge, "the only one in Meecha-gahn, and, as I understand it, one of the only three in the world," the desk clerk incorrectly told me at check-in. I told him there are more than three covered bridges in the world (I know because I've been on at least twice that many myself), but the guy was firm in defense of his ignorance.

"No, there are only three covered bridges in the world and we have one of them. Will you be staying long?"

"In the whole wide world?" I asked.

"Far as I know. Will you be staying long?"

"Dude, there are more than that."

"No, there's only three and we have 33% of all of them in the world right here in little old Michigan."

There was a long line of supersized sunburned folks behind me, so I didn't want to make too big a deal about my deep knowledge of covered bridge counts across the globe that flew in the face of the desk clerk's limited worldview. I so wanted to tell the guy about other things out there in the world like Brazil, bull elephants, fetish weekends, sailboats, the Great Barrier Reef, and the South Pole, but I hadn't the time. Other to-be guests behind me wanted to check in and eat more food, same as me. I shrugged my shoulders and mumbled, "Dude, I've been to, like, six or seven different ones. There is a state called Vermont that has an assload of the freaking things, but whatevs."

I slid the 3.37 x 2.125 inch plastic card with my name on it his way. After showering me with a whole bunch of fake "Nice to have you's", "Enjoy your stay's", and "Just call the front desk for anything you needs," he gave me my card back and a room for the night.

Before I was out of earshot I heard him say, "Total of three." I whipped my head around to deliver a sneer his way. I thought he was trying to get the last word in on the covered bridge debate, but no. The family he was checking in had three people in it.

I'll never really know for sure.

The Bavarian Lodge Inn was built in 1985, and the covered bridge leading up to it was built in 1980 or so. The whole place was engineered to look like a chalet town in Germany. (Contrary to what the folks in line behind me at check-in believed, you don't pronounce the *t* in *chalet*). Most of the village businesses had German spelling on their outdoor signage with places like the coffee house spelled 'koffee haus.' Oompah-loompah music was piped through speakers on Main Street, and all the tourists seemed happy to part ways with their money. What a racket.

I loved every minute of it.

It was a nice experience, kind of how Walt Disney might do 'Walt Germany World' without any WWII references. There were at least six "bier gartens" that came complete with busty Fräuleins dressed in white blouses and flowing skirts. Those beer maidens delivered mugs of cold beer along with their come hither smiles. I didn't fall for their cute "Yahs" and "Danka shines." Nor did I fall for the flirting that suggested under the right conditions; they might be actually interested in talking to me as a person, not just as a customer. I knew those "certain conditions" for me, personally, would include Armageddon, hell freezing over, and when pigs flew.

But hey, a small chance is still a chance, right?

Anyway, they delivered the beer with a wink, and I accepted the beer with a smile.

"Alians," Germantown, cold beers, music, and, yes, once again, clean laundry—another typical day of variety on two wheels.

The next day I left Frankenmuth via one of the only nine hundred million covered bridges in the world and rode for six hours and twenty-one minutes, with an average speed of 16.2 miles per hour. I had to wait until the end of the day before anything really exciting happened.

It finally did when I found the River Crab Blue Water Inn. As luck would have it, I got the last room in the place. Closing the book on a 104.2-mile day provided me with a huge sigh of relief. Could I have rallied and pushed on further to the other end of St. Clair, Michigan for the next available hotel room if I absolutely had to? Sure, no question. I could have dug deep and done another fifteen large the hard way, but I didn't have to call on my reserve power. My room key was my finish line.

Crusty with salt, I stood under the shower and washed the day's grime, stink, and sweat off my body and my clothing. I was my own washing machine, sudsing up and rinsing out my riding clothes and leaving them to dry on the towel rack. What a pleasure it is to have access to clean running water at the turn of a knob.

Water is awesome. I hope I never run out of it.

I got up and started riding again that next day, a Sunday.

The best part of my Sunday breakfast was the Frosted Flakes, as the eggs and bratwurst were subpar.

My next few hours in the saddle were, like the previous day, fairly uneventful. During my ride, I passed the birthplace of the motor home, appropriately named Brown City, Michigan. I also came across a dune buggy for sale. I hadn't seen one of those vehicles in decades. The Monkeys used to drive one on TV, as did the Banana Splits. My passion for the dune buggy had waned over the years, progressing from "I must have one! I'll mow the lawn every day, Dad, come on!" to "Holy crap, that's a dune buggy. Remember those death traps?"

Funny how time changes everything. "Different stages for different ages," right?

I got lost (again) and sought directions from a guy who gave me permission to take his picture. He was sitting outside a liquor store in a car that had more rust on it than the city of Detroit itself. While he enjoyed his cigarette, he was able to confirm to me that I was, indeed, on North Range Road heading south toward Yankee Road, about ten miles away. He said he spent his days smoking cigarettes and playing Keno because he liked smoking and loved his chances.

"Of all the lotteries out there, Keno is the one that pays out the most."

When I put a camera in front of him, he stopped smiling. I think he was self-conscious about the state of his teeth. Too bad: teeth or no teeth, he had a big, winning smile on his face when I first spoke to him, and for a guy in a rusty car who was a self-confessed "outta shape smoker who would die if I had to pedal a bike as far as you did so far today," he was more happy and content than a lot of tri-athletes I've met. I wish I hadn't thrown a camera barrier between us: he reduced the beam of his smile as soon as I asked to take the photo. What makes for a great smile? Heart, and he had plenty of it.

A little later in the day and for the first time in my life I had the opportunity to tell people that I got into Yale. I did. I got into Yale, (Michigan) that very day.

After arriving at Yale (I love saying that), I went to a gas station convenience store for some water (surprise, surprise), and another biker whizzed in behind me, parking his "beater bike"— his words—next to mine. Its pilot was a seventy-one-year-old guy wearing a flannel shirt and long black pants with boots in a ninety-four degree heat. He said he was "into biking too," and he stuck to me like glue.

Terrific. My first bike stalker. I wasn't being dismissive of him, just cautious.

I held the door open for him and we both stepped inside and were enveloped in the welcome cool of air conditioning. The young woman with the nose ring at the cash register knew the old guy as a regular and greeted him with a half wave and a "S'up Harry?"

Harry followed me around the store like I was a movie idol on a visit to a Girl Scout camp. It turned out the guy was as sharp as a tack and had the ability to quickly and accurately calculate time and distance in his head. He was able to figure out my days-on-the-road count after I gave him my start date of May 16, and he figured my age in a flash when, at his request, I gave him my birth year. He told me that in 1966, "three years after they shot Mr. Kennedy," he'd pedaled from his hometown of Yale (where we were standing) to Portland, Maine (where I was heading), and back, "on a ten-speed."

He continued: "I have a really nice bike at home in my living room. They call it a Specialized. It has twenty-one gears. How many gears does your bike have?"

"God, I don't even know, twenty-seven, I think, but the gear count has no real bearing on quality of the bike... Get it?" I asked. "The gear count has no *wheel bearing* on the quality of the bike? Punny, right?" When I saw the joke went nowhere, I apologized. "Sorry, I have a pun problem. I can't help myself," I said.

He cocked his head to the right and looked at me with a furled brow like I was some kind of a nut-job. Maybe I was: it was hotter than hell outside and I was probably a little punch drunk from the heat.

My "humor" sailed right over his head and out the door. The old man had completely missed it.

I'll tell you one thing, though: not much else had slipped by him. A confirmed bachelor, he'd worked very hard, saved his money, and invested it wisely over the years. He was the largest landowner in town. He owned fifteen houses in Yale alone. He also had ten acres on Lake Huron, had an apartment complex in Vassar, Michigan, and had just bought a trailer park outside of Yale. And those were just the investments and businesses he owned and operated that I could remember him mentioning. I didn't ask for any of the information he offered.

I confirmed it later with the cashier. The old guy was legit. "He owns the town. Lucky for us he's a good man."

Maybe it was me who'd missed the point. I was way, way behind him in the real estate game.

I asked him why he wore a flannel shirt on such a hot day.

"I do well with heat. It doesn't bother me. I was a distance runner in high school."

He said he ran the fastest mile in the state of Michigan in 1961 and that his record stood for a few years, but he knew when he set it was bound to be broken. "It was a record after all. I broke someone else's and then some else broke mine. That's what happens."

My new buddy first came across as an old bike groupie who was one brown bag away from being mistaken for an unshaven bum on a stolen Diamondback bicycle. He first put me off when he hovered about and fired questions my way, but his intentions were good. He was just friendly and maybe a bit lonely, but his brain shone bright as a star if you listened to him for a second. He was another example of someone I was glad to run into.

Our twenty-minute chitchat concluded with a handshake and my hard-selling the old man on the benefits and importance of always wearing a bicycle helmet when riding. I told him people don't bounce as high at seventy-one or at fifty-three as they once did at, say, twenty-one. He smiled and said he had a helmet at home and promised to try it out on his next ride.

"Thanks for talking with me. Have a good day. Be safe," he said before getting on his Diamondback and rolling slowly away past the gas pumps, using the same legs he'd set a state track record with way back when President Kennedy was still alive.

Seventy-one years old and the clear winner of the local game of real-life Monopoly in Yale, Michigan, the man was thanking *me* for taking the time to talk with *him*. Imagine that. *I* was the one who was thankful.

I have to add something to a statement I said earlier: Water *and* good company are *two* things I hope I never run out of.

Chapter Twenty-One

It's A Small World After All

The morning I was to take a short ferry ride into Canada passed without me leaving my hotel room. I was futzing around with emails and phone calls in-between catnapping and eating breakfast. I took an early lunch before checking out of the motel. It was somewhat atypical behavior for me in that I had unknowingly reached the point of being an unwelcomed guest. My unwelcome status was made abundantly clear when the front desk called my room and insisted that a noon checkout meant a noon checkout, "no ifs, ands, or buts."

When someone uses three conjunctions in a row like that, I tend to get the picture pretty quickly.

It was an atypical morning for another reason a well—a good reason this time—as it included an "It's a Small World after All" story that you might be interested to hear about. So hand over your ticket, jump in the boat, and enjoy the ride. And sure, feel free to go ahead and sing the song to yourself from this point going forward.

Here's what happened. Ed Dillon was a classmate of mine freshman year at Holy Cross and I hadn't seen or heard from him in over thirty years. He disappeared a couple of weeks into our sophomore year and never came back. I hadn't seen him since.

Low and behold that very morning I'd received word from Ed that he was still alive and well and living in LA with his wife and a couple of kids. He'd reached out to me after learning about my travels. I was in his home state of Michigan, so maybe that was it. Regardless of his motivation, it was good to hear from him. I thanked him for his "keep riding'" well wishes.

It was ten past noon by the time I shut my computer down and left the room. Off I went in an attempt to get back on the Bridge to Bay Trail that would lead me to the ferry to Canada. I was fuzzy on how to backtrack to the B to B Trail. I remembered leaving the trail the night before to cut through a subdivision so I could to get to the hotel, but I wasn't sure which subdivision it was: there were several and, frankly, they all looked alike to me.

I took a stab at one of them and lost. I was in the wrong place. I turned around and was making my way out and back to the main road when I saw a guy on a bike standing at the base of his driveway. He looked like he was about to leave for a ride, so I figured he knew his way around. I accosted him and asked how to get to the Bridge to Bay Trail.

He knew exactly where I wanted to go and gave me two options on how to get there. The first was to cut through some dense woods at the end of his road or go back out the way I came and take the next right into "The Meadows at the Pines" subdivision. That would land me back to the trail "in short order" he said.

"Oh, I see what you did," he explained. "You took one right too soon. Hey, maybe we can show you. We're about to head out for a ride ourselves. Where are you heading today?" he asked.

When I told him I was headed toward the ferry to Canada, he offered to escort me directly to it. My timing was perfect as he was just about to go on a training ride with his wife. If I arrived a minute later, they'd have left, and if I arrived a minute sooner, he would not have been standing at the end of his driveway.

His wife rolled down the driveway to join us.

"The Bridge to Bay Trail will get you to the ferry, but I have a nicer ride that will get you there in shorter time," he said.

"You had me at 'shorter.' Let's roll," I replied.

"By the way, how long have you been on the road?" the guy asked, looking over my saddlebags. "You from around here?"

"No way, man," I replied. "I'm from back east. I'm on a forty-two-hundred-mile bike ride to the Atlantic Ocean. I haven't seen a familiar face since I kissed my wife goodbye back in the middle of May."

"No way! That is awesome. I'd love to do that," he admitted.

His wife cleared her throat.

"I mean the bike part, honey," he sheepishly said, playing it up.

We all laughed.

After names were exchanged, I joined them for a ride to the ferry. We rode along and talked some more. I answered their questions about my trip. It turned out Dave was a radiologist, US Army (ret.), and a former denizen of at least a dozen states during his days in military service. Laurie was a nurse. They got married and eventually settled into life in St. Clair to raise their kids.

It was my turn. I told them a little bit about my boring self.

"I grew up in Boston."

"Hey, Boston. I love Boston. That's where I met Laurie," Dave said. "She was dating another guy when I came along and swept her off her feet. It was kind of random: she'd moved to Boston to be with her boyfriend. I was posted there for six months of training. Weird to think about, but if it wasn't for that guy and that post, we wouldn't have been in Boston to meet each other."

We were riding in single file, with Dave leading, me in the middle, and Laurie in back. It was tough for Laurie to remain within earshot during parts our conversation because the traffic and the thin shoulder prevented tight grouping.

After a few minutes, we got to the "Where did you go to school?" part of the conversation. I told Dave I graduated from Holy Cross in 1984. Laurie just happened to be close enough to hear me say the words "Holy Cross."

She took notice and asked me two questions, one of them rhetorical.

"Wait," she said, "You went to Holy Cross? Do you know a guy named Ed Dillon?"

You could have knocked me over with a feather.

"Do I know Ed Dillon? Yeah, I know Ed Dillon," I said. "I just texted him about forty-five minutes ago. I hadn't heard from the guy in thirty plus years and now twice in a day? You gotta be kidding me. Really?"

I was floored.

"Laurie," I asked, "How in the hell do you know Ed Dillon?"

(Cue the music: "It's a Small World after All...")

Without answering me, Laurie swung in for the kicker: "Honey," she asked her husband, "do you know who Ed Dillon is?"

"Nope. Never heard of him."

"Ed Dillon is the guy I moved to Boston for. I was going out with him when I met you. He was my last boyfriend."

Unreal! I overstayed my welcome at the motel because I was busy catching up on email and social media with, among other people, an old buddy I hadn't heard from in many years. Then I run into said old buddy's girlfriend less than an hour later after making a wrong turn? Dave and Laurie were off their schedules, too, when I happened by to ask directions.

Super coincidence. It turned out that Dave grew up in Rye, New York, the very town I'd moved to when I was eighteen years old. Though we'd never met before, Dave and I had twenty something friends in common. One of my brothers had a huge crush on one of Dave's sisters. Dave knew my wife's first boyfriend in middle school...and on and on. I was in Bizarre-Oh-World. I knew his wife's last boyfriend and he knew my wife's first boyfriend. It was very strange. I took their picture. Even now, I still shake my head at the sheer coincidence of it.

It *is* a small world after all.

I arrived in plenty of time for me to catch the next ferry. Dave and Laurie went on their way, as happy to make the small world connection as I was.

I caught the ferry into Canada and discovered a new pet peeve of mine. Why *Canada* we all get along? Seriously. If you want two countries to intermingle more, why not make it less expensive to call across the border? Why such big phone bills in such a small world? I spoke to my sister in Toronto and it cost like a million dollars to make the call.

I completed that day's ride in four hours flat, with a bike-com-puter-calculated average speed of 14.7 miles per hour. I covered sixty miles—even more distance if you include the ferry ride that took me from my home country (that's the good old' US of A, by God) to a quaint little country north of us that is filled with simply charming people who know how to play great hockey. It is called Canada and it is pronounced 'Canada', if that helps you in any way. Fortunately, I had the chance to brush up on the language and local customs and culture, so, by the time I stepped off the ferry and slipped into general population, I blended in to the point of being indistinguishable from the natives in the region. To this very day the most deeply covert foreign operatives can't come close to my skills and abilities to blend in. The spy guys want agents with no distinguishable facial characteristics, guys who people don't remember ever seeing. Average height, average weight, average looks. The best of the best operatives never stand out. You could meet one at a party, talk for fifteen minutes, and the very next day miss him in a police lineup. Operatives such as myself must be nearly completely forgettable. They must blend into the background.

I'm their type: I'm *built* forgettable.

So, by the time I stepped onto Canadian soil after my short twenty minute ferry ride, I had fully assimilated and was ready for my interview with the border patrol officer.

The guy was jacked. He was clean-shaven and had, as far as I could tell, the biggest biceps in all of Ottawa and had huge pectoral muscles that looked like they wanted to bust out from beneath his green flak jacket. I never understood why some people insist on lifting themselves past all reasonable measures of proportion. Mr. Border Patrol seemed like a nice enough guy, but his build made him look like a Ken doll that wanted to punch out G. I. Joe with the Kung Fu grip. Or, maybe all he wanted to do was devote his life to the dance. I wondered. If I turned up "I Will Survive" really loud on a boom box, would this guy bust out a move and tell the lady behind me that she had been "a bad, bad girl, a naughty girl who needed to be spanked?"

With no ready access to a sound system, I couldn't test my theory.

He saw my approach.

"Great," he probably thought as I came closer. "Some wimp on a bike wants in."

As a spindle-legged bicyclist, I was well aware that I registered as an exceptionally low threat level. Forget Color Level Red or

Yellow: I guessed my threat level color was more like "Lavender" or "Sea Mist" and I suppose I ranked somewhere between *Mime* and *Music-theater major* on the international terrorist threat level chart.

When he asked me "Do you have any firearms, ammunition, explosives, or chemical weapons, including Mace, something, something, or pepper spray?"

I surprised Barry the Border Barron when I replied, "Yes."

Wow. I went from being a middle-aged biker nobody to a Person of Interest pretty quickly.

He repeated the question to be sure I'd heard him right.

"Yes," I repeated, sensing somehow that I'd put myself mortal danger. I noticed the border patrol guard's right hand had moved, ever so slightly when I made a "sudden movement" and reached into my bike handlebar bag to show him the Mace I bought after the dog attack. His right hand came to rest on the butt of his Glock 9000.

"Yes. I have some Mace."

It turns out Mace is contraband and illegal to bring into Canada. For just a second there, it looked like he wanted to pop a couple of caps into my forehead, flatten the Fun Mover's tires, and toss us both into the slowly moving river we'd just been ferried across. I couldn't hear it, but there must have been a voice in his head that shouted "Stand down!" in time before he drew his weapon and ended my ride.

He took my passport and the pink lipstick case/spray vial of Mace mumbled something about a confiscation form I'd have to sign.

By the way, I knew it was illegal to bring Mace into Canada, having made that same mistake years prior—the only other time I owned Mace, purchased for the same reasons. I offered it up not that I wanted the border drama as much as I wanted to be certain the chemical agent was disposed of properly. I would miss the false sense of security that twelve-dollar sleeve of Mace had provided, but if I had to get rid of it, I'd rather hand it over to a responsible adult than have it fall into the wrong hands or pollute some landfill.

Oh and the ferry ride? It was short and sweet, much like the story I heard onboard from its owner/operator, Lowell. Lowell was an eighty-six year old man with the exclusive rights to shuttle people back and forth between the US and Canada on the Ludington ferry. Lowell's first wife had passed away back in 1998, "just sitting in her favorite chair up at the cabin." He got married a second time a few years back, this time to a Puerto Rican woman whom he loved very much as well.

I wasn't sure why, but Lowell reassured me, "It's not a sleepover thing. It is a real marriage."

Chapter Twenty-Two

THE MAN DOWN MANS UP

Back in the day in Ancient Rome, they told Caesar to Beware the Ides. I'm no Caesar, but I should have listened up. About twelve miles into my riding day on July 15th I crashed on a flat road with little wind, dry conditions, and fair skies. Pilot error was the cause of my single vehicle pileup.

How did it happen? Stupidity, laziness, and shortsightedness all got together under one roof—my skullcap, that's how. In short, human error was to blame.

I was rolling along in the great wide open between two fields at about twenty miles per hour on a two lane road with a soft shoulder and light traffic minding my own business when my right front saddlebag bounced free of one of the two mounts that affix it to the front rack. Being too lazy to come to a complete stop (and lose all that momentum), dismount, and put said front saddlebag back into place, I stupidly thought I'd try to fix the problem while still underway. So I unclipped my right foot from the pedal and tried to kick my right saddlebag back in place as I was rolling, my left leg still locked in and cranking.

The first kick didn't work, so I tried again. On my second attempt, a mighty kick, my right foot hit the saddlebag, deflected left and into the path of the spinning spokes. My right foot was force fed through the front fork when the cleat got caught in the spokes. That sent me over the handlebars, ass over teakettle.

Didn't see that coming.

I crash-landed after sailing over the handlebars in classic "endo" fashion. All four saddlebags came off the bike. Two of them opened on impact and spewed their contents all over the road. The front tire, my helmet, my left hand and left knee took most of the impact. I must have been out for a moment or two because the next thing I remembered was opening my eyes to blue sky.

I knew exactly what had happened—I'd kissed the pavement doing twenty miles an hour. Darwinism was at work here: I was an idiot for trying to kick a pannier back into place.

I wasn't sure if I was seriously hurt or not, so I did a systems check; I wiggled my fingers and toes. Having asked twenty things to wiggle, I was happy to see that all twenty things wiggled back. Next thing to watch for was oncoming traffic. I sort of sat up and looked both ways. There was no traffic at that moment, so I lay back down and continued to catch my breath.

There I was, splayed on the asphalt, arms and legs outstretched like da Vinci's Vitruvian Man or like some idiot trying to make snow angels on the pavement in the middle of July with a bike still attached to his left foot. I had been so stupid. All I had to do was stop for a second and fix the mounting of that right front saddlebag. But no, I had to give being clever a go.

Well, I suppose on the bright side I learned there is no graceful way to do an endo while your left foot is clipped onto in and your right foot is stuck in the front fork—not that I was curious.

I assessed damage: the front wheel was a pretzel, four spokes gone, and the tire flat. I wasn't going anywhere. I had no idea where the closest bike shop was or how I'd get to it. My hand began to hurt as the shock wore off. I was starting to think the accident might cost me a few days' riding time and some inconvenience.

Boy, was I in for a surprise. As I lay sprawled and blinking, a trail angel came out of nowhere and to my rescue. The driver of the very first car on the scene pulled over and got out. She helped me off the pavement and gathered my stuff up off the road. Her name was Penny and she was from Heaven. She took time on her day off to help me out. She insisted we load my bike and gear into the back of her brand new car. A real life saver, she drove me forty minutes out of her way to a bike shop where, for twenty bucks, the spokes were replaced and the wheel trued and the flat repaired in less time it took for us to finish our "thank you for not running me over and helping me instead" lunch. The Fun Mover, hand built of steel in New Market, NH, suffered no structural damage. Before I knew it, I was back in the saddle at the scene of the accident a couple of hours later with a sore left hand, a bruised shoulder, a bloody knee, a hurt ego, a scratched helmet, and a new friend.

Both my bike and I were good to go, so off we went.

I logged another fifty miles before the day was out. I fell down, got up, fixed the bike, and just kept pedaling.

The Ides of July ended with me in my tent. My left hand, head, left shoulder, and right knee were beginning to complain about things after dinner, so I popped a couple Aleve for dessert and called it a day. I thought it was going to be lights out the whole night on account of all the fun I'd had that day with the accident and all, but I was proven wrong again.

God only knew what time it was, but at some point that night, I woke up to the sound of sniffing noises. I immediately put my echolocation skills to work and after a moment or two of triangulation, I was able to detect a nose not six inches from my face just outside my tent. I considered any nose six inches from mine an invasion of my personal space. Think about it in terms of your own nose; what other noses have come that close to your nose in your lifetime? Only friendly ones, I'll bet.

Said nose was no higher than a foot off the ground and attached to...what? Was it a massive man-eating grizzly stooping in low for a sniff? Some sicko serial killer named The Nose, famous for sniffing his victims before slitting their throats? Or was it just a baby raccoon or some curious and hungry opossum? It was most likely the latter, of course, but being awoken from a sound slumber by some creature great or small was unnerving.

"*What in the hell is that?*" I thought. I lay stock-still just to be sure I hadn't been nightmaring the whole thing. Sure enough, I got confirmation and a precise location when a second, then third sniff was heard.

I weighed my options. I was a busted up old dude already flat on the ground and enclosed in rip stop nylon that rendered me just as blind as a bat to the outside world. I was all of one hundred and sixty pounds with no upper body strength to speak of. I was a midnight snack for a surprising number of nocturnal carnivores if you thought about it. Yet still, I was the most dangerous animal the world has ever known: I was a cornered man.

Before I thought much more about it, I blurted out a heartfelt "Oh, come *on!* Are you fucking kidding me?"

The sheer aggravation of being woken up by some nocturnal pest fueled my consternation. Presto! The mystery guest beat a quick retreat, scratching and scampering its way back into the void, undoubtedly with a "tale of terror from a talking tent" story to share with the folks at home. I was back to sleep in about a New York minute because I was such a tough guy at that point. (Actually, I was too tired to be worried.)

The next morning, I was up and out early (7:00 a.m.), and if you'd met me on the way back from the campsite washroom like a father and son pair had, you, too, might have been just as unaware as they were that only a few hours before, I had faced near-certain death for the second time in a month and had lived to tell about it.

I rode three wake-the-hell-up miles through some chilly ass air to get to the nearest Canadian equivalent of a VFW hall for some breakfast. (Near death experiences make me want to swear more, sorry.) That air sure got my eyes open and my blood flowing. The Canadian equivalent of a V.F.W. hall is called a "Royal Legion Hall", which, to me, sounds regal with the word "royal" in it.

Inside, they were serving love on a plate, and I happened to be looking for some, so I was a very happy customer. My breakfast cost five bucks and included a condiment selection of seven homemade jellies and jams that were available at each table. I had a second helping of toast and I taste tested all of the jellies and jams. It was a tie between the red raspberry and a green jelly from a berry I didn't get the name of.

After that intake of wholesome nutrition, I wandered down by the water to make a phone call home and look at an old submarine that was once used in war, but before I could dial came a voice out of the blue. I heard someone say, "Hey man, you are one good-looking' fella."

I looked around and instantly recognized the fellow bicycle tourist I'd shared a lunch with a week or so before. It was Pete, the ex-military guy on the Co-Motion bike, giving me a hard time. It was only about nine o'clock in the morning, but he was already twenty-seven miles into his riding day and on the lookout for a breakfast spot. I boomeranged it straight back to the Royal Legion Hall with him in tow. While he was chowing down on the stellar grub, I stepped outside with a cup of coffee to sit and enjoy the splendid sunshine.

After completing a quick phone call home, I ended up talking a while with a woman who was dying of cancer. She was sitting nearby in a wicker rocking chair in the morning sunshine outside the Hall, reading a book, waiting on a friend. A devoted chain smoker for thirty years, she had suffered a cancer scare that put her off cigarettes for two years. But, by the time I met her, she had recently learned the cancer bout she thought she'd won two years prior was just the first round in a fight to the death.

"I beat the cancer, but I had to get this knee replaced last year. I got an infection in the operating room and that took nine months to heal. Nine months! The surgeon was a doctor who couldn't decide to shit or make putty. It's all his fault. The infection weakened me and the cancer has returned to do me in."

She had another appointment with an endocrinologist later that very day who would deliver his thoughts on her chances. She wasn't kidding herself, though. She was realistic about her chances and well aware of her grave condition. She figured the second doctor would tell her there was nothing left to do.

She lit a cigarette at the end of her story.

"I thought you said you quit," I asked, and then quickly wished I hadn't. Why would I ask that? She'd just told me she was dying of cancer. Sometimes your author was just as stupid off the bike as he was on it. It was none of my damn business, but she was kind and answered me anyway.

"I did, but what's the use? What's this thing gonna do, kill me?" she asked me holding her cigarette up as Exhibit A in a watertight argument so sound it wouldn't go to trial. She knew she was a goner and smoking gave her pleasure, so why not spark up another cancer stick for old times' sake? She knew she wouldn't live long enough to see one minute of 2016.

"Smoke 'em if you got 'em," she said, and then coughed for a good minute at her own line.

Her grandson showed up to join her for breakfast, and her face lit up brighter than the match she'd used to light her cigarette.

"Here he is!" She closed the book on her lap and waved as her "grandbaby" limped across the parking lot towards us.

She turned to me and whispered, "He's so smart and so good-looking, too! I'm going to try my best to be there when he graduates high school next year. He's only limping 'cuz he's broke his ankle like six times. He's an athlete."

Well, she didn't say he was a *good* athlete…

She introduced him to me and they both limped their way inside. Pete emerged from his breakfast and we finished our coffees in the sun.

I joined Pete on an all-day ride that ended at a nice camping spot on the water for the going rate of a mere five bucks Canadian. Over the course of the week since I'd last seen Pete, he had met and paired up with a mother/daughter duo from New Hampshire who were also riding east on the Northern Tier. He had made arrangements to meet them at the waterside campgrounds we found ourselves in. Mother and daughter eventually showed up at our camp with a tale worth telling. What a pair they were, though.

I'll get to them first and their tale second.

I might have this all wrong, but this is the way I understood it: the daughter wanted to ride the Northern Tier before veterinary school got started in the fall, but, like me, the daughter had experienced difficulties finding someone else willing (or able) to join her on the ride. *Unlike* me, there may have been more reasons than calendar conflicts that factored into her challenges in sourcing companionship.

As her daughter's departure date approached, the mother's anxiety mounted. Something had to give, and it did—Mom threw her hat into the ring and declared that if her daughter was going to go, she was going to go with her—not because mom wanted to ride, but because she didn't want her daughter to go it alone. Mom, a classic type A personality was like any other self-respecting control freak that helicopters themselves into other people's business.

They were an interesting pair to say the least. To start with, only the daughter, the faster rider of the two, had a map. She would stop at every single waypoint across the United States and wait for her mother to catch up. On long stretches the daughter would end up waiting hours by the side of the road for the rendezvous. The longest wait period so far had been *four and a half hours*! Can you imagine waiting all those hours for a slowpoke that insisted on not having his or her own set of maps?

In the grand scheme of things, bike maps are inexpensive and readily available, so I wondered why each of them wouldn't prefer to have their own set. Why was helicopter mom was so reluctant to navigate? I mean for a measly hundred bucks her daughter would not have to wait at every waypoint. They could arrange to meet somewhere at the end of each day, much like they'd arranged to met with Pete that night. There were a million reasons why two riders armed with two maps are better than a pair of riders with only one map. It took me a minute, but the answer came: mom didn't want a map because if she had one, her daughter would be able to make her way in the world, free of her mother's dependency. Not having a map meant the mom would remain coupled with the daughter. I think it was a control thing. Also, I think mom lived in New York, so there was that little tidbit of info. From where I stood it looked like there was a better-than-good chance mom wasn't keen on losing things like control.

The big wow for me was when I learned Mommy Dearest had developed saddle sores after I'd asked her why she had an extra saddle.

"That's not an extra saddle," she informed me. "I use them both. I switch them every couple of days to relieve the pain. One saddle hits me here," she said, pointing to a specific point on her backside, "and the other one hits me right here, slightly higher and further back. Each seat gives me relief in different spots. I have lots of cream and some duct tape. So what happens is, I lube up every morning, bend over, and have my daughter help me duct tape the open sores on my ass, one on each side. I slather more Butt Butt'r everywhere, then put my extra thick chamois shorts on and go."

I paused. Sometimes my ability to picture things in my mind was a burden, not a gift.

"How long have you been switching seats to relieve saddle sore pain?" I asked her.

"About three thousand miles." She called over to her daughter who had her nose in a book, reading alone a few picnic tables away. Her daughter was just keeping herself busy while her mother finished cooking dinner.

"Honey, it has been about three thousand miles since we left that bike shop in Washington, right sweetie?"

"Yeah," her daughter droned. Her eyes never left the page of her book as she replied.

They had a low simmering "I hate you—Well, I fucking hate you more" type of thing going on. They hadn't taken a single zero their entire trip, maybe because neither wanted to spend a day together with nothing to do but rest and get on each other's nerves. I'm just spitballin' it here, so I might have read it all wrong. I just didn't understand those women, but I'm a guy, so there is that, too.

Strange as the whole thing seemed to me, the mom was able to laugh about her saddle sores, and Daughter didn't seem to mind ignoring all of our company. Reality is stranger than fiction. If I had to make a Sophie's Choice between the two of them, I'd give the mom the nod. I can't stand helicopter parents any more than you can, but I appreciated Mommy Dearest's iron-will and her concern for her daughter's safety; both had kept her riding through all that saddle sore pain, which was pretty impressive.

From what I saw, the biggest pain in the ass the mom had to deal with was the daughter, not the duct tape.

And as far as the daughter went, I thought she'd demonstrated a high level of self-awareness by opting to pursue a career as a veterinarian, as her future clients would be unable to provide the a poor bedside manner review that the daughter would most certainly earn.

Wait. A goat could provide a review of her bedside manner:

"So, Mr. Goat how was your visit with the vet?"

"Baaaad…Baaaad."

A goat joke. In a bike book. Who knew? Ok, enough of that. (I do have one more that is really funny. Ask me to tell you it if we ever come across each other.)

And now, the tale.

Earlier that day, the dynamic duo were biking along together when they'd happened upon the scene of a suicide attempt just moments after a forty-eight-year-old woman had driven head-on into a telephone pole. Her vehicle had hit the utility pole so hard that the impact had knocked down the two other poles adjacent to it.

As the mom pulled the driver from the smoking car, the driver mumbled an explanation for the mishap, "I must have fallen asleep—no, I can't even kill myself right. Let me drive into the woods and die."

"No," said Saddle Sore Mom. "We are going to get you out of this smoking car. You are in shock. Sit over here."

Nothing, repeat, nothing was physically wrong with the driver save for a scratch on the knee and a light concussion. It was a beautiful, sunny day with white clouds sailing above, and some nutjob had tried to off herself.

You just never know. On one hand, I met a lady at breakfast that was dying and wanted to live, and on the other hand, I heard about a woman who was living and wanted to die. The grandma wanted to spend as much time as she could with her seventeen-year-old grandson ("My grand baby who walks with a limp because he's broken his right ankle six times.") The crash dummy wanted to spend time with no one. One had been given a death sentence; the other had tried to engineer one.

Crazy.

I took some pictures of the day's seventy-eight-mile ride. The landscapes were typical of the area. Wide open with slightly rolling hills and small farms one after the other. The wind kicked up before the sun went down. It caused trees to sway as I brushed my teeth and me to stake my tent in the ground after I'd cleaned my dinner dish. Ah, but that wind! It, too, grew tired around ten o'clock and finally settled down for a calm night's sleep, which allowed me to do the same a short time later.

The ladies were late risers so their tents did not get so much as unzipped by the time Pete and I rolled away. Pete's "get up and get at it" time wasn't around seven o'clock—it *was* at seven o'clock—sharp. So off we went at seven oh dam clock in the morning, one of us following a bugle call of Reveille that wasn't there and the other following the guy hearing bugles.

Not fifteen minutes later I ran into a guy who has lived in Port Peacock for twelve years on disability.

"My heart. It's my heart," he explained in a practiced tone while pulling out his mail from the RFD mailbox so he could get his "money from the greedy government." I looked down at the bike he was riding.

"Oh…well, I have to do something every day for my heart," he explained.

Bullshit. His *heart?* The only thing he was closely monitoring was his welfare checks. Apparently fraud is alive and well in Canada. I once heard that the problem with socialism is eventually the socialists run out of spending other people's money.

One other memorable sighting occurred that day during my seventy plus mile ride. I passed a teddy-bear scarecrow, and it struck me as the pinnacle of irony. Why? Well, we all have crosses to bear in Life, right? But the cross in the picture bore an actual *bear* as its cross to bear. And on the flip side, the teddy bear's cross? The teddy bear's cross to bear was an *actual* cross. Ironic, no? Sure, that the cross itself had a cross to bear in its life is understandable, but that specific cross had an actual bear as its cross to bear. And that bear had a literal and figurative cross to bear, which was an actual cross.

To me, irony can't run thicker.

By the way, I checked. The cross was made of iron. That didn't make me cross. It made me happy. I was happy to come across that cross that bore that bear. Even the metal itself was iron-ic.

I may have lost a few of you with those last few lines, but suffice it to say that irony is everywhere. Here I go again: "Bike travel takes you further." Can I hear an 'Amen' from the few of you out there still reading this tome?

I had one more day until I was back into the good old' US of A.

That's 'Merica to you and me, dag nab it.

Chapter Twenty-Three

SOMETHING NEVER DONE BEFORE

Part of the fun of being alive is getting the chance to do something no one has ever done before. It doesn't have to be a big thing or an important thing, just a new thing. Whether it's as dramatic as setting a new world record or as simple as setting the table for dinner in a new way. It doesn't matter. What *does* matter is that everyday every single one of us still breathing has the chance to boldly step into the realm of Never Been Done Before by Anyone, Ever.

I did something new on the morning of July 20th. I'm no hero; I was forced into doing it. You see, while I was in Canada, I ran out of Chamois Butt'r or "Butt Butt'r" as it is otherwise known. Remember Butt Butt'r is the aforementioned salve that keeps the nether regions chafe-free. Running out of it is bad: I needed to replace it *statim*, as I did not want to run the risk of getting saddle sores like Mommy Dearest had. So, after running out of it, I immediately headed to the nearest bike shop—the only one in sixty-seven square miles—only to learn the one tube they had left was *Pour les Femmes* (Chamois Butt'r for Her). It said so right there on the big purple tube of lube.

I held the feminine-hygiene product in my hand and weighed my options. Sure, I needed to be frictionless down below, but I had a built-in reluctance to apply any and all feminine products onto my masculine parts. What the heck would happen down there if I did? Some very serious social, geopolitical, psychological, economic, and religious consequences could result and I didn't want to be the human guinea pig that would have to endure any such possible dire consequences.

"No Chamois Butt'r for guys?" I asked the bike shop guy.

He confirmed my worst fears. "Yah, man, this is the last tube we got. It says it's made for chicks, but I wouldn't worry none about it."

"Why don't you have any Butt Butt'R for guys?" I asked.

"Good question. We usually do, but last weekend we had a run on ass grease. A bunch of German dudes rolled through town with butt cheeks redder than the planet next to ours. Wait. You know Mars is red, right?"

"Yeah, I do."

"Good. You should have seen 'em, man. Those dudes slinked off their mounts and duck-walked in here single file, and all of them to a man asking for the same thing in their funny accents:

'Vhat kind of bum budda dew yew sell heeyah?' Love those accents, man. Hey, I couldn't blame them. It was hot as hell last weekend. The chaffing index was probably through the roof for those guys, especially when you consider the fact that all of them wore cut off jeans." The sales guy went into his impression again, putting his knees together and covering his groin with both hands. "My private pahts are keeling me!"

He laughed at his own impression. He turned and yelled back to the bike mechanic who was fixing a tire. "Hey, Gerry, how many tubes of ass butter we sell to that flock of German dudes last weekend?"

"Nine or ten, I think," answered Gerry.

The sales guy turned back toward me. "Yeah, nine or ten. We got more ordered but it won't get here 'til Wednesday. All the bicycle-touring companies roll through here and stop at our bike shop for drinks, trail bars, or whatever. It always seems to be them German dudes short on ass grease and long on duck walk by the time they pull up outside. When will they learn to wear bike shorts?"

I was laughing pretty hard at that point when the salesclerk caught himself. "Wait. You're not German, are you?" he asked.

I replied, "No, man. I'm American Irish Catholic from Boston. Go Sox. 'Short on ass grease, long on duck walk'? Dude, I'm taking that with me today. Classic."

So with the Chamois Butt'r *Pour les Femmes* the only tube left, I bought it and stuffed it into my handlebar bag like it was something to be embarrassed about, but I had no real choice. My next stop would have been to drop by a gas station for a quart of 10W40 engine oil. Desperate for something to grease the parts, I swallowed hard and channeled my inner Gloria Steinem. I accepted the fact that I needed to secure the big purple tube of lube that had kept my taint thus far mute the whole trip. After overpaying for that tube, I asked the guy what the hell the difference was between man butt butter and woman butt butter.

"*Pour les Femmes* is Ph balanced," he said.

I expressed my deep concern. I didn't master chemistry or biology in high school, but I believed anything that was expressly made to go onto a vagina and all the parts surrounding it should not go anywhere near the Angry Inch.

"Dude, don't worry," the guy reassured me. "It's probably just some marketing thing. What the hell is Ph anyway?"

"I don't know man. First two letters of the words "phallus phobia.""

Still unsure and just as desperate to grease the parts the following morning, I rolled my eyes and looked away as I applied a liberal amount of Chamois Butt'r Pour Elle onto the Twins, the Kickstand, and Le Grand Egress.

Later I crossed the border into the United States of America, arguably the best country in the world, with butt butter *Pour les Femmes* slathered all over my nether regions.

Bam!

It was my very own never done before by anyone ever moment. In the recorded history of all mankind, crossing into the United States with Chamois Butt'r *Pour les Femmes* greasing what squeaks on a man had never been done. Well, at least it had never been *admitted to being done* before in all of human history... No matter. I was alive and well and doing new things.

But, like all people ahead of their time, I paid for my transgressions. A few hours later, "the changes" began to wash over me. They came subtly at first, then more markedly as the hours wore on. As a result, I decided I had to replace the lady Chamois Butt'r tube as soon as possible.

What changes came over me you ask? Horrible, unspeakable things. I caught myself thinking that cats were actually kind of cute. I became manicure and pedicure curious. I started wondering if my bike shorts made my ass look big. Oh, and I began to see the practical sense of owning one thousand pairs of shoes and caught myself wondering when I'd last heard the song "People" by Barbra Streisand. My nipples hurt, I had a headache, I could feel myself losing the ability to parallel park. I decided I was going to vote Democratic in the next town election, no matter the candidate, and I started replying "Whatevs" to everything. Worse yet, long, terrible, lonely minutes drifted by without a single thought about sex. I forgot what wrenches do. I wanted all of my future text messages to include a shitload of unnecessary emojis. Pretty women walked by and I liked their outfits and the way their purses matched their belts and shoes. Simply put, I was slipping into the Estrogen Zone.

When I found myself *totally* wanting a cute little white VW bug convertible with a fake flower stuck in a vase on the dash, I violently threw the tube of lady butt butter away in the nearest trash can and made finding another bike shop to make the necessary replacement purchase priority Numero Uno. It took me a while for the changes to recess: my lowest point was when all I wanted to do was curl up under the covers with a pint of Ben & Jerry's Cookies and Cream and watch *Sleepless In Seattle* three times in a row.

As soon as I scratched my butt, burped, and guiltlessly farted in a public place, I knew I'd escaped from the Estrogen Zone. I was back to being an unapologetic red blooded Amerian man.

One of the things that makes America so great is the fact that Butt Butt'r *Pour Homme* is available in every bike shop in the country. As it should be.

Moving on.

Niagara Falls, baby! I couldn't believe I'd made it this far—only a little more to go.

I snapped a picture of a sign I saw right outside the Root House, a stop on the Underground Railroad. It stands as hard evidence that the world, then as now, is filled with a heady mix

of politicians, evildoers, and plain old good people trying to do
the right thing.

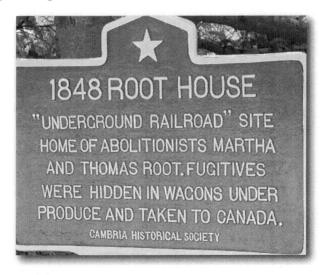

After making it back into the United States that morning,
Pete and I blasted to Lockport to meet my brother, Chris, for a
few days of riding. We met up with my brother without a hitch
and ended up riding seventy miles that first day as a trio. Seventy
miles for the first day out of the gate was a truly impressive physical feat on my brother's part. Chris came off the bench and
played a good game. That long a ride would have broken me in
half on my first day. As a matter of fact, I remembered riding *half
that distance* over similar terrain and being too tired to move by
day's end. Kudos to my bro for going the distance.

All day we rode along the flat gravel trail along the Erie
Canal. The canal itself didn't see much boat traffic; I saw only
two boats in the water over the course of the seventy miles we
rode that day. Though the path we rode was tree-lined and traffic free, our ride became monotonous and ended up being a
mundane push over loose gravel. I renamed the Erie Canal the
'Banal Canal', because that was what it looked like and that's
what it rode like.

We arrived in Holly, New York and decided to camp along the shore. On our left was a five-man tent and on our right were two single "pup" tents. The party on our left lit a bonfire, drank a ton, and pulled out two guitars—one bought from a crack head for five dollars and the other found on a road. Neither guitar stayed in tune, but that was ok because none of the singers around the campfire could stay in tune either. One of the guys, Stan, wasn't too bad a player, given the circumstances. He played some Beatles and some Dead. His drinking buddy, brother-in-law, and tent companion named Bruce had boots laced all the way up to his knees, stood about six foot two, and though he was covered in tattoos, you couldn't see them clearly because his skin was so dark and wizened by the sun.

Bruce was a lineman with AT&T and was as skinny and strong as the telephone poles he'd climbed for decades. He was also a grandfather who loved to get drunk. He got so hammered that when he stood up to return "to his woman in his tent," he almost fell face first in the fire. We all knew his woman was in the tent. We could hear her snoring over the music.

The campers to our right were an astonishingly odd father-and-son pair. The son was celebrating his thirty-first birthday. They were Scottish Wiccans, followers of the ancient religion. (The Wiccan religion, also known as the Craft, Wicca, Benevolent Witchcraft, and the Old Religion, is a diverse and decentralized religion that is part of contemporary Paganism.) When I asked the birthday boy to describe his religion, he did not explain it very well, but he was insistent Wiccans didn't kill goats or chickens and that Wiccans were not part of some weird cult. They hated the Devil and all Her dirty deeds.

"I hate it when the ignoramus non-believers call me a Satin worshiper. It ain't like that."

He said "satin" not "Satan." Classic. I wasn't a very big fan of satin, either; I'm more of an Egyptian cotton man myself. The 'satin hatin' birthday boy was a redhead who claimed when he was a school kid some bullies called him "carrot top" and the "the ginger head man."

Then he said with a satin-ic smile, "You know Tim, I didn't like it when people called me names, but they never got to me. Want to know why?"

"Sure," I said.

"Because gingers have no souls. I learned that on South Park."

I think he was trying to be funny so ok, whatevs. All I know is that two Wiccans went down to the river to fish for a birthday dinner and returned empty handed. I learned Wiccans eschewed dental hygiene, they didn't kill goats or chickens, they sucked at fishing, and one of them believed he had no soul. With all the boxes checked on my mental clipboard, I clicked my mental ball point pen closed and put it back into the chest pocket of my white lab coat, the one that I was wearing in my mind.

We were all done here.

Live and let live I always say. That father and son pair were just another example of people leading different lives and sleeping in different tents.

The next morning, we were up before the birds in Holly, New York, only because some total asshole with no sense of decency or appreciation for the letter 'z' was out hunting with his dog. That baying hound woke us all up and robbed us of all our zs. Goddamn hound barked louder than an air raid siren and when it ran right by my tent I felt the ground shake. That four pawed amp ripped by our tents twice on the way to treeing a 'coon. Hearing that commotion—a dog treeing a coon—at four o'clock in the morning was like being on the set of a horror movie the day they film the murder scene.

Once that dog simmered down and left, I thought that would be it for the early morning activity, but it wasn't. Stan and Bruce decided to strike camp at five o'clock while the "woman" went to fetch the car. She came back with it around 5:15 a. freakin' m., and they opened all the doors in the sedan and cranked the radio while they drank beer, struck the tent, and packed their sedan. They and their No Sense of Consideration for Others left at precisely 5:43 a.m.

Shortly after that the sun came up, the birds started chirping like they were all trying to win the Loudest Bird Contest, so I got zero shuteye after that. We struck camp and headed out.

After rolling through Rochester, NY, my brother Chris decided to bag the idea of continuing on. I think he was beat from the long ride the day before. He bought us a nice lunch at mile twenty and doubled back to the Rochester bus station to return to New York that very day. Lucky for him he did; right after he left, the hills showed up.

Pete and I pushed on for a total of sixty-eight miles and made it as far as Macedon, New York that night. It rained, and we were camping once again, this time on the grounds of the Macedon, NY fire station.

We were both bummed about our accommodations because not seventy yards from where we slept was a perfectly good pavilion with a big roof and a level platform covered in indoor/outdoor carpeting. It was a dream stage for a campsite. Unfortunately, it was being used by a local theater group that was putting on a really crappy play called *Only Once*. The owner of a local bookstore had written, directed, and somehow won the starring role in it. The acting, writing, set, and music—the whole thing—was absolutely terrible. Its three-day run was three days too long.

I could hear it, so I knew it sucked. Desperate for entertainment, though, I strolled over for a closer look and became an audience member for all of four minutes. After two hundred and forty seconds, I couldn't take it any longer and turned back and walked through the rain to my tent. That show should have been taken to the US Military Base in Afghanistan—not as USO entertainment for our troops, but as torture for our enemies.

"I'll tell you anything you want, just shut these people the hell up!"

It was so frustrating: a perfectly great tent site was being used by thespians intent on performing *Only Once*. I wanted to convince the stage manager to concede the play and give the bike campers the stage, but when I found out the stage manager was also the town librarian and a little old lady with a white hair bun, I hadn't the heart. Well, dear reader, *Only Once* was *Only Once Too Many*. My review? I gave the play, the players and the performance two thumbs down and the dreaded Triple A, Single C Award. That stands for "Avoid At All Costs."

Pete camped over in the wet grass with some other campers who had set up their tents under a ripped tarp that had been draped over the branches of a fallen tree. I chose to sleep on the dry cement under the short overhang above the front door of the fire station.

What sacrifices we all make for the theater.

The outlook for that Sunday morning was dry, but overcast. By day's end, it was sunny, hot and humid and I was in a flop sweat. It was so humid my forehead sweat dripped onto the inside of my sunglasses even with the skull cap/headband on. All told, we pedaled another sixty-eight hilly, against-the-wind miles and landed in a hotel called the Riverside Inn in Fulton, New York on that Sunday night.

We'd managed to find another total dump. The blanket on my bed had a hole in it the size of a small pizza pie (I replaced it), and the towel I took off the towel rack was damp and had a stain on it. Evidentially, housekeeping had folded a still moist towel from the previous room occupant and had returned it to the top of the towel rack unwashed. Gross and ew at the same time.

Nasty, nasty, nasty.

Over the course of my repeated trips to the front desk, I got to know Big Peggy, the front desk clerk. While she dutifully dug through the linens to locate a decent blanket and a clean towel, she told me a little about herself. She was new to the area, for one thing, having left her home state of Mississippi earlier that spring.

"I met a man, fell in love, sold all my things, and drove up here. 1,500 miles from Mississippi."

"How is he?"

"Who?"

"Um, the guy you moved up here for."

"Oh, him?" she said with a dismissive wave, "Yeah, the man thing just kinda turned out weird, so he's gone."

"I am sorry," I said. "How long had you guys been going out?"

"About two weeks. I met him on the Internet and I just knew."

Pause. Wait. Ok, now ask:

"You moved from Mississippi to Fulton, New York to move in with an Internet friend of yours that you'd only known for *two weeks*?" I asked. I was surprised at the very idea of it.

"Yeah, I thought I was in love, but that's more than over now," she said with a big roll of her eyes and another backhand wave. "But I'm still here. As crazy busy as the pace of life is here in Fulton, I still prefer this town to anywhere at all in the state of Mississippi. People from around here don't know it, but things are really bad down there, with the poverty and everything. People are real paw and there ain't nothing to dew."

While finding me a fresh blanket and a clean(er) towel, she offered to do my laundry for ten bucks. I accepted. When Pete learned about the deal, he was in, too.

Around eight o'clock that night there was a knock on the door and there was Big Peggy with our laundry in a basket, still warm from the dry cycle. We paid her the money and got to the two-minute job of folding clothing and stuffing it back into saddlebags. Each of us was short one sock. That might be no big deal if you are at home, but when you are on the road, all socks need to be present and accounted for.

I went back to the front desk to ask Peggy about the missing socks. She had no idea how they got lost. She went to check the laundry room and came back with a four-letter word: "Nope."

"I am so sorry about this," she said. "I will worry myself just about to death about your paw socks. Please go and double check everything back at the room and come back and tell me that you found your socks," she said, fluttering her eyes and using the fairy-light voice of a woman half her size.

I did one better: I convinced Janet Leigh to give me an all-access pass to the hotel laundry room in order to search for the damn things myself. I followed her down to the laundry room to solve the Mystery of the Missing Socks.

As we made our way to the laundry room, she came up with a handful of she's-just-a-victim excuses. "I have heard that socks fall into some kind of cortex or something, but this is the first time ever it ever happened to me."

I looked at her and decided, what the hell? *A little effort here, Tim. She's got more issues than tissues, so you may as well give her a hand with this one little thing.*

"It's *vortex* with a *v*, not *cortex*."

"Oh, OK. 'Vortex' then. Those socks of yours fell into a vortex."

I felt better knowing that I'd helped her out with a word. Maybe I should have been a teacher.

When we reached the laundry room there were several commercial washers and driers along the wall. She approached one and presented the commercial drier that had eaten our socks with a leading wave of both of her arms like she was a game show hostess showing a contestant what they could win if they guessed the right price for a can of spray starch. I opened the big round glass door and removed the dry sheets that were in there. Lo and behold, I found our socks. They were still in there, way in the back of the dryer, snagged on something. I didn't see them at first, but I leaned in for a good look and found them with very little extra effort. They were hot as molten lava, but they were fine.

Her carelessness was irksome and her Scarlet O'Hara routine annoying. Apparently the Mississippi Momma would rather sit on her behind and do her best Gone With the Wind imitation ("I hope you find your socks; I really, truly dew, God bless your sweet little biker heart. Sometimes socks just go into a cortex…") than solve the problem at hand. She said she "felt just terrible about it all and the commotion and such, good Lawd almighty sweet bay bee Jesus" when she saw the socks in my hand.

"Yew found yaw sox. God bless you! They must have been way back in there hiding on me!"

Clearly I needed to get my butt home. When losing a stupid sock ends up with me feeling that impatient towards a desk clerk, it's time to move on.

As we shared a walk back toward the front desk and the front lobby, Peggy thanked me again for the money we paid her, and said it would come in handy for gas money. "As it is right now, I can hardly afford to get to work."

Wait. So she had no money for gas?

Think about that for just a second, dear reader. Here was a woman that moved 1,500 miles to live with a guy she didn't know and in less than one month she was again single and working a "crappy job in a low-life hotel" (her words). Some people seem bound and determined to create their own problems. Maybe in this case, though, she was still better off than she was in Mississippi. It is hard to say. I wished her well and turned in.

The next day I woke up to the sound of my buddy Pete working a toilet plunger in the bathroom. The toilet had backed up and Military Man wasn't going to wait for hotel management to feel badly and do nothing about it, so he was taking the matter into his own hands. (I'm speaking figuratively here, folks.)

Eager to be free from the soundscape of plunger noises that had awoken me, I got out of my bed and walked barefoot down the carpeted hallway for a cup of morning coffee, half asleep and too lazy to bother putting my shoes on. I noticed the carpet was wet in a section of hallway, which was sort of strange because we were inside, but maybe not so strange because the wet carpet was right near the ice and vending machines. A water leak maybe? Melting ice? That was as far as I got in my analysis. I wiped the bottom of my feet off as soon as I returned to dry carpet.

I got a cup of coffee at the coffee station near the front desk. I sat in a leather chair in the lobby and grabbed a newspaper from the pile on the table. I thought I'd give my eyes an opportunity to work their way open with the caffeine hydraulic system that was beginning to pump through my veins. I figured I'd drain my cup halfway, top it off, pour one for Pete, and head back to Plunger Palace.

But there was some drama going on at the front desk that won my attention. A female guest was barking about something she felt fairly passionate about. I couldn't hear it all, so I got up off the leather chair and wandered over to eavesdrop.

She was complaining about the fact that no one had been by to "clean up the piss in the hallway those college boys musta gone and done did."

My eyes popped open wide as it dawned on me. Yuck! I inspected the soles of my bare feet. My kingdom for a footbath! When I'd first sensed the wetness of the carpet, I'd figured it was water bleed from the nearby ice machine, but that lady knew better. She said she'd smelled piss in the hallway and said her breakfast soda with the ice cubes in it *tasted* like piss.

"Those drunk boys musta pissed in the ice machine!"

Ew!

And again, ew!

Well, looking on the bright side (as I like to do), at least I wasn't drinking iced coffee and at least I didn't ruin my freshly laundered socks by wading through a shallow pond of college boy urine.

Now I had a problem: how to get back to my room without getting another urine "footbath-tism" that morning. Between the hot soapy suds that would make everything good again in my world and me was a piss swamp. I made a mental pinky promise to myself that I would soak in soapy suds until I got the word "*ew*" out of my head.

Never before had I wished so much that I had the power to levitate. I returned to my room, walking along the edge of the hallway, sliding along with my chest flat against the wall and my arms out like I was pulling some Mission Impossible move. I am happy to report there was a dry path back to the room, so less urine was pushed between my toes and absorbed into my bloodstream through the skin on the bottom of my feet.

A few short minutes later, I had the cleanest feet in all of Christendom.

Pete was more disciplined than I will ever be, so when he said he'd be ready to roll at Oh Eight Hundred, he rolled at Oh Eight Hundred. I bid him adieu from across the room. I figured my departure time was going to be more like Oh Ten Million, if at all. I was tired and I was not eager to deal with the sticky, hot, and humid outdoors.

I told Pete I might catch up to him later in Boonville, New York, but not to depend on it. I wasn't sure when—or even if— I'd leave the room anytime that day.

Four hours passed before I reached the decision to get rolling. I went out the front door of the Riverside Inn and into an invisible wall of humidity in Fulton, New York. My morning had flown by in air-conditioned comfort with some computer work done and some bike cleaning and light maintenance.

I felt a zero coming on, but I was going to try my best to meet up with Pete at Stysh's Brown Barn Campground in Boonville, NY. Like it or not, I had to face almost eighty-one hilly miles through heavy air. It wasn't a "scortchah" like my mom used to say, but someone had definitely fiddled with the thermostat, cranked the outdoor temperature, and stirred in some thick air for good measure.

Chapter Twenty-Four

WIFE IS GOOD, AND MY FRONT TIRE QUENCHES ITS THIRST

A h, but the bike gods had something in store for me: they delivered an early afternoon jab that stopped me dead in my tracks. Not four minutes after leaving my refrigerated cocoon of air-conditioned comfort, I suffered another flat tire while ascending a steep hill. Naturally, I had to fix it, but the flies and humidity made fixing that flat a more memorable experience.

"I gotta fix this flat and just keep pedaling," I whispered to myself as I dismounted and pulled over to the side of the road. By the time I had the back wheel off, I'd come up with a new game plan when facing adversity: no matter what happens, just keep pedaling.

As I toiled, two guys on Harleys pulled up. One of them asked me if I needed any help. I thanked them both for stopping, and told them I'd be back to riding in a jiffy, once the flat was fixed.

"Hey Ed," the guy in the beard shouted back to his friend over the roar of his Harley, "When was the last time you heard anyone use the word, 'jiffy'?"

"What?"

"I said when was the last time you heard anyone use the word 'jiffy'?"

Ed thought about it for a second and answered, "You did, just this morning when you were giving directions to that lady. You told her to take a right at the Jiffy Lube."

"I mean in a sentence."

"That was a sentence."

"Oh shit, Ed, forget it." The guy with the beard turned back to me and said, "Good use of the word 'jiffy' man. I will admit to you that I was not ready for that. I'm a word guy and don't get surprised too often, so touché, dude. Tell you what. We'll be even if you can't find yourself a way to seamlessly drop the word *sublime* into a conversation by the end of today. I'll bet you can't. *Sublime*'s a real bitch to dovetail into any sentence. She tends to stand alone. No one is ever ready for *sublime*, man. You ever see the movie *Shawshank Redemption*? That warden sure wasn't ready for *sublime*, either. When my man Tim Robbins's character Andy Dufresne dropped it on that old warden, he freaked and sent Andy to the box for a full month of hard time. You take it easy now," he said, and roared off.

I noticed his vanity plate was "ENGTCHR"

Somewhere out there are a couple of tough looking motorcyclists offering directions, aid to flat tire victims, and challenging people to use the word 'sublime' in a sentence by the end of the day. God Bless America, man. What a country we live in. Seriously. Let's not screw this up.

It was a hot day. After fixing the flat I was up on two and rolling along again, this time for a few hours before my on board and on back canteens ran dry. Thirsty, I swung into a quiet bait shop to find a young woman sprawled out on the front porch couch, engrossed in a book. I joined her for a sit in the shade before filling up my water bottles from a faucet out back. As I have said *ad nauseam* at this point, bikes take you places and deliver you to people you would not come across otherwise.

Nineteen years old with a winning smile, young Bree was the sole employee at the bait shop that day, pushing crawlers and baiters, flies, and hooks somewhere just outside Texas, New York. I opted for a Canada Dry club soda for $1.83 and joined her back on the front porch for a sit and a stretch. She and I shared a separate history of lower back problems and we ended up sharing stretching exercises and war stories. Not too pumped about returning to pedaling through the heat of the day, I ended up talking to Bree in the porch's shade for the better part of an hour, you know, just to make sure the adverse secondary sex characteristics and effects of the errant application of Chamois Butt'r *Pour les Femmes* had completely disappeared.

They had. I was back to my normal manly behaviors, once again making a complete ass out of myself in the presence of true beauty.

I joked with young Bree that she was like a siren in Homer's *Odyssey*, "luring" travelers to their "ugly baits—I mean fates."

I took a selfie with her and managed to step away from the siren unscathed. A reader, Bree was looking forward to a career in law enforcement. Bree was a life-long hunter who had a boyfriend who aspired to hunt different prey: he wanted to become a U.S. Marshall. It's not every day that you meet a hunter who wanted to read fifty books by summer's end. Bree was heading off to college that fall, and I sincerely hoped that whatever college she would be attending would be ready for her.

The bucolic region around Texas, New York, had lots of rolling hills and pastures. I spotted one pasture so idyllic that I stopped to take a picture of it. The bales of hay with the greenish tone were beautiful, but the color as rendered was lacking compared to the brilliance of the colors the original artist used. It is impossible to capture the brilliance and the subtleties of Mother Nature's brushstrokes with a camera phone.

A quick stop at a grocery store left me with enough food for the next couple of days including a bunch of locally grown blueberries that I just could not say no to. Shortly after leaving the store I passed a graveyard on a hill with some kids playing just outside its walls. They had made a crude jump out of a piece of plywood and were catching air. I stopped and asked if I was going the right way to the bike barn and they all pointed the same way down the road I was going.

They were good kids. I offered them some blueberries that still had some chill from the store refrigeration unit five miles back. Naturally they were reluctant to take food from a complete stranger, so I began eating them myself. I made up the excuse that I'd bought too many (which was true) and that they would be helping me out if they helped me kill the two quarts (also true). We did so and chatted a bit. I answered their questions about the bike and all my gear. They answered my questions on what it was like to grow up in Boonville. They all looked like they were in ninth grade or so and were likely enjoying their last summer without jobs. One kid lived on a farm and said, "I might not have an official job right now, but there's always work to get done when you live on a farm."

Another one of kids in the group, the shortest one, spat compulsively. He must have spat forty times during my ten-minute break. He was also the only one to shake my hand upon my departure. I had not expected him or any of the others to offer a hand of thanks, but of all the kids there, he was the only one to do so.

He came up to me, stuck out his hand, looked me in the eye, and said, "It was nice to meet you."

"Thanks, man," I replied. "It was nice to meet you, too." I told him that if he ever visited New York City, he'd better avoid spitting or he'd risk a fifty dollar fine.

"Don't ask me how I know that," I yelled over my shoulder as I rode away. I left him laughing and he shouted, "OK, I won't."

In less then five miles from the graveyard I was in the cool darkness of a barn basement in Boonville with all my bags on a three-cushion couch. I was declaring my territory, my bed for the evening. After an eighty plus mile long slog through the thickest air of the trip, that basement air felt cool and dry. Pete had been there for hours and was pretty beat, too, and before we even had dinner, we both decided to take a zero the following day. I must have really needed one because the second I agreed to take a zero, I felt a huge sense of relief. I was going to cram the following day's schedule full of nothing but consecutive nap appointments.

My zero was spent foraging food from all the various corners of my saddlebags and napping from all my efforts. I was Biking Bear enjoying the cool darkness and many splendid sleeps of hibernation. My back was feeling better and I could not remember the last time I had to take an Aleve pill. It didn't get any better for me. I figured I'd be home in about eight days, the good Lord willin'.

Oh, and I also tried my hand at T-shirt design. You saw it here first, folks. It's a trucker girl with the words 'Wife is good' underneath. Kind of like Life Is Good" but with "Wife" instead. Clever, awesome and wicked classy, no?

It was July 23rd and I have to tell you that by that point all that kept me from being at home was the distance that separated me from it. Mentally, home was where I wanted to be and the adventure, as great as it had been, was playing very distant second fiddle for the first time to a burning desire to be back with my family and have the ride over and done with. Maybe my grieving was mostly over, or maybe the road was getting more familiar and less exciting as a result. For whatever the reason, I wanted to see familiar familial faces.

The hills were coming back, and I knew the riding would get worse before I saw the coast, but that didn't bother me much. I knew I had it in me to crush the hills at that point. Whatever New England had it wasn't as bad as the Rockies.

Car license plates from VT, NH, and ME were all over the place and were the first harbingers of home like seabirds are the first sign of land that sailors can spot after a big ocean crossing. I could sense the trip winding down and my energy winding down along with it.

Regardless of how tired I was the morning following our zero, the wheels-up hour was seven o'clock. So seven o'clock found me all packed and ready to go. Pete was all about early morning starts and "getting on with getting on with it", so off we went. Rambo *For A Reason* liked leaving on time.

I didn't get the full story on Eric, the barn's only permanent resident and the overseer of all things in the barn, but I did learn he did not own a car and he really wanted to bike to Maine in September. A forty-three old easygoing bachelor, Eric did not offer any specific reasons why he had been living in the barn's basement for over a year, watching other bike travelers come and go to far flung places. He slept behind the only locking door in the building. His only mention on the matter occurred when he told me he "hadn't ever in his life expected to live in the basement of a barn."

Eric said his legs were hungry for some miles, so he joined us for the first few miles of our ride. Lucky for us he did. There was a bridge under repair and a severe lack of clear detour signage, so having Eric along to show us the way was handy: we would have been lost without him. But, with him along with us, we were out of the work zone and back on route before we knew it.

The rest of our riding day went well. We managed to outpace a trailing rainstorm most of the day. Upon our midafternoon arrival at the Hide-A-Way Campsite in Long Lake, New York, the storm we had outpaced all day overtook us. The skies opened up and I took shelter under the roof of the owner's front porch and sat on a chair and watched the summer rain come down. I fell asleep on that porch chair almost immediately and awoke about forty-five minutes later, cold, stiff and determined not to camp at the Hide-A-Way for the night.

The owner of the Hide-A-Way was an eighty-one year old man who had lived there for at least fifty-four years. He told me that there were motels down the road closer to town that might have some room if I didn't want to camp. After spending two nights on a three-cushion couch, I was after a decent bed and a good night's sleep. I bailed on very idea of staying at the Hide-A-Way as soon as I got up from that porch chair and learned I had options.

A bed, a shower, and a roof were the top three things on my wish list. Why? The grass was soaking wet, and I didn't like the neighbors. (I noticed that members of a road construction crew had pulled in while I was napping.) Road crews are pretty easy to spot: they wear hard hats, have deep tans on their faces, arms, and necks, they wear bright neon vests, big boots, and they are the only people I know of (besides German tourists) who wear dungarees in the summertime. Road crew guys are pretty easy to hear, too. They generally don't make for good camping neighbors because they tend to be loud and late going to bed, and loud and early going to work. And after two nights couch surfing in the common area of a barn basement, I wanted a solid night's sleep in a room that only had me in it.

I was delighted with my decision to leave the Hide-A-Way when I heard what happened to the guy who stayed. I met Pete for breakfast the next morning at a roadside diner and he reported his tale of woe. "The construction guys were loud and stayed loud until the cops came by and told them to shut the fuck up."

He cupped his coffee mug in both hands to help warm his fingers and hunched over the steam like he'd just returned to base camp after climbing Mt. Everest. "Though it was hot as hell when I went to sleep, it got real cold in the middle of the night, so I had to go find my sleeping bag and bring it into my tent or just lie there, freezing my ass off."

Unfortunately for Pete, during his nighttime search and rescue for his sleeping bag, he also found a big spider web...with his face. "I didn't see it, I felt it. It was wet with night dew and had some dead crusty bugs in it. That woke me up real fast. I stepped back to avoid it, but it was too late. The thing stuck all over my face. Then I tripped on a stick and went down. Hurt my elbow, but I can ride."

He took another pull on his coffee. His fleece jacket was draped over his shoulders like a shawl.

The road crew started their cars at four thirty and had their radios blaring while they struck camp. And just after they left, the sun started coming up. The first thing Pete saw in the early morning light was a spider the size of a Ping-Pong-ball inside his tent. He figured it slipped in somehow the night before when he was out looking for his sleeping bag. He checked all over: he hadn't been bitten.

"I hate spiders in my tent," he said and took another sip of hot coffee, his hands shaking. "I think that was a wolf spider. Fucking thing was huge."

Yes, I was definitely glad I'd opted for the hotel that night.

The Adirondack Hotel in Ticonderoga, New York, had been my abode the previous night. It was built in the late 1800s or so. No TV. No closets. Not much room in the rooms. Oh, and no sound insulation at all. I could hear every single piece of sound generated from the couple in the next room. Everything.

Coughs. Sneezes. Words. Let's just put it this way: when either one of those two ripped a fart, three people knew about it. I thank God above they hadn't been "in the mood for some rough-ie stuffy" that night. I didn't want to be a victim of my own very powerful abilities to visualize things.

In addition to those sixty-five miles ridden on July 25th, we traveled 3,414 vertical feet. We left Ticonderoga and hit the road at seven thirty. Not much of a day, save for the ferry ride that dropped us in Vermont and the roughest road I've experienced on the whole trip. Route 100 in Vermont was under some serious renovation for about seven miles. Two sets of flagmen acted as NASCAR starters, holding us all up then waving us all on. The problem was that Pete and I were in the front of a long line of cars and trucks that had one narrow, bumpy, scraped-up, stretch of uphill road to climb without much of a shoulder. Every driver seemed to be in a mad rush to get somewhere. It was a case of being regularly missed by inches, not feet, for several harrowing miles.

The end of the day landed us in Bethel, Vermont, a place I've traveled through countless times on the way to and from ski weekends in Warren, VT. A forlorn looking B and B called the Nestled Inn that I'd never noticed before, was to be home for the night. The man who ran it could not have been more accom-modating. Stay there if you can. It did not look like much from the road, but it is quiet and very comfortable inside. We each got our own room for thirty-five bucks. That beat camping by a mile. And, truth be told, camping was no longer an option for me; I'd jettisoned all my camp gear and unneeded items in preparation for my landing at home. For twenty-five bucks postage, fifteen pounds had come off the bike.

Less weight to carry meant less difficult vertical climb. I liked that math.

We biked seventy-eight miles from Bethel, Vermont, to Lincoln, New Hampshire, which was 5,100 feet of climb, five hours and thirty-five minutes, at about an average speed of 12.5 miles per hour. I was certainly back in New England, with the drivers not as courteous to bikers as they were in other areas of the country. Frankly, I think it comes from the fact that they are not used to seeing touring cyclists around. Or maybe we New Englanders are just poor drivers and not very courteous people. Take your pick. Both choices work for me.

As my friend Margo would say in her Polish accent, "Timmy, your trip is almost over! One final pooosh!" I was looking at the final hill, the Kancamangus Pass on the Kancamangus Highway. It would be a biggest "pooosh" I'd ridden in a while, no doubt, but after nearly four thousand miles on the Fun Mover, I knew I was more than up for the task.

Pete and I were on a break by the side of Route 112 when some guy pulled over and asked us how far we were headed. He told us he had always wanted to ride across America, but he had issues with his neck and was having an MRI done the following Monday to help decipher what was making his neck hurt and making bike riding impossible. He reached into the backseat of his car, popped open the lid of a cooler and came up with two ice-cold chocolate milks. I took one and Pete took one. I downed mine in about a minute, and Pete gave me his because he didn't drink milk. It was a hot day and the cool chocolate milk was refreshing going down. I fired down the second chocolate milk in about a nanosecond.

Not so long later, the milk caught up with me and I got a little taste of the cramps lactose-intolerant people get. Yikes, no thanks. Life lesson: stay the hell clear of cold chocolate milk on "wicked-haut daze in New Hampsha."

We rolled into Woodstock, New Hampshire, a tourist trap in full swing on a Saturday afternoon. The streets were crammed with cars, the shops were full of people, and the bars were full of hungry, thirsty folks who pumped their hard earned dollars into the hands of the tattooed members of the restaurant army willing to exchange money for food and beverage items. One glance confirmed it: all were having a good time. I wanted in on the action, but we had to secure a room first. The whole town was hopping. Unfortunately for us, once we saw the level of tourist activity, we suspected we had little to no chance of securing a hotel room in that town for the night.

We were right.

"All the hotels in town are full because of the weather and such," said the bartender who handed me a couple of beers. "Welcome to Woodstock. Place runs crazy like this for like two months. If you want to drive up and get a room without a reservation, come back in February."

Lucky for me I would not take that no for an answer. I put the beers down and accosted the restaurant's maître de and put the same question to her. Friendly, pregnant, fast-talking, Stephanie at the Woodstock Brewery came through in spades. She had a friend up the road who worked in the next town at a condo time-share place called the Pollard Inn that sometimes, with the owners blessing, had rooms to let. It was only nine miles up the road in Lincoln, New Hampshire. After a minute or two on the phone, Stephanie hung up and smiled at me. "I got you covered. Go see my friend Dawn. She'll hook you up. Tell her you know me and the room rate is seventy-five bucks."

I thanked her. If she showed that kind of concern to two perfect strangers in a busy restaurant, it was a cinch that she would be a great mom to her soon-to-be-born child. Stephanie was one of the good ones.

Pete and I mounted up and clawed away at the nine miles ahead of us and they were over before we knew it. Of course it was a hard left up a steep hill for the last half a mile or so, but at that point, I just smiled at the last jabs of the day. Last jabs didn't carry the weight they once had. I'd grown a little tougher over the course of my travels. Sure, I remained steadfast in my reluctance to kill and for that I will be a forever disappointment to Rambo for No Reason, but you put over four thousand miles on a bike under your belt and you, too, will learn to smile in the face of a jab. The grief of losing both parents had been a jab of sorts for me, and the overwhelming sense of sadness I felt at the beginning of the trip was now much more in hand.

We checked in to a four-bedroom condo for seventy-five bucks that was head and shoulders above any other accommodation I'd experienced on the trip. I had a full kitchen, my own room, my own shower, and my own reading nook. Yes, I had a reading nook. I didn't know the owner, but I appreciated the design of the place.

The place came with pool access, so I enjoyed a long swim in the outdoor pool like any other self-respecting time-share traveller would. After a long hot shower full of cleansing suds and clean water, I toweled off and dove under my covers for a nice long afternoon nap.

It was a nine-mile ride back to Woodstock, but it was mostly downhill and with all the bags off the bike, it was very easy going.

Pete was after a "descent porter and a decent meal," so we returned to the brewery for a pint and some pub grub. He also wanted to make sure the mother/daughter pair made it safely to town, so off we went, back to Woodstock to eat and greet.

Surprise, surprise: the folks we were waiting for were late. Earlier in the day they'd called and told Pete that they'd be in Woodstock, NH sometime after five o'clock. Well, that's what you get when one person has a map and the other one has duct tape covering saddle sores on her ass cheeks: things don't go as planned. We sat at the bar and nursed a couple of beers then committed to eating dinner without The Map and Mommy Dearest.

While we were nursing our beers, we met a guy named Bill who owned a construction company and claimed he had "found the Lord."

"What were you like before you found Him?" I asked.

"Oh, I was an animal," Bill replied. "I would go on Match. com and set up ten dates with ten different women in five days. I was unstoppable and very unhappy until the Lord found me."

"I thought you said *you* found *Him*," I pointed out.

"Oh, yes, that's right. I've had a couple of beers. I found him. He always knew where I was. I finally just turned to Him and accepted Him into my life."

Bill had driven to the bar in his 1962 Triumph TR4, which had won tons of awards at car shows. He was selling it for thirty grand and had gotten no hits on Craigslist or Hemming's Motor News. His Lord wouldn't let him have any Match.com hookups, but a couple of beers and some fast cars were fine. My man Bill had it dialed in, although I could tell he still struggled with his lady demons; as soon as I stood up to leave, he took my chair, a perfect perch from which to look out over the talent at the outdoor seating section and to get a clear shot of a very attractive blond woman in a tight tee shirt and cutoff shorts.

"I can still look" were Bill's parting words to me.

With only a hundred miles to my finish line in Scarborough, Maine, my adventure was very close to being over. The following day's ride would be my last ride of the trip.

Lincoln, NH, sits at the base of Kancamagus Mountain so right after getting up from a solid night's sleep and right after enjoying a cup of coffee and a couple of blueberry pancakes the size of manhole covers, I pointed my front wheel toward the final hill.

I started pedaling.

Same old, same old: I had a hill to summit and a bike to do it with.

Pete's bike was still fully loaded, so I had the weight advantage going up and over the hill. I climbed faster than he did, but not by much. He was near sixty, very fit, and he could still kick any biker's ass over the long haul, including mine. That being said, I left him behind me during the Kancamangus Highway

climb after a firm handshake and after some preemptory con-
gratulations were exchanged. We'd nearly made it to the end of
our separate finish lines. He was on his way to Bar Harbor and
planned to fly directly home to Portland, Oregon for some R and
R of his own once he hit the ocean. I pressed on to the Maine
coast farther south.

After leaving him, I cranked. My four-thousand-mile-strong
blueberry-pancake-fueled legs were good to go. At the summit,
I paused to have a picture taken of me sitting on a wall, the very
one that I'd sat on when I'd ridden the same highway on a motorcycle with my brother-in-law years before. I remember that
motorcycle ride well—it was one of only a handful we'd ridden
together. I still have a picture of the both us in full motorcycle
gear hanging in my den at home. I planned on putting the new
shot of me on a different sort of bike trip right next to it. With
that photo taken, I rolled down the other side of the hill and
into the state of Maine, determined to make Sunday my last day
of the trip.

But those pesky bike gods—they still had one final last jab for
me in the form of a rainstorm and a dead cell phone. I forgot to
charge my cell phone the night before, so it died leaving me off my
mapped route and without GPS. My seventy-two-day trip included
about sixty-eight sunny, breezy, temperate days. Weather-wise I had
nothing to complain about, save for some really nasty headwinds
that messed with my head. Wouldn't you know it? The last forty
miles of the trip, it rained "pussies and poodles" as Dave would say.
At one point it was raining so hard that I thought someone was
above me pouring tubs of water directly onto my back.

I stopped to check to make sure my rear red light was blinking: it was the only way cars could see me through the rain. After
a while the rain let up and I stopped under an awning of a closed
hardware store to warm up and have some lunch. Lunch was
a bagel smeared with peanut butter after riding eighty miles. I
could not find my spork (a camping tool that is both a spoon

and a fork) so I used my fingers. Ah, bike travel. I'd miss it, but maybe not enough to want to pedal four thousand plus miles in a row again. I had gone a long way and had a lot of fun in my ten weeks and two days on the road, but make no mistake: it was a long, *long* way.

I'd wondered what my stomach thought about bike travel. Blueberry pancakes followed by peanut butter and bagels. If I pushed it and reached home in time, the next arrival to my stomach would be lobster and a fine French red wine. I looked forward to sitting at my father-in-law's table that very night for his famous Sunday night family dinner. All I had to do was just keep pedaling to get there.

The rain slowed to a complete stop, the clouds pulled a Sunny and Cher and broke up, and a warm sun took to the sky and shone down on a lone cyclist who appreciated "Mother Sun's" return engagement.

I chewed my sandwich and looked at the people gawking at me from their cars and trucks as they waited at the traffic light. The light would change and they would drive away, only to be replaced by a new group of gawkers the next time the light went red.

A slight breeze kicked up and I got chilly. It was time for me to dry off and get out of my wet clothes and into any dry ones I could find. I was in Standish, Maine and so close to home I could taste it. I dug through my bags and grabbed some dry clothing and my camp towel. The wind was working against me even while I was off my bike: it was making me shiver. I shamelessly stripped down to my bike shorts (I always rode with mountain biking shorts over my spandex bike shorts) right then and there and toweled off as best I could. In doing so, I revealed my soft, white middle to the world, a gut so white that it glowed a bluish hue that could probably be seen from space.

Very few people on this planet have interest in seeing the shirtless Irish Pastry of Sheer Determination that had pedaled the Fun Mover across this great country of ours and none of those few people were in Standish that day. Hey, I didn't want to freeze, and they didn't have to read the menu if they didn't want to. (And, by the looks on their faces, they didn't want to.) I had more rubberneckers than a traffic accident. I needed a cop to move people along by saying, "Nothing to see here folks. Move along. Nothing to see..."

I was almost home.

I couldn't wait to see everyone and to enjoy a nice long shower in my own house. Before my phone died I'd managed to speak with Eileen. She knew I'd be home that afternoon, but didn't know exactly what time to expect me. I figured she'd assemble a welcome committee and I wanted to look presentable when I arrived, so I changed, dried off, and washed my face and arms.

Back on track and with only about five miles away from my house, I stopped again, this time outside a bike store on Route 1 in Scarborough. No, I hadn't stopped because I was tired or hungry or cold or because needed anything from the store. It was an unanticipated set of mixed emotions about my final finish line that had stilled my wheels. Sure, I was excited to see my wife and son (and dog), but the ride had been terrific and a time away that I knew was about to end. In some ways I was reluctant to have the trip over. I knew it had to end, obviously: I didn't want to bike forever, but I did want to bike a little more. Maybe more than the five miles I had left.

I got off the bike and took measure of myself. I'd gotten into the shape I'd wanted to. I'd lost some weight and said goodbye to chronic lower back pain. In addition, my left leg no longer hurt and I'd seen a beautiful country thick with a cornucopia of real characters. It had been a great ride and I was thankful to be going home more mentally and physically healthy then when I'd left. I got the Grief Monkey off my back. My seventy-two day two-wheeled therapy session had yielded strong results.

So why was I standing in a bike shop delaying the inevitable? I wasn't sure.

I recognized the guys who worked at the bike shop because I'd been there before on different occasions to grab a new helmet for my kid or a new bike light or something. One of the bike mechanics put down a wrench and came over to me.

"Need any help finding anything?" he asked.

"No, thanks," I said. "I'm just taking a final breather from a long ride and I thought I'd stop in here for a minute to gather myself before I call it quits."

"Jesus dude," he said, looking at my loaded bike out in the parking lot, "Where'd you ride from, Boston or something?"

"No, Washington."

"Right on, man. D.C. is a haul. My uncle said he did that ride once. Good on you."

"No," I said, correcting him. "I rode that bike from Washington *State*."

"Like Nirvana Washington State? Shit, that is a long way. You know, dude, they got planes for that. You need to sit down or something? Want some water? We got some GU here if you need some. The tri folks swear by GU. Man, that shit is crazy. What was it like to ride that far?"

He got me with that simple question. I had to think about it for a second. "It was great, one of the best things I ever did. Unfortunately and fortunately, it's about to end."

"Well, stay as long as you like. I feel you, man. Good going."

The bike mechanic with the bike silhouette tattoo on his calf returned to the service area and grabbed the wrench he'd put down earlier. I was left standing alone with the racks of bike shirts and shorts, helmets and cleats. I looked around the shop and sighed.

There was nothing left for me there in bike world. It was time to go home. Time to end my ride.

I took the turn down Black Point Road and pedaled faster and faster. I rode the last few miles in blazing speed. Any momentary hesitation to have it over with was gone. I was doing an unsustainable twenty-eight miles per hour by the time a bunch of little kids came into view about a mile out from the finish line. I got closer and could smell salt air. I could not wait to see that beach.

After my stop at the bike shop, I was now properly psyched and over-the-moon happy to call it quits: I couldn't wait to dunk my front tire into the Atlantic Ocean and dismount one last time.

But who were those kids and why were they standing by the road? Why were they waving at me? It was a welcoming committee chaired by my son George and populated with a bunch of buddies of his!

I slowed down and gave a wave and a shout hello, but I could not stop. Perhaps fittingly, I biked the last mile with my son.

"Can't stop George. Come ride with me!" I said.

He did. His little ten-year old legs pumped furiously to keep up, but his smile required no effort at all. George wasn't the only person I'd spoken with from my bike seat on the trip: I'd talked to my mom, my dad, my wife, Dave, Pete, Larry, and a few other people while riding the many miles under a hot sun. But George was part of the scouting committee there to greet me and that meant the world. Matter of fact, the best mile of the whole trip was the very last one I rode because I got to ride it with him. Was it ever good to see him!

I crested the last incline and saw more people gathered at the turn in the road where the yacht club was located and, of course, that long awaited beach. Other friends and family, including Eileen, greeted me. My last phone call to Eileen had lasted only long enough to let her know I'd be there sometime in the late afternoon. My phone quit just after she said, "Great! Can't wait to see you."

Since the call she'd hastily assembled a welcome committee just in time to greet me at the finish with open arms.

I rolled to a stop in front of a clapping crowd of a couple of dozen people. They started shaking my hand and backslapping me a welcome home. George was right behind me and I got two armfuls of family and held on tight. I still had one eye on the ocean, though, and excused myself from the group that had encircled me as soon as my feet touched ground.

I pushed my bike toward the beach.

"Ride's not over just yet," I explained to the small crowd.

The Fun Mover bounced over the sand and rocks and splashed in. As soon as my front wheel hit that water, I heard cannon fire, a one-gun salute that signaled the official end of my trip. Eileen had arranged it: she had instructed a trigger-happy yacht club kid to fire off a 12 gauge blank round from a small brass cannon the moment my front tire got wet. The kid was a master: the second my tire hit, the gun went off.

I was happy to hear that one-gun salute fired in my honor. It was far cry from the lonely wail of my starting gun, the Super-class ferry *MV Elwha's* "Boo Whoo" on the beach in Anacortes, Washington, the very blast that marked the beginning of my ride. Two and a half months, two days and roughly seven hours and twenty minutes after that wail, I heard that cannon.

My ride was over. My bike, my legs, my heart and my head had all done their work and I was safely home.

That Sunday ride was a doozy: up and over Kancamangus Pass and 101.4 total miles ridden. It was the last mighty push of a Herculean effort. Words cannot describe how happy I was to be back home, safe and sound, and in the company of my family once again.

My dog didn't recognize me. Maybe she thought I'd died; her ears laid flat on her head and she was reluctant to come anywhere near me for a few of days after I returned home. Every time she looked my way, her ears deflated onto her head and she, an Australian Cattle Dog, cowered behind a piece of furniture or behind someone's legs at my approach. It took her about four days to get used to having me around again.

Unlike our dog, it took me much longer than four days to slip back into a normal routine at home. "Re-entry into the world" was something the more experienced bike tourists had warned me about. "There is definitely, most certainly, a re-entry process that takes place after you return from a bike tour," Larry once said to me, and he was right. Not being constantly on the go was strange for me. I'd grown accustomed to putting my head down on a different pillow every night. Suddenly, there was no road left to ride, no hill left to climb, and the same pillow waiting for me at night just where I'd left it that morning. I felt antsy for the first few days at home, but I began to relax back into domestic life.

I'd done it, but all that pedaling had cost me. The effort I'd put forth to haul my butt clear across the States had taken a physical toll. I was, of course, feeling fit as a fiddle in some ways: I had legs of steel and not much fat hanging off me. My BMI, or body mass index, must have been the lowest it had been in a couple of decades, but I felt exhausted all the time. For months after I got back, I took hours long naps every afternoon. Something seemed wrong. I suspected that I was suffering from some sort of mineral or vitamin deficiency, but did not seek any medical help other than to ask a couple of doctors at a cocktail party their opinions on the matter.

"Probably just over fatigue," said one. "It'll take time to come back from the punishment you've put your body through," said another. Many months passed before my weight and energy returned to somewhat normal levels. My lower back problems were over for good, though: chronic lower back pain no longer ailed me.

That fall and winter I was too pooped all the time to even think about getting any regular exercise. Just the thought of riding a bike, running a mile, swimming a lap, or skiing a hill made me yawn and go in search of a place to lie down. The following spring when the weather got better I figured I'd ride again, but I didn't. The Fun Mover was all ready to go, but I sure wasn't. I joked with my friends that I'd left it all on the field.

I eventually reached the point where I felt a little guilty when I saw the Fun Mover hanging on a hook gathering dust in the garage, so I sold it. I'm not bike free, though. Soon as I sold the Fun Mover I went out and got another flavor of bicycle. Now I ride a gravel bike on the weekends and around town. It is one sexy beast that fits me like a glove. This time 'round I went through the effort of being properly sized for the bike. What a difference it makes to have an appropriately sized bike to ride. I believe that most if not all of my early travails in the ride could have been avoided simply by getting fitted properly to a bike and doing some break-in rides before leaving home for the trailhead.

Well, you live and you learn.

But let's get back to the end of my story. The first home cooked meal in seventy-three days was enjoyed the night I arrived back. Lucky for me I arrived in time for the weekly lobster dinner that included wine, baked potatoes, corn on the cob, and ice cream for dessert. My first dinner back was a family affair, just what the doctor ordered.

My poor family: I was not short of words that night. I went on and on about how hot shit wonderful I was and how great the trip had been. People were firing questions at me and I was answering them just a quickly as they came. I was feeling a little self-important perhaps as a sense of bravado crept over me. Hell, I'd crossed a continent on a bike and was enjoying all the interest and attention I was getting. "Believe you me" as my mom used to say, it wasn't often I got to be the center of attention at that table full of high achievers. I found myself rather enjoying the spotlight. The wine was delicious, the company receptive, the words flowed.

My father-in-law sat quietly at the head of the table and patiently listened to me ramble on about the places I'd stayed and the people I'd met and the difficulties of the climbs et cetera. When I boasted about the roughly 70,000 feet of vertical climb (my best guesstimate if you add up all the ups along the way), he cleared his throat and claimed the floor. He raised an index finger, and pointed it skywards, calling for my and everyone else's attention.

"Tim," he said in a lawyerly fashion, "Is it true that you rode the entire way across the United States from, where did you say? Anacortes, Washington to Prouts Neck, Maine?"

"Yes, that's what I did, George," I replied.

"So you made an ocean to ocean trip on that bicycle of yours?"

"Yes, that's right," I said with a smile on my face, knowing full well that the old man was about to drop an insight that I and perhaps everyone else there at the table had overlooked.

"Well, because you made it all the way from one ocean to the other, I would like to point out you enjoyed roughly 70,000 feet of vertical *descent* as well. You see, by definition, because you spanned the *entire* continent, all of the vertical feet both up *and down*, evened out in the end."

Laughter erupted from all sides of the round table.

My father-in-law was a gifted lawyer and a brilliant man with a keen ability to see both sides of an argument. His point was indeed a fair one and he meant no ill intent. Sure my biking bravado took a little hit, but so what? I did ride downhill a lot, too. George Gillespie was one of a kind and he had my back every minute I knew him. He was as good a man as they come. He will be missed.

And, as always, he was as right as rain: ocean-to-ocean rides have just as much uphill as downhill.

Well, uphill, downhill, or on the flats—somewhere along the way I dropped the lion's share of the grief I suffered from at the loss of both my parents. I was fortunate enough to spend some time between the ears, to ponder and wonder across this great country of ours, and to meet some memorable characters that cemented the trip as one of the all time best things I've ever done.

The people I met along made the trip. I mean, come on: the sneeze fart from the waitress with tummy issues at the Contagion Café? Pete, Dave, and Larry, my fellow road warriors? The dirty, dusty, dignified man who owned the magnificent wolf dog, Kettle? The bike shop guy who did impressions of German dudes with chaffing issues? Suzie Bee who ran an RV park from the driver's seat of a broken down camper who said I wasn't determined and who loved pepperoni pizza and Brad Pitt? The border patrol guard who wanted to beat someone up? Steve R., the financial advisor who welcomed me into his home for a cold soda? Penny, who stopped to help put my bike and me back on the road after I crashed? David and Heather inviting me along for a July 4th fireworks show? The Donny Train? Or how about the woman with the "wasband" or the jilted waiter who invented the word "relationshit"? Or the young waitress who wanted to travel to a far-away land where castles are real and not make believe? They and the many others I met during my coast-to-coast ride made all the pedal turns a little easier.

So what's the walk away from a long bike ride? Well, I got a much better understanding of just how right my brother-in-law was when he said, "There is no wrong way to grieve, and everyone grieves differently." In addition, I also picked up a little something along the way that I can use both on or off the bike:

No matter what happens, no matter how tough things get, just keep pedaling. You'll get there eventually.

About the Author

Tim Fahey grew up next to a six-lane highway outside of Boston in a large Irish Catholic family, so, naturally, he's wicked normal. He graduated from Belmont High School, Lawrenceville, and Holy Cross and earned his MBA from Boston University. He lived in Manhattan for a dozen years, in Cambridge, Massachusetts, for a decade, in Connecticut  for another decade, and eventually came to his senses and moved to Maine.

Writing is a recently discovered passion. *The Fun Mover Chronicles* is his first, and most likely, his only book if it doesn't sell well.

18791340R00214

Made in the USA
Middletown, DE
01 December 2018